Tribal Libraries, Archives, and Museums

Preserving Our Language, Memory, and Lifeways

Edited by
Loriene Roy, Anjali Bhasin, and
Sarah K. Arriaga

THE SCARECROW PRESS, INC.
Lanham • Toronto • Plymouth, UK
2011

Published by Scarecrow Press, Inc.
A wholly owned subsidiary of The Rowman & Littlefield Publishing Group, Inc.
4501 Forbes Boulevard, Suite 200, Lanham, Maryland 20706
http://www.scarecrowpress.com

Estover Road, Plymouth PL6 7PY, United Kingdom

British Library Cataloguing in Publication Information Available

Library of Congress Cataloging-in-Publication Data

Tribal libraries, archives, and museums : preserving our language, memory, and lifeways / edited by Loriene Roy, Anjali Bhasin, Sarah K. Arriaga.
    p. cm.
  Includes bibliographical references and index.
  ISBN 978-0-8108-8194-5 (pbk. : alk. paper) -- ISBN 978-0-8108-8195-2 (ebook)
  1. Libraries and Indians--United States. 2. Indians of North America--Library resources. 3. Indians of North America--Information services. 4. Indians of North America--Archives. 5. Indians of North America--Museums. I. Roy, Loriene. II. Bhasin, Anjali, 1979- III. Arriaga, Sarah K., 1986-
  E97.8.T75 2011
  025.5'4--dc23

2011016320

Contents

Preface

Unbeknownst to many people within the professions of librarianship, there are hundreds of tribal libraries and archives. There is no exact figure itemizing their existence. No single directory lists and identifies the tribal school libraries, public/ community libraries, college libraries, archives, and collections/repositories in museums in Indian country and in other rural and urban settings. Yet they exist nonetheless in villages in Alaska, on pueblos in New Mexico, in the Everglades of Florida, and in the woodlands of Wisconsin and Minnesota. These are libraries and other information centers that offer the expected services: circulation of materials, collection of singular items such as oral histories, and provision of public services such as summer reading programs. Yet, there is always something unique and special in these settings as they balance tribal protocols and infuse their settings with tribal lifeways expressions, from their footprints on the land, to their architecture and interior design, institutional names, signage, and special services such as Native language promotion.

In the late 1990s, Alyce Sadongei, then assistant curator for Native American Relations at the Arizona State Library on the campus of the University of Arizona in Tucson, managed a grant from the U.S. Institute of Museum and Library Services (IMLS) for the Five State Library Leadership Project. The Five State Project promoted discussion among those working in tribal libraries, archives, and museums in Arizona, Colorado, Nevada, New Mexico, and Utah. These successful statewide and regional meetings led to subsequent funding from IMLS to organize national conferences, the first of which took place in May 2002 in Mesa, Arizona. More recently, the national conferences were organized by the Oklahoma Department of Libraries and the Oregon State Library. The conferences have been received warmly and well attended, justifying the need to establish a continuing gathering point. In 2011, the Association of Tribal Archives, Libraries, and Museums (ATALM) will likely be established, the first national organization that will provide the continuing network and foundation for those interested in tribal information settings and the issues that affect them.

This book reflects the growing attention paid to tribal libraries and archives and provides an opportunity to share their stories, challenges, achievements, and aspirations with each other and the larger professional community. It opens with an introduction by Robert Sidney Martin, former director of IMLS who was extremely supportive of the initial Five State Library Leadership Project and observed the potential of these gatherings to serve a broader, national audience. Several other chapters reference those early meetings and witness their great impact. Martin clearly describes the role of IMLS in helping to support such initiatives and affirms that the distinctions among libraries, archives, and museums are not as great as the commonalities they share.

Part I introduces the tribal community library, providing context and case studies. Bonnie Biggs and David Ongley contribute chapters that depict the history and status of statewide tribal library development in California and Alaska. Biggs attributes some of her motivation to the Five State Library Leadership Project as she traces her involvement with California tribal issues to the mid-1980s. Her efforts resulted in a formal census and needs assessment of tribal libraries in her state, the formation of a tribal library intern project, and local training to ensure that tribal library concerns continue to be voiced—and heard. Ongley describes how efforts to advance library services in Alaska Native villages need to occur at two levels: from within the Alaskan village level with support at the statewide level. The distances involved and the rural nature of Alaskan locales have led to the development of unique funding models, including oil revenues and local collaborations such as multitype libraries that combine public and college library structures and services.

Karen Alexander describes the evolution of the Miami Tribal Library & Archives in Oklahoma, a story that illustrates how successful partnerships can extend the breadth of tribal community library services from providing consumer health information, to public access computing, recovery of tribal records, to a books-for-babies program for the youngest tribal members and their families. Unfortunately, this story also illustrates the vulnerability of tribal library services; in her postscript, Alexander describes the recent decision to close the library. Advocacy, as Sandra Littletree points out in a chapter in part IV, remains a daily need and concern for tribal library employees.

Kawika Makanani reflects on his career as an indigenous librarian through his experiences and the services he launched in the Midkiff Learning Center of the Kamehameha Schools of Hawai'i. He again illustrates how one person can make a difference in such tangibles as a new lecture series, the hosting of indigenous visitors from around the world, presentations in classes and at conferences, and producing bilingual signage in English and indigenous languages.

Amelia Flores and Susan D. Penfield recount how, through their joint efforts, the oldest tribal library in the United States supports the documentation and use of local Native language. The Colorado River Indian Tribes Library/Archives in Arizona created coloring books in the Mohave and Chemehuevi languages and worked with community members to create, copy, and archive audio recordings. Gabriella Reznowski and Norma A. Joseph also discuss winning collaborations to support language revitalization. In their case, they discuss how academic librarians can feature language materials from their collections in displays and collaborate with tribal officials in supporting Native language study through publications and courses. Participants in these efforts learned that the human attributes of trust, patience, and passion were essential in sustaining language initiatives over time.

In "International Efforts in Supporting and Advancing Library Services for Indigenous Populations," Loriene Roy expands the stage of tribal librarianship across borders to include references to activities taking place in Australia, Canada, New Zealand/Aotearoa, and Sweden. The launch of the biennial International Indigenous Librarians Forums in the late 1990s and the more recent Special Interest Group on Indigenous Matters within the International Federation of Library Associations and Organizations have provided platforms to extend discussions of indigenous librarianship issues across governmental boundaries and seek unifying themes. Following this chapter are two brief entries that document the presence and impact of the American Indian Library Association (AILA) and the newer Tribal College and University Library Association (TCULA), prepared by Kelly Webster, past AILA president, and Mary Anne Hansen and James Thull, organizers of the annual Tribal College Librarians Professional Development Institute.

Part II features service functions of tribal information centers. Here are gathered chapters that address common library services—the library facility, selection, organization, instruction, and programming/outreach—with Native clientele in mind.

Anishinabe architect Sam Olbekson provides a framework for understanding a process of consensus that adapts over time. Kristen Hogan views collection development as "a tool for social justice." She sees a librarian's professional responsibility as not only demonstrating resistance through acquiring materials by Native writers but also supporting the noncollection of materials that homogenize or demean American Indian cultures and values.

Rhonda Harris Taylor is a longtime educator in the area of organization of knowledge. In "Organizing Information Resources," she offers logical advice on not only following formal organizational models but also on creating new models or modifying existing models to best meet the needs of tribal community members. Her extensive listing of resources is a publication in itself.

Victoria Beatty's "Empowering Indigenous Students in the Learning Library" is the rare discussion that presents an indigenous interpretation of a traditional library service, that of library instruction/information literacy. She shares her experiences serving as the only instructional librarian at a tribal college, which included helping Dine/Navajo students understand the potential of their academic library and connecting the library services to a curriculum built on a Dine paradigm or worldview.

Loriene Roy's chapter on weaving partnerships provides advice for working with American Indians in developing community programs on Native culture. She describes why such programming is popular and sometimes mandated by law. She also describes how to learn more about the tribal groups within a library's service area and introduces the protocols or etiquette of such collaborations. Finally, she cites useful resources from curricular material and study guides to planning resources such as ALA's programminglibrarian.org website.

Tribal library and archives services are sometimes customized for specific clientele, one group of which is represented by older tribal members, often referred to as elders. Roy describes how to work with tribal elders in appropriate ways and identifies services that elders might especially find useful, such as providing wellness/health information and technology training. She advises including elders in developing library policies and collaborating with other social services whose clients include tribal elders. The presence of elders in a library or archive is evidence that the setting is respectful of tribal culture and acknowledges that tribal knowledge lives beyond that which is documented in print and electronic forms.

Part III includes three chapters directed toward those interested in tribal archives. Shayne Del Cohen's "Where Are the Records?" is a brief account of the types of records that tribes might collect. Amy Ziegler extends this conversation to encompass legal issues related to collecting archives and the development of policies that guide collection building and access. Loriene Roy and Daniel Alonzo's lengthier contribution discusses the physical location of archives, their functions, and approaches to bring training and education to those interested in careers as tribal archivists. They close with a sampling of funding sources and snapshot descriptions of noteworthy archival collections.

The final part covers topics of interest to those working in tribal libraries and archives. Loriene Roy opens this collection of chapters with a brief overview of steps in tribal library strategic planning including preparing vision and mission statements while identifying service responsibilities, setting goals, and using output measures to assess whether objectives are met. Included are several examples of mission statements developed by tribal librarians.

Cheryl A. Metoyer, a visionary in the area of tribal information services, shares her twenty-one steps for success in working with tribal communities. She helps us pause to recognize that these behaviors involve common sense—expressing gratitude, being aware of local issues, collaborating, listening—but are often overlooked. Sandra Littletree echoes that advice in her chapter on advocacy and marketing. Advocating for tribal libraries might involve special skills if patrons associate libraries with institutions of learning and the residual trauma that many Native students experienced in boarding schools. Librarians need to demonstrate to their constituencies that the tribal library offers more than books and serves not only children but all community members. All libraries—tribal or not—will benefit when we tell the library's story at every available opportunity and recruit a cadre of supporters who also add their stories about the importance of the library.

Loriene Roy and Janice L. Kowemy (director of her tribal community library at the Pueblo of Laguna) emphasize the need for continual acquisition of professional skills and retooling through developing a written staff development plan. Kowemy's plan has served as a model for tribal librarians in her state, New Mexico. With the added responsibilities of advocacy and continuing and extending services, the need to manage one's own time is even more imperative. Loriene Roy adds a short chapter with tips on time management that any library worker, especially one working in a one-person library, might find useful.

In the introduction, Robert Sidney Martin discusses how the differences among tribal libraries, archives, and museums are blurring; most institutions share common concerns and common collections, and in tribal lands they may be the same institution located in the same facility. Anne McCudden describes how a tribal museum, the Ah-Tah-Thi-Ki Museum of the Seminole Tribe of Florida, was fully accredited by the American Association of Museums. This is the first tribal museum in the United States to receive this recognition. The process they followed involved the museum staff reviewing their staff organizational structure, challenging traditional thinking and processes, and positioning their staff more squarely in the court of strategic thinking.

Perhaps the most suitable chapter to conclude the book is that prepared by recent graduates of the School of Library and Information Studies at the University of Wisconsin–Madison Christina L. P. W. Johnson, Catherine H. Phan, and Omar Poler, who saw a gap in their curriculum. Together, with the strong support of their recently retired director, Louise Robbins, these students created their own graduate course, which included a strong service learning component of visits and work with tribal libraries in Wisconsin. They demonstrated that work may begin independently, but to be successful and find professional fulfillment working in tribal settings, there is a need for a supportive community of peers.

We still might not know the number of tribal libraries and archives or where they all are located. But what is certain is that this is a time of exciting development. Joseph D. Horse Capture, associate curator at the Minneapolis Institute of Arts, describes not only the future but the role of tribal centers in that future: "The future is changing for Native people. Many tribes are devoting resources to construct museums and cultural centers, which gives them an opportunity to preserve and foster their history and culture."[1] This book aims to share past efforts, current accomplishments and challenges, and a view of what may come next in tribal libraries and archives.

NOTE

1. Joseph D. Horse Capture, "Foreword: Our Obligation to Our Past," in *Caring for American Indian Objects: A Practical and Cultural Guide*, ed. Sherelyn Ogden (St. Paul: Minnesota Historical Society Press, 2004), v.

Introduction: The Role of Libraries in Lifelong Learning[1]

Robert Sidney Martin

I thank Alyce Sadongei, former assistant curator for Native American Relations at the Arizona State Museum, for her leadership and hard work in putting the initial conferences together. These were important events that had lasting consequences for tribal libraries, museums, and archives. Though many other individuals contributed substantially, I think it is fair to say that without Alyce's constant inspiration and direction, the gatherings would not have taken place. And I know for certain that I would not have been there, for it was Alyce who extended to me the kind invitation to come, and I thank her for that.

I want you to know something about me and my background. I am a native of Texas. But I have deep roots here in the Southwest. My grandfather was born in Ohio, but like many families one hundred years ago, his moved west. By the time he was eighteen, the family had relocated to Hereford, Texas, where they operated the local hotel. My grandfather earned his living for a while as a cook there, but he soon got wanderlust and moved out into the world. He was soon working for the copper mining companies in Arizona as a millwright and mining engineer. He met my grandmother here—she was a nurse in the company hospital—and my mother was born not far from here, in Globe, Arizona. My grandfather was the oldest of five, and all of his siblings ended up in the Four Corners area, in San Juan County, New Mexico, and Archuleta and Montezuma Counties, Colorado. The Southwest is where I feel most at home.

GladysAnn Wells, director and state librarian, Arizona State Library and Public Records, mentioned that I was the director of the Institute of Museum and Library Services (IMLS). In that office I spent a lot of time meeting with librarians around the country, and I was surprised to learn that a great many members of the library profession did not know what IMLS is. So one of my primary responsibilities was to tell people what IMLS is and what it does.

IMLS is an independent federal agency that fosters leadership, innovation, and a lifetime of learning. It is the primary source of federal grants for the nation's libraries and museums. IMLS was created in 1996 by the Museum and Library Services Act, which merged the federal programs for supporting the nation's museums and libraries, transferring the library programs out of the Department of Education and grafting them onto what had been the Institute of Museum Services. Funding for the IMLS in fiscal year 2002 was $224.5 million. That total was divided into three categories: $168 million for library programs funded under the Library Services and Technology Act, $27 million for museum programs funded under the Museum Services Act, and $29 million in directed appropriations.

IMLS grants to museums and libraries build institutional capacity, support core library and museum services, and encourage excellence. IMLS is a catalyst for leadership. It takes an active part in championing the role libraries and museums play in our society. As a federal agency, IMLS has a responsibility to place a national spotlight on the outstanding work that libraries and museums do and on the enormous contributions they make in building communities. IMLS does this in a number of ways: through conferences, through encouraging best practices, through our website, through our National Awards program, by offering training in outcome-based evaluation, and through our publications.

The majority of IMLS funding for libraries is distributed in formula grants to the library administrative agency in each state. These funds are used in a variety of important ways. You may not be aware of IMLS's role, yet the funding provided to your state library may be very important to the services that your library provides your community.

IMLS also provides substantial funding through competitive grant programs called National Leadership Grants. These grants foster innovation and creativity and develop best practices. Probably the best examples of such grants are those that supported the Five State American Indian Project. In two initial grants, IMLS provided $468,000 to fund this innovative collaboration to explore new ways to strengthen the tribal institutions documenting and preserving American native tribal culture.

Of course the library programs in IMLS include a special program designed to support libraries in Native American communities. With noncompetitive basic grants, as well as competitive grants, IMLS provides a range of support for tribal libraries. I certainly urge you to take full advantage of the opportunities that these grants provide. The program officer responsible for the Native American grant program is Alison Freese, and I strongly recommend that you get to know Alison. Her job is to provide assistance and support to qualified tribal entities in securing IMLS funding.

President George W. Bush's FY2003 budget request proposed an additional $10 million for IMLS to support recruitment and education for the next generation of librarians. Congress's appropriation of these funds in accordance with the president's request led to a new era in federal support for library education. IMLS worked with the library profession to gather input that shaped and structured this program.

Finally, I mention that the Museum and Library Services Act of 1996 was reauthorized in 2002. Broad-based coalitions in both the museum and library communities hammered out consensus language on which a reauthorization bill could be based.

For some years now I have been repeating a refrain (to the point that it has become almost like a mantra) that "the boundaries are blurring." Originally I used this phrase when I was director and librarian of the Texas State Library and Archives Commission to refer to the blurring boundaries between and among the various types of libraries and to help explain the imperative for multitype resource-sharing consortia. Subsequently it became apparent to me that the same observation applied to the boundaries between libraries and other types of cultural agencies, especially archives and museums. From my perspective as former director of IMLS, this seems so apparent that it is a truism, but I expect that there are many in the library, archives, and museum professional community for whom it is not so obvious.

Before we can discuss the blurring of the boundaries between and among these types of agencies, however, it is probably a good idea to look carefully at the nature of the agencies and examine the boundaries in question. Let us pause then to reflect on what libraries, museums, and archives are, and what the differences between them are.

There are many definitions of libraries, archives, and museums. For the purposes of the discussion today, I would like to restrict myself to simple, heuristic definitions that focus attention on the essential characteristics and purposes. Accordingly, let me offer the following definitions:

- A library is a collection of documents that have been purposefully selected and organized to support education, research, and/or recreation. These documents may be unique, but usually they are one of many copies.
- A museum is a collection of objects and artifacts that have been selected and organized for education, research, and/or recreation. Usually, but not always, these objects are unique items.
- An archive is a collection of documents that bear an organic relationship to an organization and contain evidence of transactions carried out by that organization. These documents may or may not be unique items.

Admittedly these are very simplistic definitions, but I believe they are accurate. And it is obvious from them that the essential common characteristic of all three types of institutions is that they are collection based. The most obvious difference is that they collect different types of materials—libraries collect documents of various kinds (books, journal, maps, etc.); archives collect documents of a specific kind (those containing a specific kind of evidence); and museums collect objects.

Yet we know from history that these distinctions have not always been evident. The earliest libraries known to history were in fact archives. What are often called "temple libraries" or "palace libraries" were in fact collections of texts (usually cuneiform tablets) that documented the official religious activities of the temple or the government transactions of the palace court. Later, collections of other kinds of texts were in fact called "museums," in that they were buildings dedicated to honoring the muses. The great library of Alexandria, for example, was called the Museon, a temple to the muses. In practice, there was little practical differentiation among library, museum, and archives until the early modern period, when the development of typographic printing resulted in a dramatic increase in the volume of texts available, and these were differentiated from the collection of objects, library from museum. The practice of separating official records from other kinds of documents also arose around the same time, developing from the rational bureaucratization of governments.

My point is simply that the distinctions we now accept as common, among library, museum, and archives, are a matter of convention. And that convention appears to be unraveling under the impact of networked digital information technology. In the past two decades, libraries, museums, and archives alike have begun to use digital information technology as a valuable tool to carry out the central work that each does. The most dramatic use of this technology, beginning almost forty years ago, has been to centralize some of the work that libraries do in organizing their collections, simultaneously dramatically enhancing access to information about those collections. The work of bibliographic utilities like OCLC transformed not only the process of cataloging library collections, but also access to bibliographic information.

More recently, digital technology has enabled the creation of large-scale digital surrogate collections, which has again dramatically enhanced knowledge about, and access to, library collections. This has had an especially noteworthy effect on access to unique materials held in rare book, manuscript, and special collections.

Archives have been slower to adopt the new technology, but in recent years, with the advent of the MARC AMC format for cataloging archival materials, bibliographic information about archival materials has been significantly increased. Recent development of the Encoded Archival Description format for archival finding aids has ushered in a new era of access to information about archival materials. And now archives have joined libraries in creating digital surrogates of some of the most important and/or popularly used records series.

Museums have been slower to adopt new technology, but they too have recently joined the procession. Museum information systems are now used to register and track collections. And museums also are now creating not only online exhibitions, but digital representations of their collections, including even three-dimensional objects.

With this increasing development of digital surrogate collections accessible through the World Wide Web, a transformation in the use of materials from library, archival, and museum collections has occurred. People who formerly used such materials on-site in the respective institutions are now frequently (if not exclusively) consulting them online. More important, large numbers of individuals who heretofore made little or no use of these materials—who perhaps were even unaware of their existence—are now frequent users of the digital collections. And these new users do not care, and may not even be aware of, whether the original materials are in a library, an archive, or a museum. The boundaries are indeed blurring.

If we step back from the discussion and take a different perspective, this development should not be surprising. David M. Levy has focused much of his career, first at Xerox Palo Alto Research Center (PARC) and now at the University of Washington iSchool, on trying to make sense of the document in the digital environment. In his book *Scrolling Forward: Making Sense of Documents in the Digital Age*, Levy notes that our traditional notion of a "document" is bound up with writing and paper.[2] But now in the digital environment we are using the word "document" to refer to all kinds of other things, like text files, audio files, image files, and even multimedia presentations and web pages. The old concept of a document no longer makes sense. Levy asserts that we need to define our notion of what a document is. He offers a simple but profound definition of documents: "They are, quite simply, talking things. They are bits of the material world—clay, stone, animal skin, plant fiber, sand—that we've imbued with the ability to speak."[3]

Other writers go further. Years ago, the French librarian and documentalist Suzanne Briet asserted that a document is "any physical or symbolic sign, preserved or recorded, intended to represent, to reconstruct, or to demonstrate a physical or conceptual phenomenon."[4] Even an antelope could be construed as a document, Briet asserted. An antelope in the wild was not a document; but once it had been captured and placed in a zoo, it could be a document because it then became evidence. This striking example seems especially relevant to me, because the universe of institutions served by IMLS includes those with living collections, like zoos, aquaria, and arboreta.

If one accepts the arguments of Briet and other documentalists, then the distinctions we have drawn between libraries and museums based on the kinds of things they collect seem even more artificial. They are all ultimately documents. And from the little knowledge I have of Native American culture, I suspect that this notion would not seem strange to many of you. Native American artifacts are implicitly "talking things."

I should add that Levy does not accept this argument. He asserts that there is an important distinction between artifacts and documents in that the latter have been intentionally created to speak, whereas though artifacts (and antelopes) may indeed have interesting stories to tell, they were created for another purpose. I personally find his argument on this point unpersuasive.

When we move from the physical to the digital world, it seems to me, the distinctions diminish even further. In the digital world, all of the objects that we can access via the web have been imbued with the ability to speak. Whether the object in question is a text file, an audio file, an image file, or a web page, all have the ability to speak. They all carry a message of some significance. In converting them from physical to digital form, we have expressly delegated to them the ability to speak, undercutting Levy's reservation.

This leads, in my view, to the inescapable conclusion that, in the digital environment, the distinctions among libraries, museums, and archives that we take for granted are in fact artificial. These distinctions are not conceptual; they are conventional. If our distinctions are based on the nature of the materials they collect, and if that nature is transubstantiated in the digital environment, then the distinctions cease to have meaning.

To be sure, there are real differences among libraries and museums and archives. But those differences, it seems to me, are matters of governance, funding, and structure; organizational culture; and professional practice, not matters of concept, function, and social role. In the digital world, the boundaries between the types of institution do not merely blur—they disappear.

In 1930, Paul Tillich made the trenchant observation that "the boundary is the best place for acquiring knowledge."[5] So what can we learn from our disappearing boundaries? What are the implications for the practice of the information professions? First and foremost, it seems to me that we must anticipate a convergence, not only of terminology and practice, but also of values. We must, in short, learn from each other. At IMLS, we have a strong conviction that the primary characteristic that museums and libraries have in common is that both are social agencies that support public education. Both are about the critical work of creating and supporting learners. Both institutions invite purposeful use and forge links to the world beyond their walls. They are both embedded in their communities and frequently acknowledged as trusted content and knowledge providers.

That is one reason why your effort to bring together the agencies in your communities for preserving your unique heritage and passing it to the next generation is so important. You are forging those partnerships that will make those institutions even more effective, more central to your communities in the future. As the boundaries among library, museum, and archives blur, as these important agencies work ever more closely with each other to realize their common missions, your communities will be strengthened and your heritage ensured. I encourage you to build on what you have begun. And I pledge the support of IMLS as you carry on this important work.

NOTES

1. Robert S. Martin, "Keynote Address" (Tribal Archives, Libraries and Museums: Preserving Our Language, Memory, and Lifeways National Conference, Mesa, Arizona, May 9, 2002).

2. David M. Levy, *Scrolling Forward: Making Sense of Documents in the Digital Age* (New York: Arcade Publishing, 2001).

3. Levy, *Scrolling Forward*, 23.

4. Suzanne Briet, *Qu'est-ce que la documentation* (Paris: EDIT, 1951), 7.

5. Paul Tillich, *On the Boundary: An Autobiographical Sketch* (New York: Scribner, 1966), 13.

I

THE TRIBAL COMMUNITY LIBRARY: CONTEXT AND CASES

1

A Place at the Table: California's Tribal Libraries Take Steps Toward Inclusion

Bonnie Biggs

The Five State American Indian Project (Five State Project), funded by a National Leadership Grant from the Institute of Museum and Library Services (IMLS) and envisioned by a stellar group of leaders in the field of tribal cultural preservation and development, has sewn the seeds of success and solidarity in states beyond the targeted five of Arizona, Colorado, Nevada, New Mexico, and Utah. The regional conference drew stakeholders from outside the margins of the partner institutions and clearly achieved the goals of creating a network, articulating issues, and developing a framework for interinstitutional collaborations.

Apart from these clearly defined goals, the conference provided both a safe and stimulating environment for trust and understanding to develop and for visions to find shape. Those of us who gathered in Phoenix in 2000 and Mesa in 2002 came away inspired and rededicated to the work we had undertaken in our home states.

I was invited to deliver a paper as part of a panel at the 2002 annual conference in Mesa, Arizona. The panel, "Tribal Library Development: Statewide Initiatives," was described in the program thus: a "panel of experienced library professionals share their expertise and research on tribal library development. Their work in areas of assessment and collaboration can serve as a model for the field." I shared the honor with esteemed colleagues Alison Freese, then from the New Mexico State Library, an institution that had set the national standard for tribal library support and inclusion, and David Ongley, who has done groundbreaking work to institutionalize cultural sensitivity in Alaskan public libraries.

This chapter outlines the steps taken in California that parallel strides made through the regional and national conferences "Tribal Archives, Libraries, and Museums: Preserving Our Language, Memory, and Lifeways."

PERSONAL STEPS

In California, there has not been a formal statewide assessment of tribal libraries but rather some small steps taken by an individual, backed by an institution that has equity and outreach at the very core of its mission: California State University–San Marcos (Cal State San Marcos) and the university's library.

In the mid-1980s, I became involved in tribal library development issues when six tribal libraries, established with funds from two Library Services and Construction Act (LSCA) grants under an Indian Library Services Project, were in danger of closing due to the end of the grant cycle. My initial efforts to assess the library landscape and the information needs of San Diego County's eighteen reservations were unsuccessful, partly because a new assistant professor was unable to devote adequate time to the exhaustive study needed and partly because of the enormous geographic challenges. What tribes needed to keep their libraries afloat was money and staff. I was overwhelmed by the need throughout our region. At the same time, Cal State San Marcos was building the newest public university in the United States in twenty-five years. During the infancy of the university, I had to reconsider how my energies could best be spent. I decided what I could do was to focus on a few tribes near Cal State San Marcos and began regular monthly visits, which turned into informal gratis consultancies that included grant-writing assistance, collection and technology assessment, and general library skills development. In 1995, I set up the Tribal Library Intern Project, which placed graduate library school interns in one of two nearby tribal libraries for a 135-hour practicum class.[1] Since 1995, interns have helped set up automated systems for cataloging, acquisitions, and circulation; cataloged gift materials; designed components for a new building; moved the library; developed a patron survey; helped to develop a collection development plan and policies; and weeded the collection.

The Tribal Library Intern Project set up a win-win state of affairs. The tribal library provided the opportunity to take advantage of the emerging expertise of the graduate students. The students were exposed to a sort of minicultural immersion and wrote about life-changing experiences in their journal assignments. Cal State San Marcos met its goals of outreach and community service and had the opportunity to collaborate with another California state university. This degree-granting sister, California State University (San Jose State University/California State University, Fullerton), was able to offer a meaningful intern/practicum experience for their students. For several years during the university's infancy, I was quite happy to work locally and felt that a difference was being made, but never lost sight of the greater need beyond the university's neighboring reservations.

Fast-forward to 1998. While serving as president of the American Indian Library Association, I learned about the work that the Bill & Melinda Gates Foundation did with computers in tribal libraries in New Mexico. When I contacted the California State Library asking about the state library's plan to ensure that the

Gates Foundation included California's tribal libraries in its upcoming visit to our state, I was asked if I had a list of the state's tribal libraries!

The implications of this seemingly innocent question had a profound impact on me and framed the course of my advocacy and research from that day on.

START IN YOUR OWN BACKYARD

The Envisioning Committee for the Five State Project took a layered approach, focusing the first phase of the project on "backyard" assessment. States approached assessment in a variety of ways, depending on the number of tribes and geographic constraints. Arizona's initial printed survey of twenty-one tribes led to site visits to five tribal communities. Colorado's two tribes made it easy for the state coordinator to simply convene a meeting of relevant tribal employees. All assessment projects were undertaken to determine the current status of tribal libraries, museums, and archives and take steps toward addressing issues identified as prime factors. A minimum of one statewide conference was held in each state, but some had a second statewide conference or hosted special thematic workshops. The general result was that the Five State Project helped state libraries connect with tribes and their libraries, museums, and archives. One state library official used the term "benign neglect" to describe her state's relationship with tribal communities.[2]

In California, a less-formalized and collaborative approach characterizes first steps taken. After the query from the California State Library, I began to set my sights on the fact that California was, after a fifteen-year planning process, ushering in a statewide, multitype library network. In 1999, the Library of California was established by law:

> The Legislature therefore finds and declares the following:
>
> 1. It is in the interest of the people of the state to ensure that all Californians have free and convenient access to all library resources and services that could provide essential information and enrich their lives.
>
> To respond fully and successfully to these information needs and to the diversity of California's population, libraries of all types and in all parts of the state must be enabled to interact, cooperate, and share resources.[3]

In a letter to members of California's library community, Dr. Kevin Starr, former state librarian of California, said:

> The Library of California concept takes each library in the state, large or small, public or private, and makes it an Everywhere in terms of information services. Doing this, it equalizes all Californians in terms of their access to library and information services. Doing this, the Library of California allows each Californian to make his or her decision as to where to live without fear of falling victim to a second-class citizenship

in terms of library and information resources. In a society which is rapidly dividing itself into sectors of affluence and need, such equalization is dramatically necessary if the ideal of equal citizenship is to be sustained. A state consisting of information haves and information have-nots, in other words, cannot in the long run remain socially and politically stable, much less competitive.[4]

As someone whose radar screen is ever on the lookout for the rights of tribal libraries, I took the letter of the law to mean that the Library of California would include tribal libraries. I began asking questions about the potential for inclusion of tribal libraries in the new statewide network at a variety of statewide and regional meetings, in panels and meetings at the California Library Association conference, and at the state library. The eventual result of my queries regarding tribal library inclusion was my application for and award of a small regional grant from the Library of California to conduct a Tribal Library Census and Needs Assessment of five Southern California counties. The Library of California divides the state into seven regions. The Tierra Del Sol (TDS) region comprises Imperial, Inyo, Riverside, San Bernardino, and San Diego counties, which includes thirty-four inhabited reservations.[5]

To provide a context for the importance of this census, beyond the state library's lack of awareness, 2000 census data tell us that California's Native population is significant and deserves greater attention. California now has more American Indians than any other state. The American Indian population has risen to 333,000, up from 242,000 in 1990. Oklahoma now takes second place in terms of Native population. California has over 110 federally recognized tribes, more than any other state in the country. And the county in which Cal State San Marcos is situated has eighteen reservations, more than any other county in the United States. Given these staggering statistics alone, not to mention the horrendous history in California of genocide and relocation of tens of thousands of people, I have always felt that the university had a moral obligation to find ways to reach these isolated and marginalized populations.

THE CENSUS AND NEEDS ASSESSMENT

The grant bought my time away from the university for ten months at 80-percent time and was considered a pilot project designed to serve as a model for assessing the state of tribal libraries throughout California.

There really was no template for how to go about doing this kind of research. I was unaware that almost simultaneously with the onset of this project, five other Western states were also conducting statewide assessments under the umbrella of the Five State Project, resulting in similar findings. The steps I took were pretty much self-created. I called upon my experience in visiting tribal libraries in California, Oklahoma, New Mexico, and Arizona to guide me and consulted with noted colleagues in the field. These included the former New Mexico state librarian, Ben Wakashige; Alison Freese, then tribal libraries coordinator for the New Mexico State Library; and Dr. Lotsee Patterson, then at the University of Oklahoma, the nation's preeminent scholar on matters related to the history of and contemporary issues faced by tribal libraries.

I took a considerable amount of time figuring out who I was going to visit and where they were located on the reservation. I started with the superintendent of the Bureau of Indian Affairs for the Southern Agency to confirm reservations within the state library's regional boundaries. After sending letters of introduction to all reservation tribal leaders, I began talking with folks over the phone to find out if there was a specific library contact I should meet with. I then developed a game plan for what I wanted to find out and what I would bring on the library visits.

I knew that I could not show up empty-handed. So, I began developing a packet of information to take to each reservation that included a variety of bibliographies and information on area institutions with significant holdings of American Indian materials; IMLS grant booklets; other grant ideas; and TRAILS (Training and Assistance for Indian Library Services), Patterson's guide for setting up and maintaining a tribal library.

I developed a survey that would help me record some basic facts, based on what the laws in California require for inclusion and consideration as a "public library." Data were tabulated using the "Eligibility Standards for Libraries" in the Library of California Act.[6]

The California State Library requires the following criteria for a library to be considered a "public library." A "public library" needs to have a building or designated room with an organized, accessible collection; a posted number of open hours; stated mission and objectives; at least one paid staff member with a master's degree in library or information science or a California library media teacher credential; and a steady funding base.[7]

CENSUS RESULTS AND FINDINGS

The results of this census are staggering, yet for those who have worked in the field of tribal library development, not surprising. As I read the assessment reports of the five states, I realized that California is not unlike the states involved in the Five State Project. The following summary notes, addressing the California State Library eligibility criteria, are excerpted from the final report to the state library:[8]

- Of the thirty-four reservations that were visited, eighteen, or 53 percent, have a library facility.
- Fourteen, or 77 percent, of these library facilities have established open hours.

- Seventeen, or 94 percent, of the libraries have an organized and accessible collection.
- Only seven, or 38 percent, of the libraries have on-site, paid staff for library services.
- None, or 0 percent, of the paid library staff has a master's degree in library or information science—or a California library media teacher credential.
- Of the seven paid library staff, one person has an RN and one a BA in computer science, one is a New York State credentialed reading teacher, and one has six years of continuing experience in the same library while also pursuing a library technology certificate.
- Only five, or 15 percent, of the reservations have an established funding base for library services. Of the libraries, only three, or 8 percent, receive the majority of their funding from the tribe. Others, like most tribal libraries, are grant-dependent.

Library Facilities

There are fewer than a handful of fully operating library facilities in the TDS region. The term *library facility* is loosely defined here. It is not uncommon to find that tribal libraries are often located in a room without an education center, within the tribal hall or recreation/community hall. Most reservation children are bussed to school, precluding them from using their school library after school. The tribal library is often the only place to go for homework assistance. Some tribes have education centers that house small libraries developed to serve on-reservation schools. More often than not, education staff will serve intermittently as "library staff" for the kids using library materials. There are only two stand-alone library buildings that are not school libraries in the TDS region. The Pala and Morongo tribal libraries, while serving as the educational hub for the reservation, are fully operating community libraries. As the statistics show, there are eighteen library facilities, but only seven paid library staff. This means that though a number of tribes have a library, there is no one specifically designated to assist patrons in the use of the collection.

Typically, the idea of building a tribal library becomes the focus of a given tribal council in a given year, and a plan to seek external funding is developed. Funding may or may not be awarded during the tenure of the same council members who envisioned the library. A number of libraries in the TDS region were built in the mid- to late 1980s with Department of Education or Housing and Urban Development (HUD) block grants, back when LSCA funding allowed for "construction." Seven libraries in San Diego County were established under the Indian Library Services Project (ILSP), administered by the San Diego County Library Outreach Division. Over a period of years, many of the tribes applied for and received IMLS Basic Grant funds, usually between $3,500 and $4,500 annually. The Basic Grant has typically been used to develop or enhance collections;

purchase equipment, furniture, and shelving; and, in some cases, provide minimal staff coverage for the library for five to ten hours per week.

A number of libraries not listed as having facilities consider their collection of books to be their library. One-bookcase libraries are somewhat typical among the smaller tribes. Jamul, for instance, has a single bookcase with a collection of books and videos that are relatively current and relevant to tribal governance or used for self-education and entertainment.

Established Open Hours

Only fourteen of the eighteen library facilities have posted hours of operation. Each of the seven libraries that have paid library staff has designated open hours. Open hours in the other seven library facilities correlate with times that the school or education centers are open.

Organized and Accessible Collections

Nearly all of the library facilities have an organized collection. Typically, cataloging has been done using appropriate, broad Dewey subject area classification. Most tribal libraries receive more than their share of gift books, the majority of which are outdated and not relevant to the information needs of the community. Most tribal libraries have shelves of books that are uncataloged and yet are still utilized by the patrons. Only one library has a card catalog (Morongo), and two have electronic catalogs (Pala and Soboba). Virtually every tribal library visited has a collection of materials on American Indians, and some house primary source materials on tribal history. Appropriate materials on California's Native culture and history are limited. The packets taken to the tribes included a number of bibliographies and webographies on Native materials as well as lists of holdings at nearby institutions with significant collections on Native culture. Children's books and current reference materials were the second area of collection development concentration. Library staff noted the increasing demand for self-help, self-education, health, law, and auto repair books. Only one library (Pala) had conducted a formal survey to assess patron information needs.

On-site, Paid Staff for Library Services

The lack of paid, trained library staff is the most formidable challenge facing the TDS region's tribal libraries. Tribal library staff who are paid are managing their libraries based on gut instinct and good luck. The paid library staff in the TDS region are an innately talented group of individuals. Each has found a way to informally assess community information needs, advocate for funding through the tribe or external sources, arrange and classify materials, and develop programs targeted at the information and education needs of constituents. They are a remarkable group of people who clearly know what they do not know and want to become better library paraprofessionals. Library staff enthusiastically embraced the TRAILS manual in their packets. The need for basic library skills training in these remote, underserved populations is crucial.

As mentioned previously, many of the libraries are located in schools or education centers, yet they still serve the broader population. Education directors and/ or their staff often serve as the library staff when available. This serendipitous service model is a passive one at best and diminishes patron expectations to the point of their not seeking use of the community library. Still, reservation education staff are certainly better than no staff at all. Many reservation libraries remain unstaffed. Access to materials becomes a crapshoot. The nearest public library is usually too far away for easy access. Information needs are shelved. Reservation residents are marginalized once again.

Staff Credentials

Not one person working in a tribal library in the TDS region had an MLS, nor did anyone hold a California Library Media Teacher Credential. Morongo's former library manager was a New York State credentialed reading teacher, and Viejas's library manager has a registered nursing (RN) degree. At Soboba, DQ University's "electronic library" was overseen by a staff person with a BA in computer science. The closest anyone comes to meeting the Library of California substitute criteria for "demonstrated professional experience" is the library manager at Pala, who has six years of continuing experience managing the library. She planned to complete her coursework in Palomar College's Library Technology Certificate Program. In many cases, tribal library staff are tribally enrolled members who are given the job of overseeing the library, with no experience in libraries whatsoever. Training is a crucial need.

Established Funding Base

Ongoing funding for tribal libraries is a national problem that impacts TDS region tribal libraries equally. Most tribes did not begin establishing their libraries until the mid-1970s, and in California many did not start developing libraries until the 1980s. The transition from an oral to a print repository of knowledge came late for indigenous people. The 1984 amendment to the LSCA to include Title IV, "Library Services for Indian Tribes and Hawaiian Natives Program," opened the door for tribes to build, furnish, staff, and equip libraries.

The Indian Self-Determination and Educational Assistance Act of 1975 precipitated the need for tribes to establish an information backbone for self-governance, but also forced the need for developing sovereign social service agencies. Once established, library advocates on reservations found themselves competing with survival services such as fire and police protection for resources to keep libraries open and staffed. Since libraries have not been a part of reservation life for much longer than thirty years, tribal library advocates face an ongoing challenge in convincing tribal members of their importance. While staggering rates of illiteracy increase the need for libraries, these communities are still developing a value system that champions libraries in the face of great fiscal odds.

Many of the tribes in the TDS region are grant-dependent. Some have small agricultural concerns that yield modest income for basic tribal operations. Although several of the reservations have casinos, only a handful are established and successful. The assumption cannot be made that a successful gaming tribe provides unlimited support for the reservation library. Some gaming tribes do not have libraries but do have a museum. Others do not financially support their libraries because of access disputes between tribal council and education directors. Given these competing demands on tribal funds and philosophical differences, it is not surprising that only 15 percent of the reservations have an established funding base for a library.

CONCLUSIONS

This project was designed and funded to

- find tribal libraries in the TDS region of the Library of California,
- determine their status,
- assess their needs, and
- recommend a plan for their participation in the Library of California.

The thirty-four reservations in the TDS region either have a library, are planning to build one, or hope to have one. A value system is emerging that says libraries are fundamentally important to the success and well-being of the tribe.

Every tribal library visited:

- Is open to and actively serves the general public, which is typical nationwide. The on-reservation population in the TDS region is over 41,000 residents.
- Serves as the educational hub for the "nation," another national trend. Tribal libraries typically provide everything from Head Start story hours, to after-school tutoring programs, to GED preparation classes, to adult literacy tutoring, to computer training for seniors, to community college courses.
- Serves as a central social gathering place for children and adults living on the reservation.
- Has or is trying to acquire collections of materials that are specifically relevant to its tribe's history, culture, or sovereign governance.
- Has or plans to develop audio and video recorded oral histories.

- Has staff or users who express a deep concern for the loss of language within their own tribe, since often fewer than a dozen fluent speakers are still alive.
- Has staff or users who recognize that their library could/should play a key role in the preservation, revival, and teaching of the indigenous language.
- Needs more and newer materials.
- Has computers in various stages of currency and usability.
- Has staff who express a desire to acquire training in basic library skills.
- Has staff who express the need for a consistent, established funding base so that services and collections can continue.

Recommendations sent to the California State Library in June 2001 follow.

Change the Law

The eligibility standards outlined in the Library of California Act set the bar out of reach for almost all of the region's tribal libraries. The criterion that precludes participation more than any other is the one that defines the staff credentials requirement. The project director visited more than fifty tribal libraries and has only met one tribal librarian, in Miami, Oklahoma, who had an MLS. If the Library of California aims to become the inclusive network, as defined so eloquently by the state librarian, this standard will need to loosen a bit. The Act states that "the eligibility determination will be made by the regional library network."[9] A statewide amendment would give the networks more flexibility.

The project director suggests that the Act could be amended to create a category, similar to that of the New Mexico State Library, that recognizes "developing public libraries" in the state that are open for fewer hours and offer a basic level of library services.[10] Tribal libraries in New Mexico are eligible for small grants that encourage further development of their small libraries. Two of the Pueblo libraries at Zuni and Laguna, set up in the mid-1970s by Patterson, have achieved public library status. It is important to note that the initial library managers at Zuni and Laguna were trained in an on-site training program that Patterson developed during the establishment of tribal libraries in New Mexico.

Few tribes have an established funding base for library services. LSTA grants targeted at tribal libraries are either very small (Basic Grants average $4,500) or highly competitive (Enhancement Grants range from $50,000 to $150,000). Each year approximately fifty U.S. tribes apply for Enhancement Grants, and only around twelve are awarded. Often this means that a library established and staffed under an Enhancement Grant closes in a subsequent year due to lack of funding. Tribal libraries continue to feel and operate as though they are orphaned children. They get minimal nourishment from federal funds but do not find parents at the federal level. Federal officials think tribal libraries should be the "property or problem" of the states, yet only a few state libraries enjoy functional relationships with the libraries of their indigenous neighbors.

Training

Training is the key piece in supporting the continuation of library services on California's American Indian reservations. A trained, committed library staff will advocate for funding by the tribe, apply for funding from external agencies, develop collections and services, and build a community of library users who will share in advocacy within tribal governance and beyond. The Library of California provided basic library skills training to California's small, rural libraries through its rural initiative. The promise of inclusion in a future statewide initiative provides the greatest hope for California's tribal libraries to grow and succeed in serving the unique information needs of their isolated and often marginalized populations.

Conduct Census and Needs Assessment for All of California

Although this census and needs assessment of the TDS region paints a picture that reflects the nation's tribal library landscape, the remaining regional library networks in the Library of California should be encouraged to conduct similar projects to find and assess their tribal libraries. The process used in this project provides a general template for conducting business in an appropriate manner in Indian country. The greatest risk is in burning bridges before they are built. It is too easy to alienate and offend this historically oppressed and misrepresented group of people.

A GATHERING OF VOICES

The final official "act" of the Tribal Library Census and Needs Assessment project was to host a meeting of the tribal librarians in the TDS region. On 1 June 2001, thirteen reservation representatives came to "A Gathering of Voices" at Cal State San Marcos for the purpose of talking about issues common to tribal libraries and to begin to develop a unified voice. This historic event marked the first formal gathering of tribal library staff in this region of California. Participants were enthusiastic about meeting one another and shared information about the current state of their libraries or plans for developing a library. Discussion centered around how the group members could empower and assist one another through information sharing. The group expressed a desperate need for training in basic library skills for tribal library staff. The group came to the consensus that affiliating with the California Library Association was one way to get together to seek professional development opportunities and to find a voice at the state level. Cal State San Marcos faculty participated in a showcase that provided examples of how technology can be used to preserve and teach language and cultural traditions as well as store important images of material culture.

A powerful group of people organized that day as a formal group, calling themselves the Tierra Del Sol Tribal Libraries Group (TDSTL). Cal State San Marcos set up and maintains a TDSTL listserv. Subsequent meetings have taken place at the Pala Tribal Library, the San Pasqual Reservation Education Center, and the Agua Caliente Cultural Museum. A second "Gathering of Voices" was hosted by Cal State San Marcos in the summer of 2002. Workshops included a grant-seeking presentation by the university's grant specialist and a multimedia demonstration on uses relevant to cultural preservation projects. The group elected officers and began strategizing on how best to leverage resources for the good of the whole and how to lobby Sacramento for inclusion in future consortial endeavors.

POST-CENSUS AND NEEDS ASSESSMENT

Sadly, although the Tribal Library Census and Needs Assessment Final Report was given a warm and welcoming reception at the state library, California's budget took an unprecedented nose-dive shortly after the report was submitted. Follow-up signals from the former state librarian indicated that tribal libraries were clearly on his radar screen. Although Starr expressed an interest in and commitment to "doing something" with California's tribal libraries the year following the report, the Library of California's budget was cut by a devastating 75 percent, disabling its very core services and quashing any hopes of developing training programs for the tribes or devoting staff time to any tribal library development initiatives. State library staff quickly focused attention elsewhere due to extreme fiscal exigencies.

The momentum in California was underway and unstoppable. Considerable energy was generated at the two "Gathering of Voices" conferences, hosted at Cal State San Marcos. In retrospect, we discovered that what we were doing in California, on a smaller, more parochial level, bore a striking resemblance to the goals and objectives of the regional and national conferences hosted by the IMLS Five State American Indian Project. A sense of connection had been established by the attendees who, not unlike the Five State Project attendees, repeatedly shared moving testimonials about a new sense of belonging and courage to continue the fight for the development of tribal libraries. Tribal librarians had discovered that they were not alone and that strength could truly be found in numbers. We agreed to pursue our goals even in the absence of state library support or involvement, recognizing that the steps would be small in the beginning.

POINTS OF LIGHT IN CALIFORNIA

California's Native people suffered some of the worst documented annihilation in U.S. history, yet they persevere with grace and dignity. The libraries that do exist on their sovereign lands reflect an astonishing will to survive and rise above the past and its inequities. Several "points of light" provide some additional hope.

California State Library

Members of the California State Library's Research Bureau became involved and conducted interviews with tribal library staff in Northern California and met with tribal staff in Central and Southern California in the summer of 2003. They started a series of meetings with statewide Native American nongovernmental organizations such as the InterTribal Council of California, Northern California Indian Development Council, Seventh Generation Fund, and California Indian Legal Services to foster partnerships and support. Finally, they offered ad hoc training sessions when possible and researched alternative sources of funding for tribal library development.[11] A commitment emerged out of the ashes of the California state budget disaster that was truly heartening.

Tribal Libraries Round Table

Perhaps the best example of a formally organized group of tribal librarians can be found in the Native American Libraries Special Interest Group (NALSIG), formed under the aegis of the New Mexico Library Association nearly twenty-five years ago. Following their seminal work of setting up libraries and training library staff in the Pueblos of New Mexico in the mid-1970s, Wakashige and Patterson urged the librarians to organize and affiliate with the state's professional institution.[12] They recognized the importance of establishing a formal vehicle for the voices of tribal librarians. Drawing on inspiration from the remarkable strides NALSIG has taken in the last three decades, plans were underway to organize the first Tribal Libraries Round Table under the aegis of the California Library Association at the annual conference in November 2003. A call for action went out in an article in *News from Native California*, entitled "California Tribal Librarians Unite," urging California's tribal librarians to come together and take historic action at the annual conference.[13] At each "Gathering of Voices" conference and subsequent reservation library meetings, California Library Association first-time member applications were distributed to tribal librarians who, upon discovering that round tables exist for African American, Latino, Asian, and gay and lesbian librarians, decided it was time for them to have a voice! In 2009, the California Library Association was reorganized in a structure that permitted a few core committees and interest groups. The Native Libraries Round Table, along with three other round tables or sections, was not continued as an interest group.[14]

Tribal Digital Village

The University of California at San Diego received a $5 million grant to create a distributed tribal digital community to mirror and amplify the community and kinship networks that have historically sustained tribal communities in the San Diego region. Partnering with the Southern California Tribal Chairman's

Association, the project built a high-speed broadband connection between each of the reservations in San Diego County and to the Internet. The grant provided for connectivity, hardware, software, and training. On behalf of local tribal librarians, I served on the steering committee of this three-year project and continually suggested that this technology infrastructure provide the needed connectivity for a variety of library-specific needs, including platforms for automated systems, networking of libraries, and web-based training and videoconferencing formats. The technology infrastructure also gives the tribes the ability to develop multimedia products and projects that can serve to preserve, revive, and teach language to reservation children, who are already savvy in computer usage.

Web-Based Training

In late 2002, I was asked to meet with the library directors from University of California at San Diego and Palomar Community College, along with executive staff from the Tribal Digital Village, to discuss the role the Tribal Digital Village might play in assisting local tribal libraries and how the four institutions could work together on targeted projects. The desperate need for training quickly became the focus of our attention. Palomar Community College has one of the best paraprofessional library technology certificate programs in the state and was involved in transferring curriculum modules into web-based format. Members of the group researched funding sources to complete the format transfer so that this excellent curriculum could be exported to tribal librarians and possibly be underwritten by the grant.

ROOM AT THE TABLE?

California's tribal libraries are nudging their way to a place at the table. They seek recognition by and inclusion in initiatives undertaken by the California State Library and plan to create a context for conducting formal business under the umbrella of the California Library Association. Thanks to inspiration drawn from tribal library advocates who have fought the fight for decades and the ingenious design of the Five State Project, California's tribal libraries will prevail.

> Let us now put our heads together and see what kind of life we can make for our children.
>
> —Tatanka Iyotanka (Sitting Bull)[15]

NOTES

1. Bonnie Biggs, "The Tribal Library Project: Interns, American Indians, and Library Services: A Look at the Challenges," *College & Research Libraries News* 59, no. 4 (April 1998): 259–62.

2. Jane Kolbe, interview by Bonnie Biggs, 8 May 2002, Mesa, Ariz.

3. Library of California Act, State of California, Education Code Part II, Libraries, Chapter 4.6, sec. 18800-18802, http://law.justia.com/california/codes/edc/18800-18802 .html (accessed 17 July 2010).

4. California Library Networking Task Force, California State Library, *The Library of California—Framework* (Sacramento: California State Library, Library Development Services Bureau, 1996).

5. Bonnie Biggs and Garrett Collins, "Library of California Tierra Del Sol Tribal Library Census and Needs Assessment," http://www.csusm.edu/bbiggs/loc/ (accessed 26 August 2002).

6. Library of California Act, State of California, Education Code, Title I, Division I, Part II, Libraries, Chapter 4.5, sec. 18830, http://www.library.ca.gov/publications/librlaw_2010.pdf (accessed 17 July 2010).

7. Library of California Act, sec. 18830.

8. Bonnie Biggs, *Final Report: Library of California Tierra Del Sol Tribal Library Census and Needs Assessment* (San Marcos, CA: California State University San Marcos, 2002).

9. Library of California Act, sec. 18830.

10. "State Grants in Aid to Public Libraries," New Mexico Administrative Code Title 4, Chapter 5, Part 2, http://www.nmcpr.state.nm.us/nmac/cgibin/hse/homepagesearchengine.exe?url=http://www.nmcpr.state.nm.us/nmac/parts/title04/04.005.0002.htm;geturl;terms=developing+library (accessed 17 July 2010).

11. Kimberly Johnston-Dodds, telephone interview by Bonnie Biggs, 30 June 2003.

12. Lotsee Patterson, interview by Bonnie Biggs, 30 March 2000, Charlotte, N.C.

13. Bonnie Biggs, "California Tribal Librarians Unite," *News from Native California* (Spring 2003): 8–9.

14. California Library Association, "Interest Groups," http://www.cla-net.org/aboutcla/sectionstables.php (accessed 17 July 2010).

15. Howard J. Langer, "SITTING BULL (1834–1890) Hunkpapa Leikot, South Dakota," in *American Indian Quotations* (Westport, Conn.: Greenwood Press, 1996), The American Indian Experience http://aie.greenwood.com//doc.aspx?fileID=GR9121&chapterID=GR9121-475&path=books/greenwood/ (accessed 17 July 2010).

2

Alaska Native Village Libraries: Picking Up the Pieces

David Ongley

The struggle to build and maintain village libraries in Alaska is being fought on two fronts: getting libraries established in the villages and convincing the state legislature of the need to support them. Work is progressing on the local and statewide levels.

LOCALLY

The state of libraries in the villages of Alaska had fallen upon hard times in the 1990s. During the big-oil, big-money boom days of the 1980s, efforts were made by the Alaska State Library to bring library services to the remote riverine and coastal Athabaskan, Yupik, and Iñupiat villages as well as those Haida and Tlinget villages of the southeast panhandle and Aleut villages of the Aleutian Island chain. Some of this effort was chronicled in Gordon Hills's book *Native Libraries: Cross-Cultural Conditions in the Circumpolar Countries.*[1] By 1990, little remained of this effort, and many of the people who had initiated it became discouraged and unwilling to continue funding what they perceived as failures.

An attempt was made to provide statewide library services by mail, with centers in Anchorage, Fairbanks, and Juneau. Larger regional centers in such places as Bethel, Nome, Kotzebue, Valdez, and Barrow continued to serve their communities and to prosper in providing standard library services.

With a few scattered and singular exceptions, only the North Slope Borough in the far north of the state maintained a system whereby each of its eight villages had public library services. Barrow, a town of over 4,000 people, a majority of whom are Iñupiat Eskimo, is the center of municipal administration. The seven outlying villages of the region, with populations of anywhere from 200 to 800 people, are almost entirely Iñupiat. Due to the enormous wealth generated by property taxes assessed on the oil industry at Prudhoe Bay, the people of the North Slope are able to insist upon control of their own educational systems. As part of that effort, a community college, Ilisagvik College, was founded in the late 1980s.

A combination public and college library was established in Barrow through efforts led by Evelyn Tuzroyluk Higbee (Tuzzy, to her friends) of Pt. Hope. It was called a "consortium" library because it was to be managed by Ilisagvik College, funded by the North Slope Borough, and housed by the city of Barrow. The library was named after Ms. Higbee after her untimely death. In 1989 Gaylin Fuller, a professional librarian, was hired.

Fuller developed a funding strategy that allowed for the establishment of combination school/community libraries in the seven smaller villages. This strategy, still employed today, was supported through Alaska State Library grants to public libraries, federal Basic Grants to Native entities, and a local grant match. The entire grant-writing and reporting effort was centralized in Barrow to ensure program continuity and service uniformity. This system provides a model program for regional library operation throughout Alaska. Fuller moved to a library position in another city, and I was hired to replace her in the summer of 1996.

Every October, the directors of the fifteen largest public libraries in the state meet. The Alaska State Library hosts this directors' leadership institute (DirLead). During the early annual meetings, I learned that most of the other libraries had no programming for Native library users. I was able to visit several smaller "bush" libraries that are in Native communities or have Native villages nearby.[2] This revealed a similar situation. Few Natives work in any Alaskan libraries and, for the most part, the collections have nothing but standard Western/American books and periodicals. No effort is made by these libraries to encourage Native participation or use. Even when publications can be acquired about local Native villages or in their languages, they are seldom purchased. It is not something that most librarians even think about. For many of them, it is enough that the doors to their libraries are open and anyone who cares to can walk in.

Determined to do something about the situation in Alaska, and with the support of the director of the state library and several other key people who immediately perceived the value of what was being proposed, DirLead met in October 2000, and the issue of Alaska Native libraries was the main agenda item. This was a major departure from the type of workshops that DirLead had held in the past.

We heard first from Father Michael Oleksa, a Russian Orthodox priest known for eloquently lecturing on cross-cultural communications. Dr. Lotsee Patterson, who had been instrumental in the development of Native libraries in New Mexico, a state that actively supports its Native libraries and librarians, addressed and worked with the group. Patterson facilitated a series of directed discussions on the more specific topic of Native libraries and the information needs of Natives.

In a presentation entitled "Building a Shared Future in a Learning Organization: Providing Services to Alaska Natives," Patterson brought to bear her extensive experience and knowledge of the subject.

It was decided to create culturally responsive guidelines for Alaska public libraries. The Alaska Native Knowledge Network, which has been in existence since 1995, had featured culturally responsive guidelines for teachers, communities, and schools.[3] It seemed reasonable to base similar guidelines for libraries on what they had already developed.

Small work groups were formed to consider four aspects of libraries for which guidelines could be developed: (1) the environments in which services are delivered, (2) the programs and services offered, (3) the collections that are developed, and (4) the staff employed in the library.

Reassembling, the smaller groups brought proposed wording back. Revisions by the larger group were considerable. Patterson added a draft of the preface to the group's work. The library directors were given copies of the document to share with their libraries, communities, and Native educational organizations. Feedback was sporadic and continued to trickle in through the spring of 2001. Most changes that were proposed were minor or technical. The substantive changes that came in were forwarded to the entire group though its listserv. Almost every suggestion that came in improved the draft and was easily incorporated into the wording. By June, the document was completed to almost everyone's satisfaction. The format and style of the guidelines are similar to the other guidelines that appear on the Alaska Native Knowledge Network.

The first section, "Library Environment," deals with the physical surroundings, buildings, and décor of libraries. I have heard it said in several villages that people do not always feel comfortable entering the library because it feels too much like the boarding schools many Alaska Natives were forced to attend. Librarians are encouraged to take their libraries outside of their own walls to the places where Natives are comfortable. Although outreach is a basic precept of librarianship in the United States, it rarely seems to extend to Native Americans. Librarians are encouraged to seek out the advice of their Native communities when developing displays and decorating their public spaces.

The second section deals with services and programs designed to meet the needs of Alaska Natives. The planning and execution of programs and services is based on open and honest communication, cooperation, and respect for local Native community organizations. Frequently, librarians take the attitude that they know how to do their jobs and don't need to continually strive to get fresh input from their communities.

The third section, on collections, also emphasizes communication. It requires doing more than ordering books from publishers' catalogs. Many of the things that are requested from the villages I serve are out of print. It takes an extra effort to find and purchase these items. It may even be necessary to become involved with smaller publishing efforts or used book services to see that these materials are on the shelves. Networking with other like-minded librarians in professional organizations like the American Indian Library Association is one good way to accomplish this.

The final section, "Library Staff," is the crucial section for all libraries. A substantial leap can be made in achieving progress toward creating an environment that encourages Native use, providing services and programs that meet the needs of all local inhabitants, and developing collections that Natives wish to use, if Natives are employed in the operation and management of the libraries in their communities.

The guidelines were endorsed by the Alaska State Board of Education in September 2001 and are available on the Internet at http://www.akla.org/culturally-responsive.html.[4]

STATEWIDE

Two outstanding models for statewide organization exist in the United States today for Native libraries and librarians in New Mexico and Hawaii. Both have strengths and weaknesses. Hawaii has a separate organization, Alu Like, that receives a direct grant from the Institute of Museum and Library Services (IMLS) each year. This is essentially a parallel organization to the Hawaii State Library specifically for Native Hawaiian library services. They have done some extraordinary work and advanced librarianship throughout the islands. In New Mexico, the state library has acknowledged that libraries that may not meet the legal definition of a public library are developing and deserve support in order to continue. These libraries have created a separate unit, the Native American Libraries Special Interest Group (NALSIG), within the structure provided by the New Mexico Library Association.

One of the reasons the earlier attempt to develop libraries in Alaskan villages was less than successful may have been because it took a top-down rather than a grassroots approach. Although the "Culturally Responsive Guidelines" provide direction for individual libraries, particularly those run by librarians well versed in the operation of libraries from a Western perspective, the impetus for development and sustainability needs to come from within each village.

A small group of concerned librarians in Alaska decided to pursue a model based on the success of the libraries in New Mexico in order to create a receptive atmosphere within which these libraries could gravitate. At the 2002 Alaska Library Association Annual Conference in Anchorage in March, I convened the first meeting of the Alaska Native Special Interest Group (ANSIG). Twenty-five people attended that meeting, all of the attendees but one being white. However, of those in attendance, most were from small villages with stable libraries. A fair representation of Alaska State Library employees was also in attendance. Issues were discussed, concerns expressed, and projects and plans shared.[5]

The situation in Alaska remains far from ideal. Distances are great, and travel is only becoming more expensive. As in most other parts of the United States, rural libraries in Alaska face a bleak future. Convincing a legislature dominated by representatives from the major urban areas of the importance of rural libraries is an uphill battle. It will probably remain a losing battle without overwhelming support from the villages. With this support, it is certain that the importance of libraries will eventually prevail, and they will emerge as a force for cultural, linguistic, historic, and economic independence in the future.

NOTES

1. Gordon H. Hills, *Native Libraries: Cross-Cultural Conditions in the Circumpolar Countries* (Lanham, Md.: Scarecrow Press, 1997).

2. "Bush," in typical Alaskan parlance, is anywhere in the state except Anchorage, Fairbanks, or Juneau. To purists, it is anywhere off the state road system.

3. Alaska Native Knowledge Network, http://www.ankn.uaf.edu/ (accessed 7 September 2010).

4. "Culturally Responsive Guidelines for Alaska Public Libraries," 2001, http://www.akla.org/culturally-responsive.html (accessed 7 September 2010).

5. The following year, when the conference met in Juneau, the ANSIG, again well attended, signed a petition to the organization's executive board requesting round table status. I presented the petition and a resolution to the board at its next meeting. It was passed unanimously. Now known as the Alaska Native Issues Round Table, this status change permits fund-raising and grant application that allows the group a wider range of actions.

3

Community Collaborations
with the Tribal Library

Karen Alexander

The 2002 National Conference was a historic gathering at which it was an honor to be asked to tell the Miami story. Every tribe has its own story to tell. I am in awe of all that has been accomplished, and I am encouraged by these examples. Through attending the conference, my life was enriched and my worldview was enlarged. Our realities may be different, but our shared responsibilities brought us together. Speaking about tribal libraries with supportive audiences makes me feel like I am "preaching to the choir," as we say back in Oklahoma.

If you ever watched the *West Wing* television show, you may remember an episode in which President Bartlett, despite having muscular dystrophy, was deciding about running for reelection and asked the opinion of his staff. Each staff member stood up, one at a time, and pledged his or her support of the president by saying, "I serve at the pleasure of the president of the United States." As a nontribal member, I am ever mindful that I serve at the pleasure of the Myaamia people. Together with two other full-time staff members, all with our master's degrees in library science, we constantly strive to make whatever changes are necessary to meet the needs of the community.

Many presenters at the 2002 conference began by speaking traditionally in their native tongues, introducing themselves by telling you who they are by name, tribe, clan, or genealogy. I am unable to do that, although I may have some Cherokee ancestry if family legend is true. Like many Oklahomans, it is unproven. (But please, let me go down on record as saying that I am one Oklahoman whose grandmother was not a Cherokee princess. That I know for sure!) Because my native ancestry was denied to me, I cannot remember a time that I did not want to know if there was any truth to what my mother had told me. That created a hunger to know who I am, a hunger that cannot be filled.

Perhaps it is this feeling that connects me so strongly to the Miami people, because they have lost so much of their traditions, music, dance, language, and culture. This is very understandable in light of their history. The ancestral home of the Miami is in the Indiana/Ohio/Illinois area, the old Northwest. There, Chief Little Turtle led the Miami Confederacy, defeating the U.S. Army two times, and that really made the Anglo world angry. It is the same story that is so familiar to many of broken treaties, more battles, or "same song, second verse," as the old saying goes. The Miami, except for a selected few, were removed to Kansas around 1846 and then removed again by 1880 from Kansas to Indian Territory, which is now known as Oklahoma. Those allowed to stay in Indiana and later in Kansas gave up their federal recognition as Miami people. There were only sixty-nine names on the list of those removed to Indian Territory. By an act of Congress, these were given the right to join with the Peoria Tribe, which the Miami proper did not do, although three former bands of Miami did. Once again, the history books and some maps are wrong.

Maybe it is because of their cultural void and my own sense of cultural loss, or the fact that when I was hired as director for the Miami Tribal Library & Archives in 1989 on a one-year grant, we were given no guarantees beyond one year. Thus, from day one we operated under a sense of urgency. The mandate for program survival was clear: make the library program indispensable to the tribe. I do not know what that says to you, but to me it means you better start acting like a duck that is calm and unruffled on the top side of the water but paddling like the dickens underneath! I distinctly remember thinking that I had to work hard so that the tribe members would rather cut off their right arms than close their library doors.

For most of our existence as a library since 1987, we have been almost 100 percent grant supported. Although I do not recommend that kind of life, one advantage is that you stay very close to the money, as I call it, always pushing accountability and results, never content to stay the same. We have tried to make service our middle name, always going above and beyond what is expected. We look for innovative ways to take services beyond the library walls. But as you know, services are much more than the statistics of numbers served. Success is built in, as new programs are built on the individual professional strengths of our staff, and they must meet the needs of the community. In the process, we have had a whole lot of fun, doors have opened, and things have developed beyond our wildest imaginations. You know that when you love what you do, you can almost work yourself to death and not notice. Tribal membership or not, we are all here to serve the people. This is much more than a job. I do this because of a sense of calling. If I cannot fill my own hole, I can at least help others to enrich their lives by developing into healthy, productive, lifelong learners and contributing members of their tribal communities.

There are several steps to finding fulfillment in tribal librarianship. First, we have to define community. Because the Miamis were relatively small in numbers in recent years, there was always a lot of contact with the other tribes. Once again, what was shared in common united more than the differences divided. They shared their first office space in 1975 with three other tribes and began their first Older Americans Act Title VI nutrition facility in 1978, with a goal to serve seventy-five people a day (ages fifty-five and over, of all tribes, including spouses), in a consortium with the Ottawa and Peoria Tribes. At one time, 335 people were fed each day. That totaled 74,182 meals a year for 2,845 unique patrons. That same year, the library served 12,457 members of all tribes. Because of the location, a large number of those served belonged to the Cherokee Tribe.

A map of northeast Oklahoma shows that eight tribes in the area are within twenty miles of each other. These include the Eastern Shawnee, Miami, Modoc, Ottawa, Peoria, Quapaw, and Seneca Cayuga, plus the Wyandotte. Specifically, the total members of the Miami Tribe number about 3,530, but new names are added each month. Please note, these figures do not include the Shawnee Nation, formerly known as the Loyal Shawnee or Cherokee Shawnee, who have in recent years been finally recognized as a separate and distinct people by the federal government. There are thirty-nine tribes in Oklahoma in all.

But we are ever mindful of the need to develop services especially for Miami tribal members who never enter our Miami Tribal Library & Archives doors. For example, several years ago a needs survey was conducted, funded by an Institute of Museum and Library Services (IMLS) Professional Assistance Grant, of every tribal member over age eighteen nationwide. The results were surprising. Of the 212 surveys returned, 140 respondents had Internet access. Clearly the tribe needed to develop its online services and began to do so.

Thus, the tribal community currently served by the Miami Tribal Library & Archives consists of Miami tribal members nationwide and tribal members of all tribes who live within a fifty-mile radius of Miami, Oklahoma. The mission statements adopted are as follows: "The mission of the Miami Tribal Nation Library is to provide quality library services to all Miami Tribal members and all area Native Americans of all ages. . . . The mission of the Miami Nation Archives is to preserve the Miami's unique sense of identity as a separate people by remembering its shared past."[1]

The second step to finding fulfillment in tribal librarianship is to develop a vision. A library may have been started by a single person's vision, but it takes many people to make it happen. Besides our regular staff, in one given year we had 1,406 donated hours of service by six temporary job trainees, and thirty-three other volunteers donated an additional 395 hours. Besides these workers, it is a constant public relations job to sell the program or vision to others in and outside of the tribe. People want to be part of a successful, winning project or team.

It was several years before the tribe's economic development projects and self-governance funds provided sufficient financial support for the Miami Tribal Library & Archives. Until then, the Library & Archives was 100 percent reliant on grant funds. The tribe did not have a grant writer at first, so library staff became proficient at grant writing by necessity. No funding, no job can be a great motivator. In management terms, it is not hard to think outside of the box if you do not have a box.

Partnerships were developed to maximize any grant funds that were available; we can identify eight such partnerships. One of the strongest alliances that the tribe has is with Miami University in Oxford, Ohio. The university shares the tribe's name and has scholarships for qualified tribal members. More than that, the university regularly brought students to Miami for several weeks of classes in the summer to study a variety of subjects such as linguistics, journalism, anthropology, and archaeology. More often, research projects are developed by academic researchers, including a botany study that documents the use of plants by tribal members. Now research projects are often based on Miami tribal members selecting topics and researching them to bring the results back to the tribe. All projects are coordinated through the Myaamia Project at Miami University, with tribal member Daryl Baldwin as director.[2]

A second collaboration was in the form of advice from a library mentor, Mary Largent, from the Learning Resource Center staff at the local Northeastern Oklahoma Junior College. Particularly in the early years, because of staff isolation, projects were run by her to ensure that the best practices in the field were being considered. An unexpected result was several donations of reference materials through the years, as the college purchased newer editions.

The third collaboration was the various training opportunities available to augment the skills of the library staff. Some received grant funds to attend graduate classes at the University of Oklahoma's School of Library and Information Science for six years or until a master's degree was completed. (That should encourage others! If I can, anyone can! I am here to tell you that success or that "little diploma" goes not to the fastest or smartest, but to the most stubborn!) Staff attended archives and library workshops when travel funds were available. Added bonuses included a free computer printer and ethnography books. Free review books arrived from reviewing opportunities resulting from contacts with professors.

The fourth avenue for partnerships was the archives staff at the Oklahoma Department of Libraries. Their technical assistance helped the tribe receive a National Historical Publications and Records Commission (NHPRC) grant from the National Archives to establish a tribal archives and records management program. Another grant later helped locate historical information about the tribe, which in turn resulted in additional tribal records being returned to the tribe, after U. S. Department of Housing and Urban Development (HUD) grants enabled the library's physical area to be expanded fourfold. These same contacts in the archives world resulted in the library director being appointed to the Oklahoma Historical Records Advisory Board by two different governors, a reflection of their desire to involve tribal personnel in statewide initiatives.

The fifth partnership was perhaps one of the most unique for its time. It was the establishment of the CHARLIE Library Network, which stands for Connecting Help and Resources Linking Indians Effectively. This network, funded by grants from the U.S. Department of Education and later IMLS, connected all of the northeast Oklahoma tribes except the Wyandotte and Shawnee. (The invitation remains open for those two tribes to join.) At first, the tribal librarians purchased computer software and equipment and Internet access, and received training. A shared catalog on the Internet was a later project. Then a professional librarian rotated among the various tribes offering cataloging services or mentoring as needed.

A sixth partnership within the community resulted in grants providing a rotating storyteller, who visited day-care locations served by the Miami Tribes Childcare program. This assisted parents with funds paying for day care so they could work or attend school. At each site, regular visits would provide stories, some with native themes and Miami language. Bookmarks or color sheets were often distributed. And the hugs were free!

Our Roots and Wings program is a seventh way of reaching out into the community. The Miami Tribal Library & Archives logo features a sandhill crane silhouetted against a rising sun and a cedar tree with the complete root system showing in the foreground with the words, "Libraries gives us wings, archives gives us roots." Roots and Wings became a short way of describing the vision, so when it came time to name our books-for-babies program, that phrase was chosen. The local hospital had a similar program with the public library in town, but there was nothing for babies born at the Claremore Indian Hospital, which is ninety miles away. Initially, when they left the hospital with their babies, the mothers were given a brochure and a self-addressed, stamped postcard to sign up for the program. When the postcard was received, the tribe would mail at least two books, bookmarks, and a baby bib with the words "Roots and Wings" on it, plus suggested reading titles and a list of tribal libraries in the state so they could pick the closest library to their homes.

The original idea was to distribute more books every year around the time of each child's birthday, until the age of six. But mailing costs were a problem, as many young families would move and not leave a forwarding address, and the books would be returned. Even telephone calls proved problematic. For several reasons, the requests for the books never grew as anticipated. Still believing in the basic concept, the Miami shifted targets and began to mail materials automatically to all Miami children, six and under, nationwide as they were enrolled in the tribe. The baby bibs were sent to only the youngest members. In this particular case, the response was better. The focus was changed from serving all tribes that came to the Claremore Indian Hospital to serving Miami tribal members as they were enrolled in the tribe.

Some of the early training for the CHARLIE librarians brought medical librarians on-site from the Integris Health System in Oklahoma City. They in turn later included the Miami Tribal Library & Archives in a consumer health education grant targeting underserved populations, which is an eighth way that partnerships helped us develop community services. This grant enabled the Miami Tribe to become part of the National Network of Medical Libraries, providing up-to-date computer and fax equipment plus custom training on the use of the MedlinePlus and PubMed databases. Armed with that information, a new program was begun, coordinating with medical staff at the Northeast Oklahoma Tribal Health System next door, providing medical research on such topics as anthrax, cholera, and breastfeeding. Patients may also research diseases, medications, treatments, or pain management, making them better participants in the health process.

As opportunities present themselves, the tribe has also furnished Miami language teachers for the Miami Public Schools' after-school program for the middle school, which is a ninth form of outreach. The first language grant the tribe received was written by a librarian. It is no surprise that children learn the Miami language faster than adults do. But the same type of instruction works well with adults, too, because it is visual, very activity based, and hands on. The tribe uses several means to distribute language materials to tribal members.

The Miami Tribal Library & Archives was selected as one of the 2002 Honoring Nations thirty-two semifinalists. This awards program, administered by Harvard's John F. Kennedy School of Government, recognizes model examples of tribal governance. It was the first and only library/archives to be so honored during the first three years of the program.

We are always willing to share our experiences if they help others. From the stories that I have shared, you can tell how the partnerships or programs have developed through identifying needs and giving others the opportunity to help. As far as including non-Natives in your work, each tribe must make that decision for itself. Use the normal means for determining who is sincere in their motives. If there is no monetary benefit, perhaps that may weed some out. Some projects described here took years to develop.

Plans are continuing for future partnerships and community collaborations. In one case, four academic universities in the state of Oklahoma initiated the OKDIGITAL Project with the goal of putting original source documents on the Internet. As there was an effort to include tribal records, grants were sought to fund the work that needed to be done. Oklahoma State University has already put Kappler's Treaties on its server, which was a very welcome addition to online sources.[3]

Unfortunately, between the presenting of this material at the conference and preparing it for this publication, much has changed. In January 2010, the three current library staff were laid off and replaced with tribal members. It was further announced that once grants were complete in September 2010, the facility would be closed permanently after twenty-one years of full-time service. While it is easy to point to the bad economy or say that not having native librarians affected the end decision, tribal politics clearly paid a role. Another point raised was that the Internet had replaced the need for libraries. Another concrete factor is that freeing up the library space would allow for needed expansion of the casino. I hope that prior to this going to press, the original decision can be reversed and this paragraph can be deleted. This kind of battle is not new to the library world. Libraries of every type, size, and location are struggling. Whatever the end result, it does not minimize the value of the thousands of hours of library/archives services provided through the program, the education and training that occurred within its walls, nor the lives, primarily of the tribal elders, that were enriched.

NOTES

1. Miami Tribal Library & Archives, "Welcome," http://www.myaamia.org/ (accessed 16 September 2010).
2. "The Myaamia Project at Miami University," http://www.myaamiaproject.org/research.html (accessed 16 September 2010).
3. Charles J. Kappler, "Indian Affairs: Laws and Treaties," 1902, http://digital.library.okstate.edu/Kappler/ (accessed 16 September 2010).

4

Beyond Books and Portals: Proactive Indigenous Librarianship

Kawika Makanani

KA ʻŌLELO MUA—INTRODUCTION

Education continues to be a challenge for indigenous peoples, for it demands that we navigate through the reality of our oppression by foreigners in our own homelands. There have been many initiatives to remedy the low achievement of indigenous students, and events like the World Indigenous Peoples' Conference on Education certainly have helped our peoples to share effective ideas over the years. Curriculum, pedagogy, assessment, and leadership have rightly been the major areas of focus, but another area that is worthy of more attention is the role of libraries.

Public and school libraries that serve indigenous communities have an honorable mission. They serve the educational purposes common to all libraries, but they face even greater challenges because indigenous peoples have unique needs. Accordingly, indigenous librarians must offer more than typical services. They need to be proactive in providing creative and meaningful services that will be effective in meeting the needs of their patrons. I share below some of the activities that I conduct as an indigenous librarian. This comes at the risk of appearing to be self-absorbed, but I should share what I know best—my own work—and let others tell their own stories. Part of my mission is to inspire others to do just that.

INDIGENOUS LIBRARIANSHIP

I define *indigenous librarianship* as the provision of library services by and to patrons who are members of the same indigenous group, in libraries whose purpose is primarily to acquire, provide, and perpetuate that group's knowledge in ways it deems culturally appropriate.

Indigenous librarianship as I have defined it is rare. In the United States, at least, there seems to be a greater concern for minority education and librarianship. The needs of indigenous people are submerged in the rush to serve African Americans and Spanish-speaking Hispanics, since their numbers as minorities far outweigh those of indigenous Americans. See an article by Wohlmuth and McCook as an example.[1] It in no way minimizes that concern, but merely points out that the knowledge of Native Americans, Alaska Natives, and Native Hawaiians is indigenous to the nation, long predates that of more recent immigrant groups, and is much more fragile. Thus, it deserves more attention. For example, the World Indigenous Peoples' Conference on Education's Coolangatta Statement recognizes shortcomings in international declarations on the rights of indigenous peoples.[2] Nevertheless, minority librarianship and indigenous librarianship are complementary, and both can benefit by mutual cooperation and support.

Per my own definition, I conduct indigenous librarianship. My employer is Kamehameha Schools (KS) of Hawai'i, founded in 1887 by *Ke Ali'i* (Chiefess) Bernice Pauahi Bishop. Her intent was to educate her Native Hawaiian people and, in turn, enhance the likelihood of their survival into the twentieth century. The trustees have long maintained a Hawaiian-preference admissions policy, so very nearly all KS students are of indigenous Hawaiian ancestry. I am a graduate of the school, and returned in 1977 with a BA in liberal studies (with a Hawaiian studies focus). I taught Hawaiian history and Hawaiian culture courses for twenty-three years. Then, in 2000, equipped with a master's of library and information science (MLIS), I moved to my current position as *haku o ka Waihona 'Ike Hawai'i me ka Pakipika*, or librarian of the Hawai'i/Pacific Collection. The collection is part of the library, which itself is the main component of the Midkiff Learning Center, which serves the Kamehameha High School of the Kamehameha Schools Kapalama Campus in Honolulu, Hawai'i.

In 2000, the trustees adopted a fifteen-year strategic plan that included *'Ike Hawai'i*, Hawaiian knowledge, as a major goal. Three years later, the trustees declared that Kamehameha Schools is a Hawaiian school. *Nohona Hawai'i*, or Hawaiian life, has since been accepted as a behavioral complement to *'Ike Hawai'i*, to ensure that *'Ike Hawai'i* is actually practiced throughout the institution.

These are the contexts in which I am able to conduct indigenous librarianship, Hawaiian style. I do so with the full support of my head librarian, high school principal, and campus headmaster, all of whom are Hawaiian, the latter two also being KS alumni. My circumstances are not only unique at the global level, but also within the institution: I am the only Hawai'i/Pacific specialist among the twelve degreed librarians.

THE CASE FOR DIFFERENTIATION OF LIBRARY SERVICES

Is there a need to differentiate services among general, minority, and indigenous populations? Yes, unequivocally. As mentioned at the outset of this chapter, indigenous students have achieved in schools at historically lower levels than students of the dominant groups, and even lower than immigrant minorities in some societies. This is a grim fact; there is no need to document that phenomenon here, and background is provided in sources such as the Coolangatta Statement.[3]

I briefly mentioned previously that indigenous peoples deserve services that address their unique needs. One of the most pressing needs is the preservation and perpetuation of their language and culture. In an abstract for his paper proposing a model for an Argentine indigenous library, Edgardo Civallero expresses grave concern for indigenous peoples and calls on those working in library and information settings to "become more deeply involved in the problems, side with the helpless and struggle, shoulder to shoulder (maybe without tools, without technology, without money, just equipped with imagination, working wishes and service vocation) with other human beings, who were—and currently are—forgotten, just because they are faithful to themselves."[4] Immigrant peoples generally come from societies in which their cultures are not in danger of disappearing; on the other hand, indigenous peoples have nowhere else to turn, or return, once their cultures are terminal.

There are many educational initiatives in the United States that purport to assist indigenous citizens. The best are those created and organized by the people themselves, or in strong partnership with government agencies. Some of these initiatives reside at the level of general guidelines and may not even address libraries specifically. The Alaska Native Knowledge Network is an example, but it does link to the Alaska Library Association website and a subsite entitled "Culturally Responsive Guidelines for Alaska Libraries."[5] *Nä Honua Mauli Ola: Hawai'i Guidelines for Culturally Healthy and Responsive Learning Environments* mirrors the Alaskans' work, but is adapted to the Hawai'i case.[6] It lacks a library component, but librarians should have no trouble finding connecting points.

The American Library Association (ALA) does address the unique status of Native Americans to some degree, with its support of the American Indian Library Association. Hawaiian and Pacific Islander librarians would find few places to express their own indigeneity in ALA, but the same would be true in the Hawai'i affiliate, the Hawai'i Library Association, partly because Hawaiian librarians have yet to develop an indigenous identity. One endeavor is the Native Hawaiian Library, a service provided by the federally funded Alu Like.[7] This organization is also the primary sponsor of the website Ulukau, which endeavors to post Hawaiian-language documents, with English translations, on the Internet.[8]

Some American state library systems, such as those of Arizona and New Mexico, have taken steps to provide their first peoples with indigenous services. The latter has a well-developed Tribal Libraries program.[9] The School of Information at the

University of Texas–Austin, under the guidance of Loriene Roy, has been very active in promoting services to Native Americans, including partnering with the WebJunction website. Dr. Roy initiated "If I Can Read, I Can Do Anything," a reading club for native children, and directed the "Honoring Generations" program with initial funding from the U.S. Institute for Museum and Library Services.[10]

On the international level, *Te Röpu Whakahau*, the association of Mäori Library and Information Workers, is very active in advocating for Mäori librarianship in New Zealand/Aotearoa.[11] It helps to ensure compliance with the 1840 Treaty of Waitangi, which guarantees equal partnership between Mäori and *Päkehä*. Thus, not only do the libraries sport bilingual signage and highlight texts in *Te Reo Mäori*, or the Mäori language, but also strong efforts are made to acquire and preserve *Mäoritanga* (Mäori knowledge) and *whakapapa* (genealogy) materials, especially for use by *Tangata Whenua* (Mäori people). The Turnbull Collection in the National Library of New Zealand is a good case in point.[12] The National Museum is also leading a consortium of library-related groups to create Mäori subject headings.[13] In 1999, it probably was not a mere coincidence that Auckland happened to be the site of a meeting of concerned library professionals, from which sprang the International Indigenous Librarians Forum.[14]

Canada and Australia also have strong indigenous programs that honor their Aboriginal peoples. Further descriptions cannot be given in this brief survey of indigenous librarianship; my apologies to these and other countries, states, organizations, and individuals around the world who may also be engaged in similar programs. The point is that if these programs exist, there is an obvious need for indigenous librarianship. Its absence in other places will perhaps cause people of those areas to ask why that is so, and then initiate efforts to implement it.

DEVELOPMENT OF HAWAIIAN RESOURCES

One of the most critical needs for indigenous peoples is to tell our own stories, or at least to assert our native philosophies and understandings in materials that are being created about us. Indigenous librarians should take steps to move beyond passive acquisition, that is, waiting for others to create and publish materials, by actually producing or participating in the creation of materials that by their nature belong in our libraries. This goes a step beyond the mere support called for in *Nä Honua Maoli Ola* for schools and institutions.[15] Though cataloging an item you have produced, or contributed to, may be somewhat like an out-of-body experience, it is truly rewarding.

In 2005, I was fortunate to have published in volume 3 of *'Öiwi, A Native Hawaiian Journal,* an article honoring my late granduncle, Gabriel 'Ï.[16] A year earlier I conducted a videotaped interview of one of our esteemed Hawaiian historians and former Kamehameha Schools administrator. At the request of current administrators, I have also written pieces that serve the interests of the institution, including a legal affidavit in defense of our Hawaiian preference admissions policy, mentioned previously.

Just after completing my MLIS, I critiqued a chapter in *Princess Ka'iulani: Hope of a Nation, Heart of a People*, at the request of author Sharon Linnea.[17] I serve a similar function for several departments in the Kamehameha Schools system. In recent years, I have also been called upon to comment on film treatments that have been submitted for funding considerations. Participating in critiques is crucial, because it ensures that if the author is not a Hawaiian, or is a Hawaiian who lacks cultural depth, a carefully considered perspective can be offered, and the final product will be better for it.

Whether through direct authorship or in a contributory role, indigenous librarians can be proactive in seeing that appropriate cultural materials, produced through our own eyes and understanding, are made available to our patrons. When we encourage our *keiki*, children, to walk that path, we can then speak with authentic voices.

MIDKIFF LECTURE SERIES

When I first came into the Midkiff Learning Center as a librarian, I instituted a lecture series that was partly intended to share Hawaiian cultural and historical knowledge. This is supported by the "Culturally Responsive Guidelines for Alaska Public Libraries," which suggests that library programming involve community members in presentations, as well as recognize and communicate the heritage of the local area.[18] *Nä Honua Mauli Ola* weighs in by asking schools to "validate the knowledge of *küpuna*" (elders, especially of the grandparent generation and older) and "to provide opportunities for *küpuna* to share their knowledge."[19] Although not all of my invited speakers have been *küpuna* by generation, their degree of knowledge has earned them that respected designation.

Some of the speakers include Ramsay Taum on *lua* (Hawaiian fighting arts), Kä'ili Chun and her mentor, Wright Bowman Sr., on woodcarving, and Keoni Nunes on *uhi* (also *käkau*, or tattoo). Non-Hawaiians have also been invited, such as David Fuentes on *paniolo* (Hawaiian cowboy) saddle making, and Professor Danielle Conway-Jones, an authority on Hawaiian cultural and intellectual property rights.

This array of speakers on Hawaiian topics closely ties in to indigenous speakers from elsewhere, mostly New Zealand/Aotearoa. *Nä Honua Maoli Ola* provides space for exploring these ties in its suggestion to "create opportunities to make meaningful connections with other cultures," which is the other intent of the lecture series.[20] In 2002, Professor Graham Smith, then the Mäori pro-vice chancellor at Auckland University, spoke on his vision of Mäori tertiary education. In May 2003, a Hawaiian-language teacher asked to collaborate in hosting two wonderful women from Rotorua, Manu Nepo and Tuhipo Kereopa. They had each recently acquired a *moko* (chin tattoo), and Manu gave a moving account of why she took that step. Dear friends from Wellington came to our campus in the spring of 2004 to share their knowledge of the original Paikea, or whale rider, story. Thomas Haapu, who has family at Whangarä, and his wife, Danica Waiti, demonstrated heaps of *aroha* (affection) in the spring of 2005 to our Kapalama campus and also took their presentation to other campuses. For two other speakers, I extend a *mahalo*, thanks, to the University of Hawai'i at Mänoa for sharing these fascinating young artists, award-winning New Zealand Samoan filmmaker Sima Urale in the fall of 2004 and renowned Mäori artist and carver Brett Graham in the spring of 2005. On September 23, 2005, David Kukutai Jones, former Mäori librarian for the Turnbull Collection, National Library of New Zealand, and then president of *Te Röpu Whakahau*, discussed Mäori librarianship with my library colleagues.

HO'OKIPA 'ANA MAI—WELCOMING

The making of "meaningful connections with other cultures" intersects with the Hawaiian values of *aloha* (affection), *lokomaika'i* (generosity), and *ho'okipa* (hospitality).[21] We appreciate visitors coming because of their interest in learning about Hawaiians and our school. At the same time, we learn about them, enabling us to explore our similarities and differences. In 2002, I welcomed Native Alaskans from Nanwalek via the Alaska Native Center. We had a busy year in 2005. In April, a group from the Paskwayak Cree Nation, Northern Manitoba, Canada, made the long trek to Hawai'i. In July, I hosted the Ngaruawahia High School Kapa Haka group from New Zealand/Aotearoa, quickly followed by two groups from French Polynesia, Hälau Makalapua and a delegation led by Mme. Natacha Taurua, minister of Traditional Art and Handicraft.

HÖ'IKE—PRESENTATIONS

Delivering presentations is another way to actively share knowledge with others. I have had the privilege of addressing groups that come specifically to learn about Hawaiians and our culture. The most notable groups have come from Manchester College in Indiana and Stanford University. I have worked long distance with a graduate class at The Pennsylvania State University regarding the admissions court case; the professor and his students visited our campus in the spring of 2006.

I have also conducted presentations at local conferences, including those organized by the Native Hawaiian Education Association, the Hawaiian Historical Society, and our own Policy Analysis and Systems Evaluation. Within Kamehameha Schools, I have spoken during new teacher orientations and faculty gatherings. As part of my follow-up to a 2003 Fulbright summer tour focusing on education in

New Zealand/Aotearoa, I spoke several times on a comparison of Hawaiian and Mäori education.

'ÖLELO HAWAI'I—HAWAIIAN LANGUAGE

The *Alaska Standards for Culturally Responsive Schools*, in its "Cultural Standards for Educators," encourages educators to establish a connection with families by seeking "to learn the local heritage language and promote its use in their teaching."[22] *Nä Honua Mauli Ola* supports Hawaiian-language learning and use via guideline 7: "Engage in Hawaiian language opportunities to increase language proficiency."[23]

Although I am not fluent in my mother tongue, I am proficient enough to have conducted a conversational class for my learning center colleagues in the fall of 2005. This allowed the staff to interact with our students in the Hawaiian language, even if only at a basic level. Students seem to appreciate that their library service providers are making this effort.

I also assist other learning center staff with *'Ike Hawai'i* services, such as rewriting the "Video Production Ethics" from the perspective of Hawaiian values as opposed to Western journalistic standards. For our graphics production center, I have converted the student request form into a bilingual document. Finally, I have taken the lead on installing bilingual signage in the learning center. Since this effort has been subsumed under the headmaster's initiative to deploy bilingual signage throughout the campus, I am serving on the larger advisory committee.

THE ROLE OF NONINDIGENOUS LIBRARIANS

While indigenous peoples are rightly wary of outsiders, we need to acknowledge that some have contributed to our survival and endured their own hardships in doing so. Although their own people wrought great harm, they collected and preserved traditions that might have been lost forever. The Hawaiian people have benefited from such work. Nevertheless, it is the responsibility of such selfless individuals to consider that their best work will be to train and prepare native peoples to conduct such work for themselves. Correspondingly, indigenous peoples must accept the responsibility of being the stewards of their own knowledge.

HA 'INA 'IA MAI—THE REFRAIN

The refrain, the root of the message, is that we indigenous peoples have to take charge of our own lives and futures. Controlling and promoting our own traditions is crucial. Indigenous librarianship is one of the keys for this to happen. Indigenous librarians can be more proactive in creating cultural materials worthy of our libraries and our patrons, sharing our own knowledge with others, engaging our *küpuna* to share their experiences and skills, facilitating cultural exchanges, and promoting our languages.

What I have shared here is based on my personal experiences and makes sense within my small corner of the world. Still, I hope that other librarians will be able to identify with at least one thing that I have described. At the same time, I trust that some will educate me about what positive steps they are taking to advance their own people. When next we come together as indigenous peoples, perhaps there will be more of us sharing our stories together.

NOTES

1. Sonia Ramirez Wohlmuth and Kathleen de la Pena McCook, "Equity of Access: Igniting a Passion for Change," 2004, http://webjunction.org/do/DisplayContent?id=5507 (accessed 15 September 2010).

2. World Indigenous Peoples' Conference on Education, "The Coolongatta Statement on Indigenous Peoples' Rights in Education," 1999, http://www.win-hec.org/docs/pdfs/Coolangata%20Statement%201999.pdf (accessed 15 September 2010).

3. "The Coolongatta Statement." World Indigenous People's Conference on Education.

4. Edgardo Civallero, "Indigenous Libraries, Utopia, and Reality: Proposing an Argentine Model," in *Proceedings of the 70th IFLA World Library and Information Congress* (Buenos Aires, Argentina, 2004), http://eprints.rclis.org/3104/1/IFLA.pdf (accessed 15 September 2010).

5. Alaska Library Association, "Culturally Responsive Guidelines for Alaska Public Libraries," http://www.akla.org/culturally-responsive.html (accessed 7 September 2010).

6. *Nä Honua Mauli Ola: Hawai'i Guidelines for Culturally Healthy and Responsive Learning Environments* (Hilo: Ka Haka 'Ula o Ke'elikölani and Honolulu: Native Hawaiian Education Council, 2002), http://www.olelo.hawaii.edu/dual/nhmo/ (accessed 15 September 2010).

7. Alu Like, Inc., http://www.alulike.org/ (accessed 15 September 2010).

8. "Ulukau," http://ulukau.org/ (accessed 15 September 2010).

9. New Mexico State Library, "Tribal Libraries Program," http://www.nmstatelibrary.org/services-libraries/programs-services/tribal-libraries (accessed 15 September 2010).

10. "If I Can Read, I Can Do Anything: A National Reading Club for Native Students," http://sentra.ischool.utexas.edu/~ifican/activities/index.php (accessed 15 September 2010); "Honoring Generations: Developing the Next Generation of Native Librarians," http://sentra.ischool.utexas.edu/~hg/ (accessed 15 September 2010).

11. "*Te Röpu Whakahau*," http://www.trw.org.nz/ (accessed 15 September 2010).

12. National Library of New Zealand, Te Puna Matauranga O Aotearoa, "Alexander Turnbull Library Collections," http://www.natlib.govt.nz/collections/a-z-of-all-collections/alexander-turnbull-library-collections (accessed 15 September 2010).

13. "Ngä Üpoko Tukutuku; Mäori Subject Headings," http://mshupoko.natlib.govt.nz/mshupoko/index.htm (accessed 15 September 2010).

14. "International Indigenous Librarians Past Forums," https://sites.google.com/site/indigenouslibrariansforum/past-forums (accessed 15 September 2010).

15. *Nä Honua Mauli Ola*, 46.

16. R. Kāwika Makanani, "Gabriel Kapeliela 'Ī," *'Ōiwi, A Native Hawaiian Journal* 3 (2005): 106–9.

17. Sharon Linnea, *Princess Ka'iulani: Hope of a Nation, Heart of a People* (Grand Rapids, Mich.: Eerdmans Books for Young Readers, 1999).

18. Alaska Library Association, "Culturally Responsive Guidelines for Alaska Public Libraries."

19. *Nä Honua Mauli Ola*, 46, 48.

20. *Nä Honua Mauli Ola*, 46.

21. *Nä Honua Mauli Ola*, 48.

22. Assembly of Alaska Native Educators, *Alaska Standards for Culturally Responsive Schools* (Fairbanks: University of Alaska Fairbanks, Alaska Native Knowledge Network, 1998), 11.

23. *Nä Honua Mauli Ola*, 49.

5

Mohave Language Projects and the Role of the CRIT Library

Amelia Flores and Susan D. Penfield

INTRODUCTION

Amelia Flores is the tribal librarian and archivist for the Colorado River Indian Tribes (CRIT) of Parker, Arizona. Susan Penfield is a linguistic anthropologist from the University of Arizona. For many years they have collaborated in various ways to promote the revitalization of Mohave, a highly endangered Yuman language and the heritage language of the Mohave members of CRIT. This chapter describes several of these efforts and offers encouragement to other tribal libraries that support endangered indigenous languages.

ORAL HISTORY AND LINGUISTICS

The CRIT Library/Archives has been responsible for supporting a number of oral history projects. Many of these valuable efforts have focused specifically on language preservation. In 1995, Dr. Penfield launched a translation project involving some tapes of Mohave coyote stories she had first recorded in 1969. With the help of Ms. Flores, the library/archives became the focal point for the work in several ways. It functioned as a meeting place for the elders involved and offered staff to help with recording efforts who carefully aided in copying and archiving both video- and audiotape material. This project was deemed to be oral history and linguistics, in that it involved a number of elders jointly translating the tapes and discussing both their linguistic and historical content. These sessions were video- and audiotaped, generating a kind of oral history.

Somewhat later, this project took on a different aspect, also with the support of the tribal library. Building on the addition of computers provided to the CRIT Library/Archives through the Bill & Melinda Gates Foundation, experiments began with Mohave language translating of these same tapes online using educational technology available through the University of Arizona. This experimental project was the first of its kind to allow linguists to work at a distance with tribal elders. Using MOO (multi-user, object oriented) software, Dr. Penfield was able to work online in a synchronous format with Ms. Flores and two tribal elders. In this way, the translation and transcription of the coyote stories could continue from a distance, and Ms. Flores was able to use her computer skills to begin practicing her literacy with the Mohave language.[1]

THE COLORING BOOK

In 1999, the CRIT Library/Archives was awarded funding from the Arizona Department of Library, Archives, and Public Records for a coloring book project in the Mohave and Chemehuevi languages. Key resources in the project were local fluent speakers of those languages. The elders' primary goal was to select various animals and objects relating to each respective tribal culture. Importantly, funding was provided for hiring a local Native American artist. The consultant for the project was linguist Dr. Susan Penfield. The overall purpose of the project was to accomplish the primary goals, which were to preserve and further document the endangered languages of the Mohave and Chemehuevi, create a bilingual coloring book for each respective tribe, utilize the CRIT Library/Archives as a resource, engage tribal elders in the preservation of their culture, use a Native artist to accurately create cultural artwork, increase public awareness of culture and traditions of CRIT, familiarize all young children with their Native languages, and linguistically strengthen the Mohave and Chemehuevi languages.

THE GATES GRANT

In the spring of 2003, with the support of the Bill & Melinda Gates Foundation's Native American Access to Technology Program grants to tribal libraries, the CRIT Library/Archives began collaborating with the University of Arizona on a project to train tribal members to work with endangered languages. This grant specifically promoted the use of technology in indigenous language revitalization. As the head of the CRIT Library/Archives, Amelia Flores was named as on-site coordinator and was responsible for maintaining contact with the chosen participants. She also was responsible for archiving any materials generated as part of the project.

This project provided a new laptop computer and a week of training spread over a semester for six members of the CRIT community. Included were three

Mohave and three Chemehuevi tribal members. Both of these languages are still spoken at CRIT but are considered highly endangered in that Mohave, a Yuman language, has just forty speakers left and Chemehuevi, a southern Paiute language, has just five fluent speakers.

The focus was to train tribal members to use the software that is available on the library computers and encourage them to train others. The goal has been to provide some immediate support to both languages and to encourage the use of technology generally.

Computer-assisted language learning is effective and a well-established mode of self-instruction. Where tribal languages are concerned, computer technology can enhance established language programs and/or provide individual instruction. In any case, the library can become the center of work with technology where both equipment and training are available.

ADVICE FOR OTHERS

Language preservation in a tribal community does not happen overnight but over time. It involves many years of working with the elders of the community and building a relationship of respect and trust to begin language programs or activities. Likewise, having the opportunity to collaborate and to have a long-standing association with a linguist who is very supportive in language preservation is an advantage. Advocacy for endangered languages takes place both inside and outside the community. Tribal libraries, like the one at CRIT, often serve as a bridge and thus help create space for broader collaborations.

Many factors contribute toward language revitalization. For most individuals, it takes passion, patience, and trust for them to step out within their own tribal community. For some, it will take the interest and desire to be academically trained in order to carry on the work in public arenas. For others, keeping the language going on a daily basis at home is the goal. Any effort should count as a success. The place of the library is to network with and for anyone who is engaged in these efforts.

NOTE

1. University of Arizona, "Online Language Environments," http://www.ole.arizona .edu/ (accessed 9 September 2010). More information about MOO and other supportive software is available through the University of Arizona's Learning Technology Center, at http://www.ole.arizona.edu/.

6

Out of the Archives: Fostering Collaborative Environments for Language Revitalization

Gabriella Reznowski and Norma A. Joseph

Academic libraries in the Pacific Northwest have been collecting language materials since the appearance of the first dictionaries and grammars by missionary linguists. However, as tribes continue to develop new language materials and to seek venues for their dissemination and preservation, are academic libraries serving as collaborative partners in supporting language endeavors? As levels of language endangerment become more severe, the role of libraries and archives becomes increasingly important. Where appropriate, libraries should strive to meet a twofold goal: building endangered language collections to encourage student learning and supporting tribal libraries in revitalization efforts.

The complex issues surrounding language endangerment and revitalization are often difficult for those outside of linguistic communities to understand. University librarians may feel at a loss for establishing their role in the preservation and promotion of endangered languages. Academic librarians may know little about the native cultures in their region, resulting in a lack of understanding of the historical and cultural complexities related to a community's revitalization efforts. Achieving cultural awareness is an ongoing process that may develop through sustained dialogue, community interaction, and attendance at community events, where appropriate. A wider appreciation of the sociocultural issues related to community language endeavors may inform the protection of materials related to linguistic and cultural knowledge.

BUILDING AWARENESS AND CAMPUS ENGAGEMENT

Academic library collections often contain important archival language materials that have been collected over time, including wax disc recordings, early phrase books, grammars, papers related to linguistic documentation, and first dictionaries. Shifting the focus from a warehouse model to one that supports and encourages language learners today is still unresolved for many institutions. Aside from merely collecting materials, are there other ways that academic libraries can be involved?

Campus activities to increase awareness of language issues might include inviting speakers and hosting a film series. Currently preparing for its fourth season, Mushkeg Media offers an affordable documentary series, *Finding Our Talk*. The films initially explored language issues within First Nations communities in Canada, but the company has expanded its scope to examine indigenous communities in New Zealand, Australia, Norway, Bolivia, and Guatemala. As each documentary examines a specific community of speakers, *Finding Our Talk* allows the outsider to see that endangered languages face multidimensional challenges, with each community confronting its own obstacles, goals, and issues related to revitalization efforts.

The benefits of increased awareness, and an understanding of language endangerment levels and revitalization efforts, can be significant. It is important for librarians to continue to learn about the complexities of revitalization, particularly for languages that are local to the regions they serve. An understanding of language issues is key to supporting tribal endeavors and remaining viable partners in language preservation. Librarians should seek information about the protocols of the individual tribes that are represented within the language materials of the library collection. A greater appreciation of tribal language history is paramount in managing existing materials, promoting campus awareness, protecting the integrity of cultural materials, and supporting endangered language instruction.

Some libraries maintain close contact with language programs and, where language instruction is taught through the campus, with language instructors. The librarians at Evergreen State College, for example, work closely with campus Lushootseed instructors to ensure that students have access to materials that support language goals and foster learning. Librarians at institutions of higher learning that offer endangered language classes have specific reasons to acquire a greater understanding of the language communities they serve.

Many academic libraries are located in urban centers, and the move away from the home community is often related to a decline in language use.[1] Native American students attending college campuses may be removed from both opportunities for intergenerational communication and access to tribal language materials. Furthermore, since today's students will inherit leadership roles related to language revitalization, the university setting is an ideal environment for establishing relationships with tomorrow's language leaders. As Susana Mota Roboredo Amante states, "It is an undeniable fact that languages are a key to identity, because they convey the values and the worldview of one's culture."[2] Therefore, it is important that librarians seek an understanding of tribal language issues and take inventory of campus networks of support. Do library language collections support the curriculum? Do students have an opportunity to engage in language learning outside of formal class time? Does the library convey support to students by providing access to and promoting the language materials within its collections? Has the library contacted the tribal language program to inquire whether there are additional, updated materials that would be appropriate for the collection? Are there materials that could be made available online and, if so, what protocols must be adhered to? In addition, does the library own archival language materials that might be of benefit to tribes? Could copies of these materials be provided to tribal language officials?

In order to work through some of these issues, the Washington State University (WSU) Libraries partnered with the WSU Native American Students Center in an effort to both explore and build awareness of language-related issues. The center and the WSU Libraries engaged in ongoing collaboration for establishing tribal contacts, promoting campus understanding, and developing the library collection. Among other collaborative activities, the following two exhibits developed as a result of the partnership.

Case One—Endangered Native American Languages: Reclamation, Restoration, and Revitalization

Curated in 2008 and coinciding with a showing of the film *Huchoosedah: Traditions of the Heart*, this display examined Vi Hilbert's contributions to Lushootseed language revitalization.[3] Celebrating Hilbert's efforts, the display also included current items developed by the Tulalip tribal language program. Also featured were materials from the personal collection of Norma Joseph, acquired during her studies for her WSU First People's Language, Culture, and Oral Traditions Certification. The exhibit highlighted the research of linguists Greg Anderson and K. David Harrison about the Northwest Pacific Plateau as a hotspot for language endangerment.[4] As Harrison explains of the worldwide language loss, "small islands of languages are being submerged in a rising sea of English."[5]

Case Two—Making Dictionaries: Recording the Languages of the Plateau People

Coinciding with the 2009 Pah-Loots-Pu Powwow, this display was inspired in part by Haruo Aoki's essay "Writing a Nez Perce Dictionary," in *Making Dictionaries: Preserving Indigenous Languages of the Americas*.[6] Recruited for linguistic field work while a student at the University of California, Berkeley, Aoki initially stayed in both Lapwai and Kamiah, Idaho, where he sought elders within the Nez Perce community who would teach him the language. As Aoki relates, "I learned that it was impossible to find someone who could drop everything for three months in the summer to teach their language to a beginner."[7] After working with Nez Perce elders Harry and Ida Wheeler, Aoki also eventually met Elizabeth

P. Wilson, who spent many hours teaching him the Nez Perce language, culture, and customs:

> We traveled to Musselshell to dig camas and camped for days. After the morning's digging, she cleaned camas as I asked her questions about words and their meanings. She was well aware of the pitfalls of one-to-one translations. Typically, we would come across a Nez Perce word and spend some time pinning down its correct pronunciation. Then she would give an English equivalent. Finally, she would ask me to come up with some synonyms for that equivalent until she picked a few candidates that were more or less close to the Nez Perce original. Talk about a "walking dictionary"![8]

With clarification from the Wheelers and Wilson, Aoki incorporated words from both Archie Phinney's *Nez Percé Texts* and Morvillo's *A Dictionary of the Numípu or Nez Perce Language* into his 1,280-page dictionary.[9] *Nez Percé Texts* was recorded as told to Phinney by his mother, Wayi'laptu, who was perfectly fluent in the Nez Perce language. Giving both a literal and a free translation, Phinney's collection is an authentic and stunning contribution to Nez Perce linguistics, providing a firm basis for the construction of Aoki's dictionary.

Similar to Aoki's, Morvillo's 1895 dictionary would never have materialized had it not been for the guidance and assistance of a Nez Perce speaker who spent several hours each day assisting him in learning the language.[10] A polyglot, Morvillo had great admiration for "the wealth and beauty" of the language, referring to Nez Perce as "a big giant" in comparison to other languages.[11] Other missionary linguists expressed awe for Nez Perce, including Cataldo, who provides this stunning quote: "It was only after three years that I began to grasp the genius of the Nez Perce language, whose active verb has a million inflections."[12]

As have many Native American languages, Nez Perce has been described as a polysynthetic language, in which "a single word can encode a meaning which would require a fairly elaborate sentence in many other languages."[13] Note, for example, the beauty inherent in the word *liyayaya*: "describes the sound of icicles hitting each other."[14]

DOCUMENTATION AND HOLDINGS FOR FOUR LANGUAGES OF THE PACIFIC NORTHWEST

During the course of developing the library displays, it was apparent that, though the WSU Libraries owned significant language materials, knowledge of current tribal endeavors and publications had not been maintained. A comprehensive report detailing the depth and scope of endangered language collections in the Pacific Northwest would foster collaboration among librarians in ensuring that our collections serve the needs of Native language communities. Using four Washington State tribes as examples, following is a sampling of the type of information that might be included in such a report.

Example One: Coeur D'Alene

The tribe is currently involved in continued revitalization efforts, including the ongoing development of curriculum materials. The most complete linguistic studies include Lawrence Nicodemus's 1975 grammar and textbook, which is held by over twenty-seven libraries, according to WorldCat.[15] WSU's physical proximity to the tribe has resulted in the publication of several theses related to the language. WSU anthropology graduate Jill Marie Wagner's work "Language, Power, and Ethnicity on the Coeur D'Alene Reservation" provides a unique record of the triumphs and challenges of tribal language revitalization efforts.[16] Audiovisual materials held by OCLC libraries are mainly in antiquated formats such as cassette and VHS. With the guidance of elder Lawrence Nicodemus, the Coeur D'Alene Tribe produced updated materials in 2000, including a high-school-level textbook.

Example Two: Kalispel

Tribal officials are establishing partnerships with academic institutions for preservation and revitalization efforts. Cusick School District provides language classes to elementary, junior high, and high school students. Eastern Washington University (EWU) offers college-accredited language classes at the Kalispel tribal language center. EWU's Department of American Indian Studies held classes in Kalispel language and culture at the postsecondary level. Important linguistic materials include Vogt's *The Kalispel Language: An Outline of the Grammar with Texts, Translations, and Dictionary*, held by over seventy OCLC member libraries.[17] Limited audiovisual materials are currently available; however, the tribe is involved in significant language efforts. Although a joint project between Gonzaga University and the Kalispel Tribe resulted in the digitization of early linguistic work by Giorda and Mengarini, *A Dictionary of Kalispel or Flat-Head Indian Language* and *A Dictionary of the Kalispel Language*, the hosting website currently has limited functionality.[18]

Example Three: Nez Perce

Postsecondary instruction is taught through Lewis and Clark State College, where students have the opportunity to practice with elders at Lapwai, Idaho, on a regular basis. Nez Perce language classes for school-age students are held through the Lapwai School District. Significant documentation includes Aoki's *Nez Perce Dictionary* and *Nez Perce Grammar* and Phinney's *Nez Percé Texts*, all widely held by WorldCat member libraries.[19] Current research by Nez Perce linguist Phil Cash Cash will form a basis for future language programming.[20]

Example Four: Lushootseed

The Tulalip Lushootseed language program has produced many current materials, some of which are also available online. Tribal language instructors teach through the Tulalip Montessori School and at Tulalip Elementary; college-level classes are available through the University of Washington and Northwest Indian College. Holding institutions for Lushootseed language materials include WSU, the University of Washington, and Evergreen State College. Thom Hess and Vi Hilbert are among the scholars who have made significant contributions to documentation, grammars, and texts, which have been disseminated and are widely held by OCLC member libraries.

ENVISIONING COLLABORATION

As tribal language programs continue to develop materials, academic librarians should be working with tribal communities to ensure that, where the tribe so desires, current language resources are added to academic collections. Although it is unreasonable to imagine that every academic institution would be able to develop comprehensive collections for each language of the Pacific Northwest Plateau, it would be ideal if each academic library serving a language community would take responsibility for one or more of the fifty-three languages of the region. Collaborative relationships might include one or more of the following recommendations.

Recommendation One: Collect Materials and Establish Relationships with Local Tribal Communities

Librarians should be keenly aware that language materials exist primarily to serve speakers and tribal communities. However, the goal of the library should not be to serve as a mausoleum for dead languages, but to contribute to the tangibility and accessibility of languages. Compared with commonly taught languages, endangered languages are often less privileged, and there may be limited multimedia resources for them. Opportunities for language exposure that commonly taught languages enjoy are not often available to students of endangered languages. Contact with tribal language managers can inform our understanding of current language projects and needs.

Recommendation Two: Establish and Maintain Contact with Tribal Language Managers, Ensuring That Protocols and Agreements Are Followed and Respected

Historically, academic institutions have not always maintained appropriate contact with tribal communities. Broken relationships between academic institutions and tribal communities have resulted from a lack of respect for tribal stewardship when researchers completed projects purely for their own ends. Rightly protective of cultural materials, tribal authorities may choose not to make locally produced dictionaries, grammars, texts, and workbooks available to the world. The

Administration for Native Americans has published *Native Language Preservation: A Reference Guide for Establishing Archives and Repositories*, which is useful for alerting librarians to issues of tribal stewardship and protocols.[21] Because each tribe is unique, librarians should not assume that a policy employed by one tribe will be acceptable to another. Each community has its own mandate, vision, and policies for language revitalization. The tribal community governs which materials to make available to the library, whether the materials may be digitized, and what level of access to employ.

Recommendation Three: Librarians and Archivists Work Together to Ensure That Materials Are Being Properly Preserved and That Access Is Provided According to Tribal Agreements

Once contact is established, librarians need to sustain communication with tribal officials and language program managers to ensure that policies and protocols remain up-to-date and are adhered to according to the desires of the tribe. Language resources should be treated as precious materials, not to be taken for granted, and their integrity protected. Past errors stemming from relationships that were not maintained and procurement without gratitude should be amended.

Recommendation Four: Continue to Work with Tribes in a Supportive Fashion to Assist with Digitization Projects and to Identify Opportunities for Online Engagement According to the Tribe's Wishes

News media provide opportunities for the preservation, development, and dissemination of materials. The level to which a tribe wishes to pursue such exposure varies and, although opportunities are endless, nothing should be assumed in engaging online and digitization projects.

Some communities embrace the use of technology in revitalization efforts, placing downloadable materials online to be accessed from anywhere. Tribes are also taking advantage of social networking software to foster communication among language learners. For example, there is a *Nêhiyawêwin* (Cree) Word/Phrase of the Day Facebook group, where members share information about upcoming language events, assist in translating words and phrases, and promote awareness of additional online learning tools.

Other tribes are more protective, with strict measures in place to safeguard materials for community use only. Some protocols stipulate that the language remain unwritten, calling for oral-based instruction in keeping with tribal traditions. In her discussion of Keres language programs, Christine Sims explains: "From a Pueblo perspective, opening tribal languages to the outside risks potential exploitation and desecration of what they hold as sacred and private elements of their internal traditions."[22] The complexities and issues vary, yet the intricacies of tribal language policies are often unknown to outsiders. Therefore, building awareness of the issues surrounding language endangerment in general, and of individual tribal protocols in particular, is extremely important.

CHALLENGES TO REVITALIZATION

The current language situation in North America is astounding for a region described as "a land of linguistic extravagance."[23] K. David Harrison and Gregory Anderson identify twelve distinct genetic language units in the Pacific Northwest, within which are found fifty-three separate languages.[24] Speaking to language diversity in the region, Alexander Ross supplies perhaps one of the earliest and most amusing quotes exposing the fact that early fur traders and explorers were frustrated, and even overwhelmed, by the linguistic abilities of the plateau. Ross, an employee of the Northwest company, had been exposed to many native languages during the forty-four years he spent in the regions of the Columbia and in the Red River Settlement. In describing the languages heard at Fort Nez Perce, he stated:

> Having given a short vocabulary of the principal language spoken by the tribes about Fort Nez Percés, we must next advert to the annoying fact, that the natives of that place differ somewhat from most other Indian tribes. Not contented with one language, they must have a plurality of languages; this, however convenient to them, is certainly embarrassing to the trader, who finds it no easy task to acquire one, and still more difficult to acquire two or three at the same place.[25]

Although Ross's sentiments speak to the multilingual nature of the region at the time, his frustration with linguistic diversity continues to be echoed in contemporary American society. An English-speaking majority is both awed and annoyed by environments of linguistic diversity, as seen in present-day attitudes toward speakers of other languages.

The establishment of comprehensive language immersion programs in the United States has been a difficult process because of government and institutional policies, political pressures, and the perceived economic benefits of assimilation. For new citizens, the fluent acquisition of English is often set as a priority, even if it means sacrificing the heritage language for greater fluency in the dominant tongue. Among recent immigrants, it is not uncommon for the heritage language to be shed, often over the course of one generation. It is therefore not surprising that Native American languages face additional challenges. As Fredrick White states:

> Would most people determine that English has become a first and only language for many Native American communities? The issue of English language dominance is all too common among the First Nations communities and Native Americans in the United States. Ancestral language loss, prevalent in most Native American and First Nations communities, has been occurring since European contact began.[26]

In what White refers to as "the dark period of assimilationist efforts to annihilate all vestiges of ancestral language,"[27] Native languages faced violent and rapid destruction, through policies of forced English acquisition and a residential school system designed to stunt intergenerational communication and expedite the shift to English.

There is no shortage of articles arguing that language loss is a natural, even evolutionary process. Despite a fierce historiography of forced conformity, some insist that assimilation is merely a normal course of the development of one's national identity. Furthermore, many feel that language programs that do not produce new speakers are irrelevant and categorically unsuccessful. Though the recruiting of new speakers is always paramount, linguists have learned that there are additional benefits to language programs. As Claire Bowern and James Bentley state: "Language revitalization should not be judged successful or otherwise purely on the basis of linguistic outcomes; it is possible for such programs to have good outcomes for all concerned even if they do not increase the number of speakers of the language."[28] Bowern and Bentley further point to beneficial outcomes that are often overlooked with regard to revitalization efforts, including changing the linguistic habits of the remaining speakers, raising the profile of the language in the community, and opening the door for the study of the language as a heritage language.

Although the Internet, digital media, and open source models provide new opportunities for less commonly taught languages, the global reach of English continues its trajectory. Certainly, libraries alone cannot solve the obstacles facing revitalization programs; the success of such programs comes from within each language community, through the determination, will, and strength of the tribal members themselves. Even through successful programming, institutions such as libraries can do little in comparison with community-driven efforts. As the report of the Task Force on Aboriginal Languages and Cultures states, "The focus of language conservation and revitalization efforts must shift from formal institutions to communities, families and social networks."[29] Nevertheless, as institutions charged with both safeguarding and promoting the cultural record, libraries should consider Native language materials and language health a key concern.

CONCLUSION

Successful language revitalization is accomplished through integrated strategies that involve communities, institutions, and support networks. Wider collaboration and involvement among academic libraries is needed to ensure that, collaboratively, collections include both academic and community revitalization materials to reflect each of the fifty-three languages of the Northwest Pacific Plateau. Libraries should remain responsive to the needs and challenges inherent in revitalization efforts through endeavors that engage and foster collaboration among language learners, speakers, scholars, elders, and communities. Ellen Gabiel, illustrator for Mohawk curriculum material, expresses this need well:

> As far as our traditions go, we say that we are responsible for the next seven generations and the work we do now will affect those generations. So if we give up, and seven generations from now children only hear it on a tape recorder or on a video, then we fail.[30]

NOTES

1. Task Force on Aboriginal Languages and Cultures, *Towards a New Beginning: A Foundational Report for a Strategy to Revitalize First Nation, Inuit, and Métis Languages and Cultures* (Ottawa, Ont.: Department of Canadian Heritage, 2005), 7.

2. Susana Mota Roboredo Amante, "Native Identity Quest: Am I Canadian?" *Canadaria: Revista Canaria de Estudios Canadienses* 3 (2007): 24.

3. *Huchoosedah: Traditions of the Heart*, directed by Katie Jennings (Seattle: KCTS, 1995).

4. See Living Tongues Institute for Endangered Languages, "Global Language Hotspots," 2007, http://www.swarthmore.edu/SocSci/langhotspots/features.html (accessed 17 January 2011).

5. K. David Harrison, *When Languages Die: The Extinction of the World's Languages and the Erosion of Human Knowledge* (New York: Oxford University Press, 2007), 11.

6. Haruo Aoki, "Writing a Nez Perce Dictionary," in *Making Dictionaries: Preserving Indigenous Languages of the Americas*, ed. William Frawley, Kenneth Hill, and Pamela Munro (Berkeley and Los Angeles: University of California Press, 2002).

7. Aoki, "Writing a Nez Perce Dictionary," 288.

8. Aoki, "Writing a Nez Perce Dictionary," 289–90.

9. Archie Phinney, *Nez Percé Texts* (New York: Columbia University Press, 1934); Anthony Morvillo, *A Dictionary of the Numípu or Nez Perce Language* (St. Ignatius, Mont.: St. Ignatius' Mission Print, 1895).

10. Gerald McKevitt, "Jesuit Missionary Linguistics in the Pacific Northwest: A Comparative Study," *The Western Historical Quarterly* 21, no. 3 (1990): 294.

11. McKevitt, "Jesuit Missionary Linguistics," 291.

12. McKevitt, "Jesuit Missionary Linguistics," 295.

13. Andrew Spencer, *Morphological Theory: An Introduction to Word Structure in Generative Grammar* (Malden, Mass.: Blackwell, 1991), 38.

14. Haruo Aoki, *Nez Perce Dictionary* (Berkeley and Los Angeles: University of California Press, 1994), 420.

15. Lawrence G. Nicodemus, *Snchitsu'umshtsn: The Coeur d'Alene Language, A Modern Course* (Coeur d'Alene, Idaho: Coeur d'Alene Tribe; Washington, D.C.: United States Bureau of Indian Affairs, Office of Education Programs, Research and Cultural Studies Development Section, 1975).

16. Jill Marie Wagner, "Language, Power, and Ethnicity on the Coeur E'Alene Reservation" (PhD diss., Washington State University, 1997).

17. Hans Vogt, *The Kalispel Language: An Outline of the Grammar with Text, Translations, and Dictionary* (Oslo: Norske Videnskape-Akademi, 1940).

18. Gonzaga University and Kalispel Tribe of Indians, "Language of the Kalíspel," http://guweb2.gonzaga.edu/kalispel/dictionaries.html (accessed 18 January 2011).

19. Aoki, *Nez Perce Dictionary*; Haruo Aoki, *Nez Perce Grammar* (Berkeley and Los Angeles: University of California Press, 1970); Phinney, *Nez Percé Texts*.

20. "Phil Cash Cash," http://www.u.arizona.edu/~cashcash/ (accessed 18 January 2011).

21. U.S. Administration for Native Americans, ACKCO, Inc., and National Museum of the American Indian, *Native Language Preservation: A Reference Guide for Establishing Archives and Respositories*, 2007, http://www.aihec.org/resources/documents/NativeLanguagePreservationReferenceGuide.pdf (accessed 18 January 2011).

22. Christine Sims, "Assessing the Language Proficiency of Tribal Heritage Language Learners: Issues and Concerns for American Indian Pueblo Languages," *Current Issues in Language Planning* 9, no. 3 (2008): 331.

23. Frederick H. White, "Language Reflection and Lamentation in Native American Literature," *SAIL: Studies in American Indian Literatures* 18, no. 1 (2006): 84.

24. K. David Harrison and Gregory Anderson, "Global Language Hotspots: Northwest Pacific Plateau," 2007, http://www.swarthmore.edu/SocSci/langhotspots/hotspots/NPP/index.html (accessed 18 January 2011).

25. Alexander Ross, *The Fur Hunters of the Far West: A Narrative of Adventures in the Oregon and Rocky Mountains* (London: Smith, Elder and Co., 1855), 321–22.

26. White, "Language Reflection," 83.

27. White, "Language Reflection," 89.

28. Claire Bowern and James Bentley, "Yan-nhaŋu Revitalization: Aims and Accomplishments," Proceedings from the Annual Meeting of the Chicago Linguistic Society 41, no. 2 (2005): 61.

29. Task Force, *Towards a New Beginning*, iii.

30. *A Brighter Future: Mohawk, Finding Our Talk: Season Two*, DVD, directed by Paul Rickard and Paul Chaput (Montreal, Que.: Mushkeg Media, 2002).

7

International Efforts in Supporting and Advancing Library Services for Indigenous Populations

Loriene Roy

One of the most exciting developments since the late 1990s is a growing awareness of and activity in international indigenous librarianship. There are several reasons for this emergence.

Native identity does not stop at artificially imposed boundaries such as national borders, usually the result of land cessions afforded by Native peoples to colonizing governments. Indigenous nations have their own traditional lands reflecting life patterns based on seasonal movement and relocation. In this era of self-determination, many tribal communities are asserting their rights. As some tribal communities achieve levels of economic stability, they can devote more resources to cultural heritage initiatives such as support for museums or information centers. This is also a time when tribes are attending to large-scale challenges such as Native language recovery and wellness. They look to their own tribal members as well as other indigenous nations for support, encouragement, and ideas. Sometimes this support takes the form of connections made long afield with tribal members from Canada, Sápmi (the traditional Sámi land in northern Scandinavia), Hawai'i, Australia, and New Zealand/Aotearoa. Native librarians who are often isolated in the workplace even if they are working on tribal lands find solace and support in gathering with other indigenous librarians to whom they turn for answers, questions, networking, and friendship.

Indigenous issues are moving to the front stage in a number of international venues, including the United Nations where in 2007, the General Assembly adopted a Declaration on the Rights of Indigenous Peoples.[1] There has been growing attention paid to issues of intellectual and cultural property rights. The question is whether or not librarians are included in these discussions.

Thus, there are a number of positive energies converging to bring increasing support to international indigenous librarianship. These energies are seen in a growing shared discussion within an environment of increasing stability and a desire by many Native librarians to acknowledge their heritage in the workplace.

ENTER TE ROPU WHAKAHAU: MAORI IN LIBRARIES AND INFORMATION MANAGEMENT

Roy's article "The International Indigenous Librarians' Forum: A Professional Life-Affirming Event" provides background and description to the events leading up to and taking place at the First International Indigenous Librarians' Forum at the Waipapa Marae cultural longhouse on the campus of Auckland University in November 1999.[2] Since then the forum has occurred every two years.[3] In 2001, Peter Sarri, library consultant to the Sámi Parliament, carried the workload in organizing the second forum in Jokkmokk, Sweden, just north of the Arctic Circle. The third forum was developed by a subcommittee of the American Indian Library Association and was held in Santa Fe, New Mexico, in November 2003. Aboriginal and non-Aboriginal library staff members of LSSAP, Library Services of Saskatchewan Aboriginal Peoples Inc., hosted the fourth forum in Regina, Saskatchewan, Canada, in September 2005. The State Library of Queensland took the lead in delivering the fifth forum in Brisbane, Australia, in May 2007. The forum returned to its origins in New Zealand/Aotearoa in early 2008 at the Wananga o Raukawa tribal college near the town of Otaki on the North Island.

Each forum carries some elements of tradition and a legacy of discussion, agreement, and dissent. Te Ropu Whakahau, the original hosts, purposefully chose to call these biennial events forums. This decision was made in order to place emphasis on debate, exchange, and the production of key statements or documents. While each subsequent forum host was given the freedom to adapt the format to local cultural traditions, the aim was not to create the familiar academic type of conference at which papers are read. Each forum has achieved this aim to varying degrees of success. Though the forums share a common purpose, each has asserted its contribution to the ongoing discussion, depicted in the conference themes:

- First International Indigenous Librarians' Forum (New Zealand/Aotearoa) Theme: "*Toi te Kupu, Toi te Mana, Toi te Whenua*: Affirming the Knowledge and Values of Indigenous Peoples in the Age of Information"
- Second International Indigenous Librarians' Forum (Sweden) Theme: "Continuing to Affirm the Knowledge and Values of Indigenous Peoples in the Age of Information"
- Third International Indigenous Librarians' Forum (United States) Theme: "Closer to the Fire: Ensuring Culturally Responsive Library Practices"

- Fourth International Indigenous Librarians' Forum (Canada) Theme: "Keepers of Knowledge"
- Fifth International Indigenous Librarians' Forum (Australia) Theme: "Culture, Knowledge, Future"
- Sixth International Indigenous Librarians' Forum (New Zealand/Aotearoa) Theme: "*Māku Anō e Hanga Tōku Nei Whare*: Determining Our Future"

Several traditions are carried across the forums. All forums have offered opportunities to share time on the land, gather with local indigenous people, and sample local community lifeways. In New Zealand/Aotearoa, this meant a trip to the Arataki Visitors' Center to learn about Maori art expressions and share time in the bush. Attendees spent a day at a reindeer camp in Sweden, at the San Diego Feast Day at the Pueblo of Jemez in northern New Mexico, at a pow-wow in Canada, and with an Aboriginal community on Stradbroke Island off the coast near Brisbane, and walked through the community of Otaki in New Zealand/Aotearoa.

The forums have developed their own protocols, from a gift exchange with program leaders to a shared stone carving, a Maori stone, that represents the spirit of the gathering. This Maori stone is a round river rock that is cared for by each host nation. Each host also adds something to the stone, enabling the stone to acquire the representation of each tribal community. The Sámi created a birch bark box to hold the stone. American Indian delegates endowed the stone with a beaded strap to the box handle. The First Nations hosts created a leather carrying bag, and the Aboriginal hosts relined the bag and unveiled their contribution to the Maori stone at the sixth forum, which took place in 2008. Stone caretakers convey the stone to sites of relevance during their two years of hosting, respecting the stone as a living object that desires human contact.

Each forum has resulted in the production of supporting key statements.[4] The Forum Vision Statement was accepted at Forum I:

> We, as unified indigenous peoples who work with libraries and information, will ensure the appropriate care, development and management of the indigenous knowledge of generations past, present, and future.

Forum goals were an outcome of Forum II in Sweden:

Goals: International Indigenous Librarians Forum (2001)
1. The indigenous librarians of this forum recognise the importance of language in relation to cultural identity and will inspire progress within our professions, whilst advocating for self determination and control of indigenous knowledge.
2. This forum proposes that international guidelines and protocols be developed to guide libraries, archives and other information providers to assure that culturally responsive practices for indigenous people are implemented in their environment, services, programme, collections and staffing.

3. We as indigenous librarians seek to form alliances with other international indigenous bodies committed to nurturing indigenous youth.
4. We as indigenous librarians affirm our commitment to utilise our collective skills, values and expertise in both cultural and professional spheres to strengthen indigenous youth.
5. As indigenous librarians, we state that the use of intellectual and cultural property in any medium, especially in light of the global instantaneous impact of the electronic environment, without the approval of all appropriate indigenous authorities is unacceptable.

A draft manifesto was developed by organizers at Forum III in New Mexico. The text reads as follows:

International Indigenous Librarians' Forum III (2003)
Draft Manifesto
International indigenous librarians believe as keepers of the record library information providers are a force for cultural and intellectual survival of indigenous people and that there exists a need for policies, procedures and practices within libraries, museums, archives and educational institutions that acknowledge the value of indigenous culture. Further, that these institutions should adopt culturally responsive guidelines to assure appropriate information services are provided.

International Indigenous librarians support partnerships with library and information agencies in order to assure global initiatives are undertaken which emphasize the value of adopting culturally responsive guidelines for use by all library information providers. To implement these guidelines librarians and information providers must:
- Mobilize and bring together those who can translate guidelines into action
- Convince library information providers of the need for these guidelines
- Assure that culturally responsive guidelines become policy and standard practice

Issues faced by indigenous people are much broader than matters of policies, practices, and guidelines, however. Initiatives to exert control over their intellectual and cultural property, to retain language, to preserve cultural practices are equally important goals shared in common. Therefore, the need to understand these issues in relationship to library information services, the following set of principles apply:
- Traditional knowledge is the intellectual property of indigenous peoples
- Protection of their cultural heritage is a right of indigenous peoples
- The primary rights of the owners of a culture must be recognized by library and information providers which should adopt strategies proposed in *Aboriginal and Torres Strait Islander Protocols for Libraries, Archives and Information Services*.[5]

International cooperation is essential for finding solutions faced by indigenous people. The International Indigenous Librarians' Forum should be established as a permanent Forum creating a global network for sharing information, ideas and practices.

Forum IV in Canada contributed an action plan:

International Indigenous Librarians Forum Action Plan (2005)

Delegates to the Fourth International Indigenous Librarians Forum offered to contribute their energies to the following efforts.

1. They will develop a Forum planning document to assist planners of future International Indigenous Librarians Forums.
2. They will develop a strategy for continuing to include indigenous information workers from around the world in Forum gatherings.
3. They will collaborate with International Federation of Library Associations and Institutions' (IFLA) initiatives related to indigenous information services.
4. They will take steps to document the history of the International Indigenous Librarians Forum.
5. They will work to review and, if appropriate, revise the initial documents arising from previous Forums, including the Vision, Goals, and Manifesto.

Proposal: Representatives to each Forum would bring with them to the next gathering books about the indigenous peoples of the country that they represent. These books would be presented to the host country committee at the conference. The host country would choose which library(s) these books would go to in the host country. For example, representatives from Alaska could bring with them books about their indigenous cultures to donate to the Australian host committee. This would help to enrich the understanding of those cultures in Australia.

Book Acquisition: Forum representatives could acquire books through direct purchase, grants, tribal, corporate or personal donations or donations from the authors.

Delegates in Australia reviewed documents and, through focused discussions, provided future forum planners with suggestions and questions. Most forums also produced published proceedings and sometimes other publications.[6]

As the forum approached its ten-year anniversary, it became apparent that some redirecting and reaffirming were in order. Two lingering questions relate to the qualifications of those organizing and attending the events. Te Ropu Whakahau, the first hosts, followed a protocol more common in New Zealand/Aotearoa. The forum was planned and attended by indigenous peoples. Nonindigenous supporters joined the indigenous delegates at the opening and closing social events, whereas the indigenous attendees presented the content and participated in deliberative workshops and discussions. When one nonindigenous delegate arrived at the forum from North America, he was welcomed, allowed to observe, and asked not to engage orally with the proceedings.

Subsequent forums created alterative ways to balance indigenous and nonindigenous presences. The Sámi hosts scheduled an indigenous council that met for one hour each day of the forum. The council reported out to all delegates on the last morning of the forum and was responsible for creating the forum goals and objectives. The forum in the United States was planned by a group including indigenous and nonindigenous delegates, reflecting the active membership of the American Indian Library Association. This planning model was continued in the forums held in Canada in 2005 and in Australia in 2007. The forum held in New Mexico made no provision for indigenous-only deliberation. The forums in

Canada and Australia organized content into two segments, with one track open to all delegates and another track open only to indigenous delegates. The reality is that nonindigenous delegates have attended all forums.

Another concern relates to the national origins of forum delegates. Only one delegate has attended all forums. Over time, organizers have observed a disconnect on behalf of newer attendees and a sense of loss of purpose by those who attend the occasional forum. Although the forums are touted as international gatherings, delegates represent only a handful of developed countries: New Zealand/Aotearoa, Australia, Canada, Sweden, and the United States. Efforts need to be extended to include delegates from other countries, especially from Latin and South America. Te Ropu Whakahau contributed the initial working definition the forum uses for the word *indigenous*: "those who have become minority peoples in their places of cultural origin."[7] Though this definition suits many environments, it might not be flexible enough to include representation by indigenous peoples who are in the demographic majority. This ignores the potential appearance and contributions by Black Africans and, someday, the Maori themselves as they become the majority culture in their country.

These experiences lend themselves to deep discussion. While some see an indigenous-only gathering as endorsement of segregation, others see this format as respectful of indigenous-centered debate and a step away from diluting content to accommodate nonindigenous viewpoints. Others note that separate tracks based on racial/cultural affiliations do not recognize the reality of work environments in which Native and non-Native library staff work side by side. A counterargument is the belief that an indigenous-only discussion forum provides a safe platform of trust from which to explore and share comments without fear of appropriation or reprisal. It remains to be seen whether the International Indigenous Librarians' Forum will continue in its present state, providing an impacting mix of intellectual stimulation and pleasantry with lingering unsettled issues.

There are other international efforts that point to the evolving stature of indigenous librarianship internationally. Three indigenous librarians' events have taken place in Latin America. Some librarians attend the World Indigenous Peoples' Conference on Education (WIPCE), held every three years in various locations around the world.

THE INTERNATIONAL FEDERATION OF LIBRARY ASSOCIATIONS AND INSTITUTIONS (IFLA)

Three tangibles emerged from this attention to indigenous issues in IFLA. First was the formal endorsement of the IFLA Statement on Indigenous Traditional Knowledge. Former IFLA president Dr. Alex Byrne appointed a temporary Presidential Commission on Indigenous Matters from 2006 though 2008. This led to the establishment of the IFLA Special Interest Group (SIG) on Indigenous

Matters. The presidential commission held public programs and discussions at IFLA conferences from 2005 through 2008. In addition, the Library Service to Multicultural Populations Section of IFLA wrote a Multicultural Library Manifesto.[8] The document divided content into seven key areas: (1) guiding principles; (2) missions of multicultural library services; (3) management and operation; (4) core actions; (5) staff; (6) funding, legislation, and networks; and (7) implementing the manifesto. In 2009, the manifesto was endorsed by UNESCO.[9]

At the Seventy-Fourth IFLA General Conference and Council in Quebec, Canada, in August 2008, attendees discussed the establishment of the SIG on Indigenous Matters. According to IFLA governance procedure, the prospective SIG needed to be placed under an existing section. The Library Services to Multicultural Populations Section welcomed the SIG and approved of the proposal, which was submitted, according to IFLA policy, to the IFLA Professional Committee for discussion and possible approval, which was granted in December 2008. The SIG is guided by a convener who must be an IFLA member. Others participating in the SIG need not be members of IFLA. The SIG has the potential to be the first truly international communication vehicle on indigenous librarianship. Since the approval of the SIG, the convener has worked diligently on assuring an indigenous voice and to make sure that indigenous matters are afforded their own platform and not subsumed under the topic of multicultural library services.

NOTES

1. United Nations, General Assembly, "United Nations Declaration on the Rights of Indigenous Peoples. Resolution 61/295," 13 September 2007, http://www.un.org/esa/socdev/unpfii/en/drip.html (accessed 8 September 2010).

2. Loriene Roy, "The International Indigenous Librarians' Forum: A Professional Life-Affirming Event," *World Libraries* 10, nos. 1/2 (Spring/Fall 2000): 19–30.

3. Loriene Roy, "The International Indigenous Librarians' Forum: A Personal and Professional Life-Affirming Event," *International Leads* 13, no. 4 (December 1999): 4; Loriene Roy, "Second International Indigenous Librarians' Forum," *International Leads* 15, no. 4 (December 2001): 6; Loriene Roy, Sandra Littletree, and Robert L. Yazzie Jr., "The Keepers of Knowledge: Fourth International Indigenous Librarians' Forum," *American Indian Libraries Newsletter* 28, no. 1 (Fall 2005): 1–2.

4. Wendy Sinclair-Sparvier and Hinureina Mangan, "Outcomes: International Indigenous Librarians' Forum 1999–2009," November 2008, https://sites.google.com/site/indigenouslibrariansforum/outcomes (accessed 8 September 2010).

5. ATSILIRN, Aboriginal and Torres Strait Islander Library Information and Resource Network, "ATSILIRN Protocols," 1995, 2005, http://www1.aiatsis.gov.au/atsilirn/protocols.atsilirn.asn.au/index0c51.html?option=com_frontpage&Itemid=1 (accessed 8 September 2010).

6. Chris Szekely, ed., *Issues and Initiatives in Indigenous Librarianship: Some International Perspectives* (Auckland, New Zealand: Te Ropu Whakahau, 1999); Robert Sullivan, ed., *International Indigenous Librarians' Forum Proceedings* (Auckland, New Zealand: Te

Ropu Whakahau, 2001); *International Indigenous Librarians' Forum 2002: Report From a Seminar at Ajtte, Sweden, Swedish Mountain and Sámi Museum, September 5–8, 2001* (Jokkmokk, Sweden: Ajtte, 2002); David Ongley, ed., *Closer to the Fire: Ensuring Culturally Responsive Library Practices: International Indigenous Librarians' Forum III* (Norman, Okla.: American Indian Library Association, 2006).

7. Bernard Makoare and Chris Szekely, *International Indigenous Librarians' Forum 1999* [Preliminary Program] (Auckland, New Zealand: National Library of New Zealand, 1999), 8.

8. International Federation of Library Associations and Institutions (IFLA), Library Services to Multicultural Populations Section, "Multicultural Library Manifesto," 2008, http://www.ifla.org/VII/s32/pub/MulticulturalLibraryManifesto.pdf (accessed 8 September 2010).

9. Mijin Kim, "Chair's Column," *Library Services to Multicultural Populations Newsletter* (December 2009): 1.

8

American Indian Library Association

Kelly Webster

The American Indian Library Association (AILA) was founded in 1979, at a time when the library needs of American Indians were gaining national attention. A meeting was held in 1978 to inform the White House about the need for improved library services on or near reservations. New tribal libraries were being established, and the possibility of federal funding was being explored. Several dedicated professionals involved in raising awareness at the national level helped to establish AILA. The organization has undergone many changes since its birth, but remains the only national organization in the United States to focus on the needs of tribal libraries.

AILA became an affiliate of the American Library Association (ALA) in 1985 and holds its meetings in conjunction with ALA's annual conferences and midwinter meetings. Members include tribal and Alaskan village librarians; Native librarians working in academic, public, and special libraries; and other individuals and institutions interested in the library-related needs of Native peoples. In 2001, AILA gained nonprofit status.

When AILA began, the establishment and funding of libraries on or near reservations was a crucial issue. AILA members were integral to the process of raising awareness of tribal library needs, guiding the drafting of legislation, and lobbying Washington. Over the years, priorities have shifted. Although funding for tribal libraries remains an important issue, AILA's goals have broadened to include advocacy in the profession for the information needs of American Indians and Native Alaskans, recruitment of Native librarians into the profession, and building relationships with other indigenous librarians on an international level.

Every year, AILA sponsors a program held in conjunction with the ALA annual conference. AILA members work to ensure that the issues affecting Native populations are kept on the radar of the profession, remaining visible in ALA programming and priorities. AILA-L, the organization's electronic list, allows members to network; share information about grants, projects, and pressing issues; and participate in organizational business even when travel to meetings is not an option.

AILA awards a scholarship annually to American Indians or Alaska Natives entering library school. Many AILA members are known for their efforts to recruit and mentor new librarians. Other recent efforts include the establishment of a Youth Literature Award and the Honoring Our Elders Award, which gives recognition to the distinguished service of active and retired AILA members.

To continue building relationships on an international level, AILA hosted the third International Indigenous Librarians' Forum in Santa Fe, New Mexico, in 2003. There are many issues common to indigenous librarianship around the world, such as cultural property issues, self-determination, funding, and battling the misinformation about indigenous peoples that remains in society and even the library profession. AILA plans to remain an integral part of continuing this dialogue.

9

Tribal College and University Library Association (TCULA)

Mary Anne Hansen and James Thull

In June 2004, tribal college librarians meeting for their annual professional development conference in Bozeman, Montana, decided to form their own association to help serve their unique professional needs: The Tribal College and University Library Association (TCULA) was born after several years of informal discussions. The tribal college librarians had been interacting with one another for many years through various meetings and training workshops, including the annual Tribal College Librarians Institute (TCLI) hosted by the Montana State University Libraries. They also had been communicating virtually with one another over the course of ten years through an e-mail discussion list. After a decade of networking and group problem solving informally, the librarians decided their own professional organization would serve them well in a variety of collective efforts and give them more of a voice in the profession and at their own institutions.

In its first formal actions, the association adopted a mission statement and passed a resolution seeking financial support for the American Indian Higher Education Consortium (AIHEC) Virtual Library. The virtual library provides guided access to resources on the World Wide Web as well as access to various expensive databases, but the grant funding for it has expired. Efforts to obtain ongoing funding and support for the AIHEC Virtual Library are still underway.

The first TCULA Executive Board elected included the following tribal college librarians: president, Rachel Lindvall, formerly at Sinte Gleska University; vice president, Holly Ristau, White Earth Tribal and Community College; secretary, Clyde Henderson, Crownpoint Institute of Technology; and treasurer, Elaine Cubbins, Tohono O'odham Community College. TCULA has created a Native American children's book award. Members continue to convene at each annual

TCLI at Montana State University in Bozeman, Montana, and also gather at annual AIHEC meetings.

At the AIHEC 2007 Conference, TCULA members convened to discuss a draft Tribal College Library Standards and Best Practices that included discussions of information literacy, collections, and staffing policies and practices. They also discussed the following topics: images of Native Americans in children's literature; how we can help teachers, parents, and school librarians identify resources; library hybrids: how tribal college libraries serve the public sector of their communities; how legislation supports or discourages library services; TCULA grant-seeking priorities for group funding; rural library sustainability; Bill & Melinda Gates Foundation grant funding, WebJunction.org, and TechAtlas; AIHEC Virtual Library updates and other online resources for tribal college libraries; the possibility of starting a student writing award for children's literature; and the possibility of starting a TCULA library drill cart team.

II

SERVICE FUNCTIONS OF TRIBAL INFORMATION CENTERS

10

Indigenous Architecture for Tribal Cultural Centers

Sam Olbekson

Many of the central issues facing leaders in contemporary Native American society involve self-determination; cultural survival; health; education; and efforts to strengthen the economic, social, and physical fabric of our tribal communities. In order to be effective, leaders must address these issues comprehensively. Passing on traditions such as language, stories, dance, and spirituality is essential to the cultural survival of Native peoples. These traditions are a key factor in creating identity, cultural bonds, a connection to our ancestors, and defining our future. As Native people, we are taught to embrace our elders and respect the earth. We celebrate our storytellers, artists, and dancers. We stress the learning of our languages as a vital component to cultural survival. We proudly persist by keeping alive the key aspects of our culture that define who we are as Native peoples. We are also able to transform and respond to new technologies and outside cultural influences without losing our identities. Taking active control of how we adapt, grow, and innovate within a continuing framework of change will continue to empower Native communities to preserve cultural traditions and control our future identities in the context of contemporary society. Cultural loss will persist only if we allow it.

We continue to lack full control over one fundamental component of our culture, though: our capacity to directly understand, influence, and ensure that cultural traditions are expressed in our architecture and built environment in an appropriate, respectful, and inspiring manner. The design and construction of a building is a process too complex to address here in any significant depth. Rather than being a "how to" for designing tribal facilities or presenting specific examples of architecture to debate, this outline offers a framework for discussing and exploring critical design components that can inform any tribal project. I outline a number of essential design concerns and strategies to consider, by focusing on how culture can influence the design process to allow for relevant architectural principles to surface and guide meaningful design.

A FRAMEWORK FOR NATIVE CULTURAL ARCHITECTURAL DESIGN

Contemporary tribal buildings have been primarily modeled after non-Native building types and designed by architects from outside cultures that have different conceptions of how space and community should reflect our culture. This has facilitated a lack of control by Native American communities in the recent past over what structures are built, who designs them, and who decides how they are operated. It has allowed outside non-Native cultural influences to define our architectural identity and inadvertently control and limit access to a critical element of our own traditions. Native people have been historically denied choices and input on the structures that have been built for them. Too often community members have been passive observers in the design process rather than active participants and form-givers.

Although this paternalistic model of development is slowly being replaced by a growing sense of self-determination and tribal control, it continues to reflect a severe cultural disconnection and break in architectural continuity that has allowed contemporary buildings to be largely removed from indigenous concepts of space and form. Native American architects still lack adequate representation in academic and professional settings, are frequently alienated and labeled as "others," and are often separated from the larger design community by distinct conceptual boundaries. Although well-intentioned, most recent expressions of contemporary Native American architecture have been produced by non-Native designers who have caricaturized, mimicked, parodied, or misinterpreted traditional form, idea, and cultural principles to varying degrees. Many Native American architects trained in Western architectural practices and educational settings also continue to perpetuate and apply misguided models of design. This practice has resulted in a visual landscape of sprawl, tacky decoration, stereotypical imagery, and culturally vacant structures in tribal communities. Look around your community and you will likely see many examples of this. What buildings do you see that truly reflect who you are? Native architecture has frequently been reduced to the equivalent of culturally diluted trinkets and chicken-feather crafts sold to unsuspecting tourists. These missed opportunities have resulted from many factors, including a lack of knowledge by tribal leaders who do not have experience working with architects; designers with little familiarity or deep understanding of Native culture; and design processes that focus on superficial distortions, mimicry, and exaggerations of Native cultural aesthetics.

In contrast, culturally stimulating and inspiring approaches to design can emerge through observing and understanding the relationships among tribal culture, the landscape, materials, climate, light, form, our bodies, and programmatic purpose. How we approach design is as important as what we design. Appropriate architectural responses stem from research, exploration, and innovation by those intimately involved in the creative process. Appropriate design solutions will arise from avoiding the use of culture as a set of trite afterthoughts and applications of iconic symbols or reliance on staged imagery that outside cultures have come to perceive as looking Native American. These approaches have provided a watered-down and often offensive architectural identity. A more respectful and meaningful approach recognizes subtle cultural principles and promotes connectivity to both traditional and contemporary cultural traditions. Design can either positively reinforce a Native world viewpoint or underline continued cultural loss by reflecting stereotypes and misinterpretations of cultural knowledge. Collaborating with Native American architects who are committed to creativity, innovation, and quality will lead to successful and respectful design solutions.

As tribal communities gain further economic stability and control over development, our leaders need to value design as a key contributor to community revitalization and stability. We must understand and acknowledge how the design of our buildings and the physical planning of our towns, reservations, and urban neighborhoods influence how we interact and engage each other as a community. Buildings not only provide basic shelter from the elements, they also directly shape how we live. Divisions of space reinforce or inhibit social structures and have a profound impact on human interaction. The design of our homes, cultural facilities, work environments, and other structures informs our ability to gather and interact as families and individuals. Tribal libraries, museums, and other important cultural institutions play a vital role in preserving language, memory, and lifeways for Native communities and have both the opportunity and responsibility to demonstrate a commitment to culturally appropriate design that encourages access and community engagement. Each tribal community or organization must develop its own design goals and aspirations through intensive research, self-reflection, and explorations with qualified Native architects skilled in critical design thinking and cultural interpretation.

As a Native architect and urban designer with deep-rooted concerns for culture and the environment, I am frequently confronted with balancing the relationship between traditional architecture and the requirements of contemporary society. Searching for an architectural expression appropriate for contemporary Native American communities has guided much of my creative exploration and research in design, and I have found that there is no single or straightforward answer. Invention and innovation are critical to the future success of tribal communities. Native cultures have never been static; they continually adapt and respond to changes when necessary, and architecture must gracefully evolve with these transformations and cultural shifts. We have the responsibility to maintain and preserve our preexisting cultural knowledge, but we also have the freedom to create new knowledge and expressions of culture that bridge the gap between modern architectural technology and tradition.

From recent discussions with a community leader asking for guidance on how to approach the process of designing a tribal museum, it is clear to me that there is a strong commitment by contemporary tribal leaders to promote quality design and a demand for architecture that responds to cultural tradition in innovative ways. A lack of experience in planning a construction project based on an indigenous point of view, or even a broader awareness of what is possible, often leaves tribal organizations without a clear path on which to move forward. There is no single way to approach the design of a tribal library, museum, archive, or other cultural institution. A collaborative design process, an understanding of a project's role in contemporary society, a recognition of precedent, and a deliberate and respectful approach to cultural symbolism are key factors to successfully designing culturally significant buildings.

CONCERNS AND STRATEGIES ESSENTIAL IN CULTURALLY CENTERED DESIGN

Establishing a collaborative design process that involves key stakeholders and developing a framework for design exploration are critical early steps. A collaborative process brings together, in an atmosphere of mutual trust, the appropriate team members at the right times to respond to the most significant issues within a framework of open dialogue and shared mission. This type of critical discourse, when done well, will force central issues to surface that allow for design solutions to be generated from well-researched and culturally founded consensus. The collective wisdom of elders, tribal leaders, designers, and other community members far surpasses the wisdom of individual stakeholders or professionals. Various consultants, such as landscape architects and engineers, are also important team members to engage early in the design process in addition to architects. Bringing together a comprehensive, responsive team during the early formative stages of design is critical for projects to stay on schedule and within budget.

Before addressing form and aesthetics, the client and design team need to reveal and respect the heart and larger purpose inherent in tribal facilities. Providing space that inspires, educates, and bonds our children, elders, families, and the rest of our relations are common goals shared by cultural institutions and Native architects. Some of the broader types of questions that should be asked include the following:

- What role in tribal society will the project assume, and what patterns of activity will it support or hinder?
- How can the building promote social interaction, strengthen tribal bonds, and define space where visitors can thrive in the context of their own culture?

- How can we design and program these spaces to complement rather than inhibit our culture?
- In what ways can this facility best affirm and develop cultural values while instilling a deeper understanding of community members' pride and understanding of tribal culture?
- How can we ensure that this project will be unique, exceptional, culturally inspiring, and intellectually engaging?

Successful design requires intense research, exploring history and precedent in the traditional architecture and customs of using space in your tribal community. This research should also include the exploration of relevant contemporary models of space and place making as well. Traditional forms, our architectural "elders," can inform how we approach the design of space today and reveal timeless inspirational generators of spatial principles and material qualities. We must reestablish an awareness of our architectural history to understand the power of architecture as a conveyor of cultural identity. Investigate how contemporary architects and artists innovate, create, and reflect culture to explore new directions and how these explorations can inform your design process. Looking at examples of poor design strategies will help to develop an understanding of how caricature, mimicry, parody, and other perpetuators of stereotypes are harmful. Successful design requires an understanding of the powerful relationships that connect people and place and how a traditional respect for landscape and environment can inform contemporary methods of sustainable construction and respectful use of natural resources.

Cultural identity and indigenous concepts of space can be influential generators of meaning and expression in architecture when used respectfully and as a starting point for further study. Explore what the appropriate cultural responses for this project type could be and refrain from forcing unnecessary cultural references. Such an exploration includes considering the following:

- Which uses of symbolism and iconographic language in design are appropriate for this project?
- Can and should references to traditional form, materials, colors, and textures be woven into the project?
- How can expressing culture help create an architecture that will bring about an emotional response and be a positive and constant reminder of Native values?
- How can the building embody the practical and the spiritual and express a connectedness to the earth while functioning for its intended use?
- By being culturally specific, we can create architecture that emerges from strong regional, cultural, and traditional sources that are closely rooted in the land, environment, and people of a specific place.
- Once the project's underlying cultural objectives are clear, the client and design team need to explore the most specific physical ways these goals

can be achieved using the concepts and objectives established. There is no right answer to how form emerges from the design process, but the most successful buildings delay an expression of form until many considerations and viewpoints are taken into account. This delay eliminates the struggle to fit a tight program of spaces into a predetermined form that might not work well for a desired function. Clients will too often have an assumption of shape for a building based on a precedent of typology or history that reflects past experiences and expectations: "A house should look like this" or "a museum should be this shape" or "a library should be made out of these materials." This approach can limit the possibilities of expression in architecture. An example of this approach is to base a new design on a traditional dwelling or gathering space and attempt to precisely reproduce its formal qualities as much as possible in an attempt to be "authentic." An approach that imitates historic structures should be reserved for those instances in which a clear cultural need is met by replicating a traditional form. Another metaphorical approach is to base design on a visual or aesthetic goal inspired by an important cultural object, idea, or point of view abstracted from its initial form or purpose. An example of this strategy is a design that reflects and honors an important cultural object or symbol such as a drum or a circle. Another, more contemporary approach would be to develop the form of a building through design studies that respond to specificities of aesthetic, cultural, programmatic, climate, and site considerations. An example of this approach would be to develop the shape of a building by allowing the function or cultural customs of using space to determine the shape, rather than the shape of the building determining or limiting a space's use.

Many other methods and hybrid approaches to design may be employed to reveal the form, details, and aesthetic qualities of a project. There will always be a push and pull among user needs, available funds, and design goals throughout the design process. A thorough predesign study involving the development of several different approaches, configurations, and building footprints for the design team to debate, discuss, and refine is an effective way to resolve these issues. Exploring multiple options can give rise to other relevant ideas that might be more suitable to project goals. Design investigations and research must be intensive and culturally specific to produce high-quality buildings that reflect an indigenous point of view. When designing cultural facilities we must always keep in mind, however, that libraries cannot replace our storytellers and that museums cannot replace our elders for keeping our traditions alive. We should focus less on memorizing our traditions than fully immersing ourselves into and actually living out our culture. Buildings can only play a supportive role in our effort to maintain culture, and they can never replace the oral tradition of passing down knowledge to our children.

Architecture is a vital component of Native culture and a powerful conveyor of identity. Like other cultural and artistic traditions, it inherently reflects a community's values and beliefs and can transmit vital knowledge and customs from preceding generations to the next. Architecture can engage all of our senses and interweave cultural meaning with the built environment to create meaningful spaces. Design solutions developed from a local and deep understanding of cultural values, aesthetics, and tribal identity can generate buildings that are culturally relevant and specific to the needs of contemporary Native American communities.

Buildings are physical manifestations of complex constructs of cultural meaning, social relationships, and community needs. Our own architects, tribal governments, and community leaders must embrace this responsibility as a critical component of sovereignty and self-determination. This authorship will allow us to control the transformation of living and social patterns that are producing new community, family, social, and architectural demands. The importance we place on the design of our structures now will tell future generations what we value as a society today. Our buildings can be inspiring, educational, and motivational, helping to promote rich cultural ways of living life. New materials, spatial organizations, and building types can be part of a positive natural growth that achieves a balance among the traditions of the past, the necessities of the present, and the opportunities for the future.

11

Tribal Libraries as the Future of Librarianship: Independent Collection Development as a Tool for Social Justice[1]

Kristen Hogan

> This is the way it goes: These Indian women warriors walk into the tribal library. There are more than three of them. They keep showing up. They are growing in number, and they are gravitating toward the glow of the computer-screen campfire in the farthest recesses of this modern sweatlodge.[2]

Ojibwe author Lois Beardslee offers this brilliant reappropriation of institutional space in her book *The Women's Warrior Society*. The women claim the library as sweatlodge; take it back from racist white librarians; take it back from the pamphlets and cardboard cutouts of army recruiters; take it back from unused, irrelevant periodicals where, Beardslee notes, *Dry Lips Oughta Move to Kapuskasing* by Thomson Highway should be, where Lois Beardslee's books should be.[3] Beardslee restores tribal libraries to the spaces Elizabeth Peterson describes in her directory *Tribal Libraries in the United States*, spaces "created and maintained by American Indian people."[4] This chapter speaks with both indigenous and nonindigenous librarians at tribal libraries to explore the power of collection development as a practice of making place. For Beardslee, finding indigenous materials in the library means validation, invitation, and the possibility of a different future. Her community in the library imagines recording one girl's story of resisting colonial teaching practices and finding it on library shelves: "What library is gonna have a book about Cinqala's story?" "How about all the libraries?"[5]

I begin this chapter with a survey of the current field of collection development in tribal libraries and of indigenous materials; this survey takes the form of a review of writings about collection development in tribal libraries in connection with writings about American Indian literature collection development in public and academic libraries. Next, I review central concerns in American Indian collection development about authorship resisting appropriation and collections resisting homogenizing American Indian identity; in connection with these discussions, I reflect on my own identity as a white antiracist ally to position my approach to this chapter as a conversation with American Indian authors, theorists, publishers, and librarians. Because responsible collection development takes place as dialogue and affects what gets published, I also include text from conversations with authors who also work as scholars, editors, publishers, and organizers: Daniel Heath Justice (Cherokee), Kateri Akiwenzie-Damm (Anishinabe), and Kimberly Roppolo (Cherokee, Choctaw, Creek). Finally, I gather a resource list of materials for collection development as well as for collections of magazines, fiction, nonfiction, poetry, children's literature, young adult literature, and reference/homework preparation resources. Although I reference a few classics of the field, my resource list focuses on American Indian–authored or –supported texts published over the last decade in order to emphasize the vitality of contemporary authorship and the exciting role tribal libraries serve in supporting and generating the next decades of American Indian authorship and storytelling.

Throughout the chapter, I engage with U.S. and Canadian indigenous authors, publishers, and libraries. In working to speak with indigenous peoples across the U.S.-Canadian border, I attempt to identify speakers as they identify themselves. Recognizing the vital significance of naming as an act of sovereignty, I draw on current writings and correspondence and use the terms *American Indian* and *indigenous* to identify North American indigenous peoples, even while recognizing the need to eradicate borders.[6] I look forward to engaging in responses to this chapter, and I hope that it serves as a resource guide to existing collection development literature, as a tool for conversations about and acquisition of contemporary indigenous literature, and as a tool for grant writing and other advocacy by arguing that tribal libraries are central to the future of American Indian literature.

WRITINGS ON COLLECTION DEVELOPMENT IN TRIBAL LIBRARIES

A survey of the library literature on collection development reveals few articles or books addressing collection development specifically in tribal libraries. In the existing literature, tribal librarians interested in colleagues' collection development practices may look to bibliographies addressing American Indian audiences, a few articles addressing collection development in and profiles of specific tribal libraries, and articles about tribal college and university collections. In "Collection Development in California Tribal Libraries," Elizabeth Peterson explains, "There is little mention of tribal library collection development in the literature, and most of the articles that do exist are more than ten years old."[7] She cites examples of such studies.[8] Although they do not specifically identify the tribal library as the site of collection, these authors notably create bibliographies with an American Indian audience in mind; they also reflect a focus of the literature on children's books, significant for the field with a focus on supporting indigenous youth who face an often damaging curriculum in the schools.

Peterson's 2004 article is itself a unique resource in the field, because it explores in detail the process of collection development for a specific tribal library. "In 2002," Peterson explains, "I was hired as a consultant to the Owens Valley Paiute tribe to help build the library collection in the Indian Education Center in Bishop, California."[9] She found useful information in region-specific bibliographies like Lauren Teixeira's 1991 master's thesis, "Access to Information on the Costanoan/ Ohlone Indians of the San Francisco and Monterey Bay Area: A Descriptive Guide to Research."[10] For Peterson, Teixeira's guide is useful as a model that "suggests pathways about California Indians in general."[11] Such a guide is "missing from the literature" not only for California Indians but for tribal libraries at large. Peterson's article thus documents one method of developing a collection specific to a local indigenous community; it lists local indigenous publishers and gives a brief list of reference, university press, and indigenous press titles Peterson finds key to the Owens Valley Paiute Library.

Literature for nontribal libraries on developing collections of American Indian literature may be of limited use to tribal librarians; however, the growing number of these bibliographies indicates the significance of tribal libraries as collections that, as Reegan Breu points out, could influence the holdings at public and academic libraries.[12] As one significant example of this advocacy work, indigenous librarian Lotsee Patterson continues her innovative and vital work shaping American Indian collections and advocating for tribal libraries. Having drafted a training manual for tribal library staff, generated a directory of tribal libraries, and authored numerous articles and chapters, Patterson has highlighted the significant work of tribal libraries.[13] In "Exploring the World of American Indian Libraries," she reviews the current state of tribal libraries in the United States.[14] Though she uses a descriptive tone that implies an audience unfamiliar with tribal libraries, Patterson offers information about the work of tribal librarianship that will be useful to tribal librarians as a way of connecting with a network of tribal libraries.

With coauthor Rhonda Taylor in 2004, Patterson emphasized the significance of local community (and limited budgets) to American Indian collections: "To meet local needs, the institution might want to limit the scope of Native American materials acquisition to specific tribes, topics, levels of interest, or time periods."[15] This article includes an extensive overview of library literature bibliographies of American Indian materials. Significantly, the authors move from the local to the (trans)national in their closing recommendations: "Effective acquisition/selection in this specialized arena requires being informed about resources and also being willing to continue learning about the complex political, historical, and cultural realities, current and historical, of the many diverse peoples called Native Americans. Is it time for the development of a national or trade bibliography devoted to the topic of American Indians?"[16] This closing question suggests that activist indigenous librarians can further influence the field of librarianship by calling for an aware and engaged collection development practice and by creating and writing about their groundbreaking collections.

Recent profiles of tribal libraries similarly provide a brief view of practices in the field of tribal librarianship and may be useful when formulating or updating collection development policies. A 2006 profile of the Cow Creek Tribal Library provides a general description of how a small tribal library can serve patrons with a variety of books in a select range of sections. Kelly LaChance, education director for the Cow Creek Band of Umpqua Tribe of Indians, explains how the Cow Creek Tribal Library uses annual Institute of Museum and Library Services (IMLS) Native American Library Services Basic Grants to "increas[e] the holdings in the Native American section of the library collection. Native American books and videos for adults, teens, and children are a high priority."[17] Other foci for the collection are periodicals and featured sections including "nature, gardening, crafts, health, parenting, and educational materials."[18] Other useful profiles include a 2006 overview by Marion Mercier, tribal librarian, Confederated Tribes of Grand Ronde Tribal Library, of her library and its 5,000-volume collection, as well as Rayette Sterling's review, also in 2006, of three tribal libraries, including a mention of the Yakama Nation Library's collection and creation of educational materials.[19]

Finally, although there is a range of articles about tribal colleges, few such articles specifically mention library collections at tribal colleges. These articles with information about tribal college libraries also offer useful information for tribal librarians about the field. As Peterson notes, many of these articles appeared over fifteen years ago, for example, Marjane Ambler's 1994 "Releasing Reservations from Isolation: The Tribal Library as Storyteller" (part of an excellent "Media and Information" issue of *Tribal College Journal of American Indian Higher Education*), and Holly Koelling's 1995 "A Model Collection Process for a Specialized Environment: Recommending Reference Titles for Tribal Community Colleges."[20] More recently, Loriene Roy and Arro Smith coauthored a 2002 overview of tribal library development that includes references to collection development resources such as the Alaska Library Directors' "Culturally Responsive Guidelines for Alaska Public Libraries" and the national reading club program, "If I Can Read, I Can Do Anything."[21] Roy's 1997 article on indigenous material collection development for academic libraries is a related tool, though not specifically for tribal libraries.[22] More recently, Juris Dilevko and Lisa Gottlieb's 2004 article on Canadian tribal college librarianship offers a good literature review as well as narrative descriptions of collection development strategies, general ideas about what collections should provide, and key differences between tribal college and other academic libraries.[23]

COLLECTION DEVELOPMENT AS
ADVOCACY FOR SOCIOECONOMIC JUSTICE

At the risk of stating the obvious, I take a moment here to participate in the ongoing discussion about indigenous collection development as a strategy for resisting misrepresentation and intellectual oppression of indigenous peoples. I raise this here because Beardslee's *The Women's Warrior Society* suggests that tribal libraries are not exempt from harmful collection development strategies originating in a white, middle-class library establishment. In Renee Tjoumas's 1993 article (still a good overview of the history of collection development for American Indian material), she asks mainstream public librarians to consider their participation in oppression: "To what extent does the profession pay lip service to the concept of multicultural collections but in reality uses selection criteria and sources formulated by the white-oriented establishment?"[24] The alternative, a self-reflective and activist librarianship, is already practiced in many tribal libraries. Breu suggests that the explicit "political goals" of tribal libraries unmask the ways in which damaging public library claims to an impossible neutrality result in librarians who practice "neutrality" by refusing to take action, thus "creating 'a value vacuum that is easily being filled by the prevailing political and economic ethos.'"[25] "[B]y supporting cultural survival and self-determination, band [or tribal] librarians do not adopt or claim to reflect a neutral position," Breu points out, and this kind of advocacy models the (antineocolonial) future of librarianship.[26]

Collection development is at the center of this work, because collection development practices have the capacity to generate and support diverse authors and publishers. Shiraz Durrani and Elizabeth Smallwood explain that the too-general language of the ALA and intellectual freedom advocacy for "neutrality" policies result not in actual (impossible) neutrality, but in a collection and practice defined by corporate interests. Globally, they argue, libraries have "become increasingly isolated from the majority of people in their local communities. Forces of corporate globalization then push them even further from their communities by offering to save staff time and mental effort by supplying pre-packaged 'best sellers,' guaranteed to meet the wants of 30 percent of the population—and to boost the profit margins of transnational publishers and booksellers."[27] Tribal libraries' autonomy from many public library systems' centralized buying arrangements makes them uniquely able to advocate for a diverse indigenous press in resistance to a homogenized mainstream.

WORDS WITH KATERI AKIWENZIE-DAMM

Since tribal librarians' ordering practices can support vital indigenous publishing, I contacted Anishinabe author and publisher Kateri Akiwenzie-Damm to ask her a few questions about tribal librarians' support of indigenous authors and publishers. She generously made time to respond, and I include her words here as a key resource. Because she consistently uses literature and texts to create indigenous community and to support new indigenous authors, Akiwenzie-Damm's work also models for librarians the practice of community activist literacy. She has authored numerous essays, journal articles, and poems, including the book of poetry *My Heart Is a Stray Bullet*.[28] She has created space by editing anthologies, including *Without Reservation: Indigenous Erotica* and *Skins: Contemporary Indigenous Writing*.[29] She has connected her writing with performance through productions including the spoken word CD *Standing Ground*, with Joy Harjo and other collaborators, and has served on numerous boards and committees to support indigenous work.[30] Akiwenzie-Damm is also managing editor of Kegedonce Press, an award-winning indigenous publishing house. Here's what she had to say to tribal librarians:

> KH: What would you most like to share with tribal librarians in the United States and Canada as they select and purchase materials by and about North American indigenous peoples?

> KAD: Librarians should know that there are indigenous publishers in Canada who are striving to develop a viable indigenous publishing industry and this includes developing indigenous literatures, supporting emerging writers, creating awareness through promotional activities, contributing to indigenous literary scholarship, expanding the perception of what "indigenous literatures" are, and creating and expanding markets. We bring the voices of indigenous people to the world in a way that larger, mainstream publishers never have and simply won't. Their concepts of our literatures are narrow and focused on the bottom line, rather than on ensuring that the diversity of our voices are heard.

> As for us, since it began in 1993, Kegedonce Press has been committed to the development, promotion, and publication of the work of indigenous writers nationally and internationally. We strive to foster the creative cultural expression of indigenous peoples through the publication of beautifully crafted books which involve indigenous peoples in all levels of production and by supporting activities which promote indigenous literary development and the development of indigenous publishing.

> Kegedonce Press works with indigenous people in all aspects of our work. Not only are our writers indigenous but we work in a culturally appropriate way that respects the writers and their creative work not only as personal creative works but as forms of literary cultural expression. We edit in a more informed and respectful way—and this is essential in ensuring that our books "speak true." We believe in forming partnerships with our writers to involve them actively in the development and promotion of their own books and their individual careers. Some become great promoters of their own work and the work of other Kegedonce Press writers. What we employ is a type of long term thinking and a form of activism that does not enter into the thinking or activities of mainstream publishers.

> We can't compete, at this point, with mainstream, resource-rich, national and multinational publishers, so we need active support from librarians who understand the value of what we're doing.

KH: How can librarians support indigenous authors?

KAD: Buy our books. They can arrange automatic delivery and billing for all new releases. Arrange for paid readings by Native American authors published by indigenous publishing houses. Run a reading series that focuses on indigenous authors and include lectures on issues on indigenous literatures and indigenous publishing. When I call for librarians to set up reading series focusing on indigenous authors, I am not suggesting a kind of ghettoizing of those writers and their works if they are running another series. What I am suggesting is that they not simply add an indigenous author in the mix and call it a day, but that they really make an effort to highlight the work of indigenous writers and help to bring awareness, understanding, and context to the audience. They can do it within their regular series or, if they run more than one, they can do it as a separate series if it is equally resourced and done with care and thoughtfulness. (For example, I have had the experience of such things being separated out and called "storytelling," instead of "readings" and all indigenous authors included called "storytellers" which is obviously not only erroneous and problematic but also reflects profound ignorance.)

Help to create awareness through displays in the library.

Host and promote book launches.

Form a relationship with indigenous publishers. There aren't many of us (three or four in Canada—one Metis publishers and one national publishers and maybe only one or two that I'm aware of in the USA) so it's quite possible to do so.

Start or expand a Native literatures (or indigenous literatures) collection focusing on the literature of local indigenous peoples.

KH: What else would you like to share?

KAD: Buying our books is essential. We need sales to keep operating and to stabilize our industry. We make beautiful books. We pay great attention to the aesthetics and quality of our books from the inside out. The design and cover art is as beautiful as the writing inside. For more information about our books check our website at www .kegedonce.com.

Existing literature has focused on the checklist strategy for assisting (especially nonindigenous) librarians to challenge their own unearned privilege and to "reject books that contain misinformation on American Indian life."[31] Tjoumas and Kuipers both collect lists of questions to guide collection development. Taking this strategy one step further, Kay Marie Porterfield and Emory Dean Keoke emphasize supporting American Indian authors, review press, and communities on their website, "Resources for Selecting Fair and Accurate American Indian Books for Libraries, Schools, and Home."[32]

This support for indigenous authorship is not a search for "authenticity," as Donna Norton and Saundra E. Norton suggested in 1993 when they urged librarians to "be equally concerned with the quality and authenticity of the literature and the references."[33] In this context, "authenticity" transforms the author into an object, readable by others and not self-reflective.[34] Instead, to prioritize indigenous authorship is a strategy to create social justice by validating readers' shared experiences with authors and by generating space for the next generations of indigenous authors by supporting indigenous authors and publishers.[35] Cherokee literary scholar and author Daniel Heath Justice explains the significance of indigenous literary analysis: "Cherokees are in the first and best place to speak about who we are and what's important to us; to deny these voices, or to marginalize them in favor of those whose assumed authority is embedded within the ideologies of colonialism, is to add strength to the Eurowestern assimilationist directive from within."[36] "To privilege Indian perspectives in discourses by and about Indians," Justice explains, "is . . . to insist on the ethical repositioning of Indian voices from the margins of that discourse firmly to the center."[37] Similarly, it is important for indigenous collections not only to include indigenous-authored primary materials in fiction, poetry, and children's literature, but also to include indigenous-authored reference and analytical materials that create a framework for reading the primary materials.

WORDS WITH DANIEL HEATH JUSTICE

Prioritizing indigenous authors is a strategy for working against marginalization and toward social justice, and the daily work of librarians can provide vital support to indigenous authors. Cherokee author and literary scholar Daniel Heath Justice uses his work to articulate the importance of using indigenous intellectual and cultural traditions to understand and make connections among ongoing indigenous literary work. Part of the tradition mapped by scholars of indigenous literary nationalism, this approach to reading American Indian writing draws on an awareness of diverse indigenous histories and calls for indigenous intellectual sovereignty as well as tribal sovereignty.[38] Exploring the power of literature to do this work, Daniel Heath Justice is professor of Aboriginal literatures in the Department of English and affiliate faculty of Aboriginal studies at the University of Toronto. In addition to creating space for conversation in his classroom and advocacy work, Justice also coedits *Studies in American Indian Literatures*, published through the University of Nebraska. Author of the award-winning essential book *Our Fire Survives the Storm: A Cherokee Literary History* as well as of the indigenous fantasy trilogy *Way of the Thorn and Thunder*, Justice's work embodies the connections librarians can make between indigenous fiction and indigenous analysis.[39] Here's what he had to say to tribal librarians:

> KH: What would you most like to share with tribal librarians in the United States and Canada as they select and purchase materials by and about North American indigenous peoples?

DHJ: Primarily that they seek [to] highlight diversity—in authorship, geographical region, community affiliation, genre, form, and publisher. Some texts come from established publishing houses, whereas others emerge from publishing initiatives in communities themselves, and more tribes, bands, and nations are developing their own publishing houses to ensure the accuracy and broader distribution of both cultural and artistic materials.

KH: How can librarians support indigenous authors?

DHJ: Buying their books would be one way, and supporting those presses and publishing initiatives that support indigenous literary expression. Corresponding with publishers about either the strong quality of their indigenous works or the lack of indigenous content would also be good, as it would help to show that libraries are interested in more of these works—and more interested in works that are written and produced by Native peoples themselves. Encouraging reading groups to read Native authors would also be good, as would, when possible, sponsoring writing groups, public readings, and other opportunities for emerging and established Native writers to share their works with a broader audience. If there are writer-in-residence or workshop opportunities at the library, considering Native writers for these experiences (and making space for sustained contact between the community and the writer via lectures, discussions, readings, and workshops) would be useful, both in terms of establishing important and long-lasting relationships and in creating interest in Native literary production.

This practice of progressive collection development also requires self-reflection on the part of librarians and library studies authors. At the start of "The Problem of Speaking for Others," feminist philosopher Linda Alcoff recounts a significant intervention of indigenous feminist authors in publishing in which Anne Cameron, a white Canadian author, "writes several semi-fictional accounts of the lives of Native Canadian women. She writes them in first person and assumes a Native identity. At the 1988 International Feminist Book Fair in Montreal a group of Native Canadian writers decide to ask Cameron to, in their words, 'move over' on the grounds that her writings are disempowering for Native authors. She agrees."[40] White publishers saw Cameron's writing as filling the "niche" for indigenous writing, which meant that Cameron was preventing mainstream publishers from publishing work by indigenous authors. This narrative of privilege is significant for librarianship. Lotsee Patterson,[41] Loriene Roy,[42] Monique Lloyd,[43] and others have written about the lack of American Indian librarians and the need to support American Indian library students and new librarians. This activist support is crucial for shifting power distribution and realizing social justice for indigenous peoples and other marginalized groups.

As I urge librarians to reflect on their own positions, I turn briefly to reflect on my own identity and position as author. As a white, middle-class lesbian, I acknowledge my own unearned race and class privilege and draw on my experiences with queer and antiracist activism and teaching to engage in this article as an antiracist ally. I believe, as does Alcoff, that choosing not to speak can also be an act of privilege, since one feature of white privilege is that white people may choose to not engage with discussions of race.[44] Rather than not write this chapter, I seek to engage in conversation with indigenous authors and publishers both through their work and in direct discussion. My passion for the potential of collection development as an antiracist and progressive transformative process grows from my experience writing about feminist antiracist bookstore histories and working in feminist and antiracist feminist bookstores, including BookWoman in Austin, Texas, and the Toronto Women's Bookstore in Ontario. I bring my experiences with dialogue building as a teacher and as a bookwoman to my strategies in writing this chapter. Breu explains, "Band [or tribal] libraries teach us that programs and services for Aboriginal peoples cannot be created in isolation from Aboriginal peoples. Librarians working in the mainstream have a responsibility to build relationships with Aboriginal peoples."[45] Though I am not yet a librarian, I work to build relationships with indigenous literary activists as I read and advocate with the words and works of indigenous librarians and authors.

COLLECTION DEVELOPMENT
RESOURCES FOR TRIBAL LIBRARIES

The following lists are separated into tools for the collection development process and suggested titles for collections. Each of the subsections includes a head note with a strategy for supporting indigenous authors as a way of supporting indigenous readers and brief references to classic titles. Following the head note, each subsection includes a list of titles from 2000 to 2009. I focus on these years to illustrate the exciting and innovative work of contemporary indigenous publishing and reference projects. Because I can include here only a brief sampling of titles, I consider these to be seed lists that will grow in various directions for every collection. With this overview, I hope to gather tools for and invite further discussion about the power-shifting, reparative work of tribal library collection development as a method of supporting indigenous authors and publishers as well as readers. Tribal affiliation, when known, is listed for authors.

Tools for the Collection Development Process

Awards

Classic awards used for collection development of indigenous materials include the American Booksellers Association and Before Columbus Foundation's American Book Awards, as well as various American Library Association awards. These awards recognize a range of books, so they require searching through to find out if an indigenous author has been included in an award cycle.

The following book awards recognize excellence in writing by indigenous authors and indigenous organizations or individuals involved with award administration. Librarians can both look to the awards as references and nominate indigenous literature for these awards as a way of supporting authors and participating in literary communities.

1. The Labriola Center American Indian National Book Award, administered by the Labriola National American Indian Data Center at the Arizona State University Libraries, recognizes multidisciplinary texts with relevance for contemporary North American Indian communities.
2. The Native American Youth Services Literature Award, administered by the American Indian Library Association, recognizes books in the categories Best Picture Book, Best Middle School Book, and Best Young Adult Book.
3. The Native Writers' Circle of the Americas Awards, administered since 1992 by the Native Writers' Circle of the Americas, recognize books in the categories First Book Award for Poetry, First Book Award for Prose, and Lifetime Achievement Award.
4. The Wordcraft Circle Awards, administered since 1997 by the Wordcraft Circle of Native Writers and Storytellers, recognize authors, publishers, books, and film in a range of genres and achievement categories. Both the Native Writers' Circle of the Americas and the Wordcraft Circle of Native Writers announce their award winners at the annual Returning the Gift Conference.

In the lists below, the following abbreviations indicate resources that have earned recognition from indigenous organizations:

(NWC) Native Writers' Circle of the Americas Award
(WCA) Wordcraft Circle Awards
(NAY) Native American Youth Services Literature Award

Words with Kimberly Roppolo. Recognition of American Indian literature by indigenous award-granting organizations works to support indigenous authors and publishers as well as to influence mainstream publishers and distribution systems. The vision of the Wordcraft Circle of Native Writers and Storytellers articulates this project, "to ensure that the voices of Native writers and storytellers—past, present, and future—are heard throughout the world."[46] I contacted Kimberly Roppolo, former national director of the Wordcraft Circle of Native Writers and Storytellers. Along with the associate national director, Jay Goombi, and the National Caucus, Roppolo coordinated the Wordcraft Circle Awards, which promote, publicize, and sustain Native authors, publishers, and publications in multiple genres. Roppolo is also an assistant professor of English at the University of Oklahoma. In addition to organizing literary networks that cross national borders, Roppolo builds connection through her writing. Her poetry has been published in journals including *Red Ink* (University of Arizona) and *Studies in American Indian Literatures* (University of Nebraska), and her scholarship includes collaborations as part of the Native Critics Collective, with whom she cowrote the anthology *Reasoning Together* (University of Oklahoma, 2008).[47] Here is what she had to say to tribal librarians:

> KH: What would you most like to share with tribal librarians in the United States and Canada as they select and purchase materials by and about North American indigenous peoples?

> KR: Research carefully what materials they are purchasing. I think joining ASAIL [Association for the Study of American Indian Literatures] and the list [ASAIL listserv] is a wonderful way to do just that and keep up with what is coming out in terms of new literature. Also, buy the works of First Nations authors and Mexican Indian authors as well who do publish in English. These borders are only imaginary, after all.

> KH: How can librarians support indigenous authors?

> KR: Buy books by Native authors, bring in Native authors for readings, encourage reading groups, bring in elders for storytelling, find local tribal communities, and get tribal folks involved directly (though I would assiduously avoid all tribal politics while doing so).

> KH: What else would you like to share?

> KR: Get on Debbie Reese's blog on American Indians in children's literature and contact John [Berry, associate librarian in the Ethnic Studies Library at the University of California, Berkeley], the best Indian librarian in the world for more advice.

Books

Classic texts for collection development of indigenous materials include, by nonindigenous authors, Libraries Unlimited's *American Indian Studies: A Bibliographic Guide* (White 1995) and *American Indian Reference and Resource Books for Children and Young Adults* (Kuipers 1995).[48] Indigenous advocacy in collection development includes collection development literature itself. In order to avoid adding "strength to the Eurowestern assimiliationist directive from within," as Daniel Heath Justice puts it, it is imperative not to marginalize indigenous literary theorists and librarians (and library students) "in favor of those whose assumed authority is embedded within the ideologies of colonialism."[49] Although it is only partially possible to address this in my own authorship, I model the ideal work of indigenous collection development by working to look to indigenous authors of collection development tools.

1. Seale, Doris (Santee/Cree), and Beverly Slapin, eds. *A Broken Flute: The Native Experience in Books for Children*. Walnut Creek, Calif.: AltaMira Press; Sonoma, Calif.: Oyate, 2005. (WCA)
2. Shaffer, Christopher. "Native American Literature in Collection Development." *Collection Building* 26, no. 4 (2007): 127–29. This resource addresses histories and attends to connections between African American and Ameri-

can Indian histories and cultures. Though it is by a nonindigenous author, I include this resource because of Shaffer's advocacy and his support for American Indian literature: "Improving Native American collections can also have a positive side effect in the publishing world in that with an increased demand, more books will be created and produced."[50]

3. Collection development workshops through Tribal College Librarians Institute provide an interactive tool for building skills.[51]
4. Varela, Elizabeth, Laura Gonzalez, and Mary Jo Godziela. "Expanding Horizons in North American Indian Literature." *Illinois Libraries* 8, no. 3 (Summer 2000): 202–8. Useful for considering support for collection development, this article overviews a 1999 grant for American Indian literature collection development and programming.

Websites

Though online materials can change quickly, that is a strength when authors reliably update resources. In addition to classic general resources through the American Library Association's web interface, these websites prioritize indigenous authors.

1. Cubbins, Elaine. *Useful Websites for Tribal Libraries.* http://www.u.arizona .edu/~ecubbins/useful.html (accessed 2 September 2010).
2. Reese, Debbie (Nambe Pueblo). *American Indians in Children's Literature.* http://americanindiansinchildrensliterature.blogspot.com (accessed 2 September 2010). (WCA)
3. Strom, Karen. *Storytellers: Native American Authors Online.* http://www .nativewiki.org/Storytellers:_Native_American_Authors_Online (accessed 2 September 2010). This resource includes lists of authors by tribal affiliation, mp3 downloads of indigenous authors reading their work, excerpts of books, and virtual greeting cards with pictures of American Indian authors.
4. When easily accessible, recent acquisitions at other tribal libraries also serve as a useful resource. For example, the Chickasaw Nation Library lists its recent acquisitions online.[52]

Publishers

Rhonda Taylor and Lotsee Patterson point out that "current reviewing sources often lack expertise or extensive knowledge on the topic of American Indians. Such tools tend to cover only mainstream publishers, often not picking up small press or entrepreneurial publishers/producers."[53] Such erasures also suppress American Indian authors since, as Shaffer pointed out, supporting indigenous publishers in turn supports the ongoing publication of indigenous authors. Though mainstream publishers and distributors may offer library-friendly book-processing features, they do not provide all the books necessary to support social justice and indigenous authorship in our communities. In addition to the classic resources of the University of Nebraska Press, the University of Oklahoma Press, the University of New Mexico Press, the University of Minnesota Press, and the University of Arizona Press, the following indigenous-run publishers provide excellent contemporary resources.

1. Gabriel Dumont Institute of Native Studies and Applied Research, in Saskatoon, Saskatchewan, publishes books and resources including websites, CDs, and interactive CD-ROMs by and for the Métis community, with a focus on educational and cultural resources, including Michif language resources for children and youth, with some materials for adults.[54]
2. Kegedonce Press, located on Cape Croker Reserve, Chippewas of Nawash First Nation, Wiarton, Ontario, focuses on poetry, fiction, and creative nonfiction; it involves "Indigenous Peoples at all levels of production."[55]
3. Oyate, located in Sonoma, California, offers books and videos. Oyate describes itself as "a Native organization working to see that our lives and histories are portrayed honestly" with a focus on resources for children. It also conducts workshops on "Teaching Respect for Native Peoples" that may be useful for librarians; the workshops "guide participants through the murky world of 'children's books about Indians.'"[56]
4. Pemmican Publications, Inc., promotes "Canadian Metis writers and illustrators through stories that are informed by Metis experience."[57]
5. Sun Tracks, a series of the University of Arizona Press, is edited by Tohono O'Odham poet and scholar Ofelia Zepeda. The Sun Tracks series started in 1971 as "one of the first publishing programs to focus exclusively on the creative works of Native Americans."[58] It continues to publish poetry, prose, art, and photography. In 2000, the Wordcraft Circle of Native Writers and Storytellers named the University of Arizona Press as Publisher of the Year for "demonstrated commitment and significant contributions as a University Publisher ensuring that the voices of Native writers and storytellers—past, present and future—are heard throughout the world."[59]
6. Theytus Books, located in Penticton, British Columbia, also runs a U.S.-based distribution house in Oroville, Washington. Open since 1980, Theytus was "the first First Nations owned and operated indigenous publishing house in Canada. Theytus's root begins within its name, a Salishan word meaning 'preserving for the sake of handing down.'"[60]

Periodicals

Classic review periodicals used in collection development of indigenous materials include *MultiCultural Review* and *MELUS: Multi-Ethnic Literature of the United States*. The following periodicals include useful review sections and are run by indigenous editors; in addition to serving as collection development tools, these periodicals are also good resources to include in a tribal library collection. For more information about magazines, see Peterson.[61]

1. *American Indian Quarterly*, from the University of Nebraska Press, has also published H. Henrietta Stockel's "An Annotated Chiricahua Apache Bibliography—Selected Books," *American Indian Quarterly* 25, no. 1 (2001): 153–76.
2. *Redwire Magazine*, from Redwire Native Youth Media.
3. *Studies in American Indian Literatures*, from the University of Nebraska Press.
4. *Tribal College Journal of American Indian Higher Education*, from the American Indian Higher Education Consortium.
5. *Wicazo Sa Review*, from the University of Minnesota Press, has published Charles F. Wilkinson and Anna Nikole Ulrich's "Annotated Bibliography of the Basic Literature Needed for an Understanding of Tribal Governance," *Wicazo Sa Review* 17, no. 1 (Spring 2002): 7–12.

Suggested Titles for Tribal Library Collections

Nonfiction

Following Robert A. Warrior's call for indigenous peoples' "intellectual sovereignty" over analysis of and writing about indigenous literature, this list includes well-reviewed contemporary nonfiction by indigenous authors.[62] For a review of classics in this genre, see John Burch's 2002 review of books, including the pivotal *Custer Died for Your Sins: An Indian Manifesto* (Norman: University of Oklahoma Press, 1988).[63]

1. Dion, Susan D. (Lenape/Potawatami). *Braiding Histories: Learning from Aboriginal Peoples' Experiences and Perspectives*. Vancouver: University of British Columbia Press, 2008.
2. Justice, Daniel Heath (Cherokee). *Our Fire Survives the Storm: A Cherokee Literary History*. Minneapolis: University of Minnesota Press, 2006.
3. Kipp, Woody (Blackfoot). *Viet Cong at Wounded Knee: The Trail of a Blackfeet Activist*. Lincoln: University of Nebraska Press, 2004. (WCA)
4. LaDuke, Winona (Anishinabe). *Recovering the Sacred: The Power of Naming and Claiming*. Cambridge, Mass.: South End Press, 2005.
5. Miller, Robert J. (Eastern Shawnee Tribe of Oklahoma). *Native America, Discovered and Conquered: Thomas Jefferson, Lewis and Clark, and Manifest Destiny*. Lincoln: University of Nebraska Press, 2006. (WCA)
6. Native Critics Collective (Janice Acoose, Lisa Brooks, Tol Foster, LeAnne Howe, Daniel Heath Justice, Phillip Carroll Morgan, Kimberly Roppolo,

Cheryl Suzack, Christopher B. Teuton, Sean Teuton, Robert Warrior, Craig S. Womack. *Reasoning Together: The Native Critics Collective*. Norman: University of Oklahoma Press, 2008.

7. Ortiz, Simon J. (Acoma Pueblo), ed. *Beyond the Reach of Time and Change: Native American Reflections on the Frank A. Rinehart Photograph Collection*. Tucson: University of Arizona Press, 2005.

8. Smith, Andrea (Cherokee). *Conquest: Sexual Violence and American Indian Genocide*. Cambridge, Mass.: South End Press, 2005.

9. Smith, Paul Chaat (Comanche). *Everything You Know about Indians Is Wrong*. Minneapolis: University of Minnesota Press, 2009.

10. Work, L. Susan (Choctaw Nation). *The Seminole Nation of Oklahoma: A Legal History*. Norman: University of Oklahoma Press, 2010.

Fiction

Classics in this genre include books by Sherman Alexie, Vine Deloria, Louise Erdrich, and N. Scott Momaday. I focus here on contemporary indigenous-authored fiction with an emphasis on that published by independent and indigenous presses.

1. Akiwenzie-Damm, Kateri (Anishinabe), and Josie Douglas, comps. *Skins: Contemporary Indigenous Writing*. Wiarton, Ont.: Kegedonce Press, 2000.

2. Beardslee, Lois (Ojibwe). *Women's Warrior Society*. Tucson: University of Arizona Press, 2008.

3. Eagle, Philip Red (Dakota/Salish). *Red Earth: A Vietnam Warrior's Journey*. Cambridge, England: Salt Publishing, 2007. (WCA)

4. Highway, Tomson (Cree). *Ernestine Shuswap Gets Her Trout*. Vancouver, B.C.: Talonbooks, 2005. (WCA)

5. Hogan, Linda (Chickasaw). *People of the Whale*. New York: Norton, 2008.

6. Howe, LeAnne (Choctaw Nation of Oklahoma). *Miko Kings: An Indian Baseball Story*. San Francisco: Aunt Lute Books, 2007.

7. Justice, Daniel Heath. *Kynship: Way of the Thorn and Thunder, Book One*. Wiarton, Ont.: Kegedonce Press, 2005.

8. Justice, Daniel Heath. *Wyrwood: Way of the Thorn and Thunder, Book Two*. Wiarton, Ont.: Kegedonce Press, 2006.

9. Justice, Daniel Heath. *Dreyd: Way of the Thorn and Thunder, Book Three*. Wiarton, Ont.: Kegedonce Press, 2006.

10. King, King (Cherokee). *Truth and Bright Water*. Toronto: HarperFlamingo, 1999.

11. Rustywire, Johnny (Navajo). *Navajo Spaceships*. Phoenix: Canyon Press, 2006. (WCA)

12. Smith, Judy R. (Quinnipiac/Mohican). *Yellowbird*. Lewiston, Idaho: Lewis-Clark Press, 2007. (NWC)

13. Womack, Craig S. (Oklahoma Creek/Cherokee). *Drowning in Fire.* Tucson: University of Arizona Press, 2001. (WCA)

Poetry

Authors throughout these lists have written widely, and I suggest searching out their other works as well.

1. Allen, Paula Gunn (Laguna Pueblo/Sioux). *America the Beautiful: Last Poems.* Albuquerque: University of New Mexico Press, 2009.
2. Coke, Allison Hedge (Wendat/Huron, Metis, Tsalagi/Cherokee, Mvscogee/Creek). *Off Season City Pipe.* Minneapolis: Coffeehouse Press, 2005. (WCA)
3. Howe, LeAnne (Choctaw Nation of Oklahoma). *Evidence of Red: Poems and Prose.* Cambridge, England: Salt Publishing, 2005. (WCA)
4. Maracle, Lee (Salish/Cree). *Bent Box.* Penticton, B.C.: Theytus Press, 2000.
5. Morgan, Phillip Caroll (Choctaw/Chickasaw). *The Fork-in-the-Road Indian Poetry Store.* Cambridge, England: Salt Publishing, 2006. (NWC)
6. Ortiz, Simon J. (Acoma Pueblo). *Out There Somewhere.* Tucson: University of Arizona Press, 2002.
7. Rancourt, Suzanne S. (Abenaki). *Billboard in the Clouds: Poems.* Willimantic, Conn.: Curbstone Press, 2003. (NWC)
8. Shuck, Kim (Cherokee). *Smuggling Cherokee.* Greenfield Center, N.Y.: Greenfield Review Press, 2006. (NWC)
9. Wood, Karenee (Monacan). *Markings on Earth.* Tucson: University of Arizona Press, 2001. (NWC)
10. Zepeda, Ofelia (Tohono O'odham). *Where Clouds Are Formed: Poems.* Tucson: University of Arizona Press, 2008.

Young Adult

This list follows the strategy of focusing on indigenous authors and builds on classic titles like N. Scott Momaday's *Owl in the Cedar Tree* (Lincoln: University of Nebraska Press, 1965).

1. Alexie, Sherman (Spokane/Coeur d'Alene). *The Absolutely True Diary of a Part-Time Indian.* New York: Little, Brown, 2007. (NAY)
2. Bruchac, Joseph (Abenaki). *Hidden Roots.* New York: Scholastic, 2004. (NAY)
3. Bruchac, Joseph (Abenaki). *Skeleton Man.* New York: HarperCollins, 2001.
4. Medicine Crow, Joseph (Crow). *Counting Coup: Becoming a Crow Chief on the Reservation and Beyond.* Washington, D.C.: National Geographic, 2006. (NAY)

5. Smith, Cynthia Leitich (Muscogee Creek). *Rain Is Not My Indian Name.* New York: HarperCollins, 2001.

Children

1. Boyden, Linda (Cherokee/United Lumbee Nation). *The Blue Roses.* New York: Lee & Low Books, 2002. (WCA)
2. Bruchac, Joseph (Abenaki). *Crazy Horse's Vision.* New York: Lee & Low, 2000.
3. Bruchac, Marge (Abenaki). *Malian's Song.* Middlebury: Vermont Folklife Center, 2006. (WCA)
4. Confederated Salish and Kootenai Tribes. *Beaver Steals Fire: A Salish Coyote Story.* Lincoln: University of Nebraska Press, 2005. (NAY)
5. Erdrich, Louise (Anishinabe). *The Game of Silence.* HarperCollins, 2005. (NAY)
6. Harjo, Joy (Muskogee). *For a Girl Becoming.* Tucson: University of Arizona Press, 2009.
7. Nelson-Moody, Aaron, Debbie Sparrow, Deborah Jacobs, Gary Fiegehen, Johnny Abraham, and Zach George. *People of the Land: Legends of the Four Host First Nations.* Pendicton, B.C.: Theytus Books, 2009.
8. Ortiz, Simon J. (Acoma Pueblo). *The Good Rainbow Road.* Tucson: University of Arizona Press, 2004. (WCA)
9. Tingle, Tim (Choctaw). *Crossing Bok Chitto: A Choctaw Tale of Friendship & Freedom.* El Paso, Tex.: Cinco Puntos Press, 2006. (NAY)
10. Van Camp, Richard (Dogrib).*What's the Most Beautiful Thing You Know about Horses?* San Francisco: Children's Book Press, 2003

Reference Resources

In *Trails: Tribal Library Procedures Manual,* Patterson mentions key reference texts from the 1990s, including Malinowski's *Encyclopedia of Native American Tribes* (Detroit: Gale, 1998) and *Notable Native Americans* (New York: Gale Research, 1995).[64] Recent well-reviewed reference texts include Todd Leahy and Raymond Wilson's *Historical Dictionary of Native American Movements* (Lanham, Md.: Scarecrow, 2008) and Joy Porter and Kenneth Roemer's edited collection, *The Cambridge Companion to Native American Literature* (Cambridge, England: Cambridge University Press, 2005), a WCA recipient. Just as Warrior's intellectual sovereignty informs my list of resource texts for tribal librarians, the concept also informs my short list of reference texts for youth and adult community members to use in tribal libraries. In order to support and offer examples of indigenous self-definition, it is essential to prioritize reference texts authored or recognized by indigenous peoples. In this section, I list a few recent reference resources by indigenous authors and/or recognized by indigenous organizations.

1. *The American Indian Experience: An American Mosaic Online Resource* (http://aie.greenwood.com, 1 January 2010), a subscription online database. *School Library Journal* rates this resource one of its "10 Best Digital Resources" for 2009 and commends the reference as "possibly one of the best digital resources available for school and public libraries serving patrons interested in Native American cultures."[65] After her tenure as the first American Indian President of the American Library Association, Loriene Roy (Anishinabe) worked with "a team of American Indian librarians and scholars" to guide the development, design, and indexing of *The American Indian Experience.*[66] The resource is a full-text database including 150 reference books, "763 primary sources (e.g., treaties, speeches, and captivity and traditional tales), 868 images, photographs, maps, a time line, topic guides to follow school curricula, and links to vetted web sites, as well as a Tribal Communities Resource with information on over 500 American Indian nations."[67]

2. Keoke, Emory Dean (Standing Rock Sioux Tribe), *American Indian Contributions to the World*. 5 vols. New York: Facts on File, 2005. (WCA)

3. Mihesuah, Devon A. (Choctaw). *So You Want to Write about Indians?: A Guide for Writers, Students, and Scholars*. Lincoln: University of Nebraska Press, 2005. (WCA)

4. Noori, Margaret. *Noongwa e-Anishinaabemjig: People Who Speak Anishinaabemowin Today*. http://www.umich.edu/~ojibwe/ (accessed 4 September 2010). (WCA)

5. Southern Oregon Digital Archives. First Nations Collection. http://soda.sou.edu (accessed 1 January 2010). Mary Jane Cedar Face and Deborah Hollens, librarians at the Hannon Library of Southern Oregon University, review their library's twenty-first-century project "to develop a digital archive of documents on the peoples and ecology of the Siskiyou-Klamath-Cascade region that would serve the scientific, environmental, tribal, and business communities regionally, nationally, and internationally."[68] The Southern Oregon University project team utilized "collaboration with tribes represented in the First Nations Collection" with the goal of "[m]aking the digital archives useful and sensitive to tribal concerns."[69] The still-growing collection includes "treaties and agency reports" as well as "explorer and missionary accounts, native language dictionaries, linguistic texts, legal documents, monographs, ethnographies, and journal articles. Publication dates range from 1843 to 2002."[70] Future stages of the project include adding regional materials.[71]

6. Veronica E. Velarde Tiller (Jicarilla Apache), ed. *Tiller's Guide to Indian Country: Economic Profiles of American Indian Reservations* (CD-ROM). Anita Scheetz, library director at Fort Peck Tribal Library in Poplar, Montana, advises, "Since the content of this CD remains mostly the same as the 1996 version, our library will keep using that version. Libraries that did not purchase the original print version might consider this updated CD version."[72]

NOTES

1. With gratitude to Loriene Roy for her mentorship and analysis and with sincere thanks to Kateri Akiwenzie-Damm, Daniel Heath Justice, and Kimberly Roppolo for their generous sharing of their time, words, and work.

2. Lois Beardslee, *The Women's Warrior Society* (Tucson: University of Arizona Press, 2008), 54.

3. Thomson Highway, *Dry Lips Oughta Move to Kapuskasing* (Saskatoon, Sask.: Fifth House Books, 1989).

4. Elizabeth Peterson, *Tribal Libraries in the United States: A Directory of American Indian and Alaska Native Facilities* (Jefferson, N.C.: McFarland & Company, 2007), 1.

5. Beardslee, *Women's Warrior Society*, 120.

6. Gloria Anzaldúa, *Borderlands/La Frontera: The New Mestiza* (San Francisco: Aunt Lute Books, 1987).

7. Elizabeth Peterson, "Collection Development in California Tribal Libraries," *Collection Building* 23, no. 3 (2004): 129–32.

8. Ruth Blank, *What Shall Our Children Read? A Selected Bibliography of American Indian Literature for Young People* (self-published, 1981); Elaine Goley, "United States: Native Americans," in *Our Family, Our Friends, Our World: An Annotated Guide to Significant Multicultural Books for Children and Teenagers*, ed. Lyn Miller-Lachmann (New Providence, N.J.: Bowker, 1992); Barbara J. Kuipers, *American Indian Reference Books for Children and Young Adults* (Englewood, Colo.: Libraries Unlimited, 1991, republished 1995); Elizabeth Weatherford and Emelia Seubert, *Native Americans on Film and Video* (New York: Museum of the American Indian/Heye Foundation, 1981–1988).

9. Peterson, "Collection Development in California Tribal Libraries," 129.

10. Lauren Teixeira, *Access to Information on the Costanoan/Ohlone Indians of the San Francisco and Monterey Bay Area: A Descriptive Guide to Research* (Banning, Calif.: Malki-Ballena Press, 1997).

11. "What is missing from the literature," Peterson notes, "is how to develop a tribal library collection for California Indians, namely, what to purchase, and where to obtain the materials." Peterson, "Collection Development in California Tribal Libraries," 129.

12. Reegan D. Breu, "Band and Tribal Libraries: What Mainstream Public Libraries Can Learn from Them," *Feliciter: Linking Canada's Information Professionals* 49, no. 5 (2003): 254–57.

13. Lotsee Patterson, *TRAILS: Tribal Library Procedures Manual*, 3rd ed. (Chicago: American Library Association, Office for Literacy and Outreach Services, 2008); Lotsee Patterson and Rhonda Harris Taylor, *Directory of Native American Tribal Libraries* (Norman: University of Oklahoma, School of Library and Information Studies, 1995).

14. Lotsee Patterson, "Exploring the World of American Indian Libraries," *Rural Libraries* 28, no. 1 (2008): 7–12.

15. Rhonda Harris Taylor and Lotsee Patterson, "Native American Resources: A Model for Collection Development," *The Acquisitions Librarian* 31/32 (2004): 41–54.

16. Taylor and Patterson, "Native American Resources," 50.

17. Kelly LaChance, "Cow Creek Tribal Library: A Tribal Library That Grows Every Year," *OLA Quarterly* 12, no. 4 (Winter 2006): 10.

18. LaChance, "Cow Creek Tribal Library," 10.

19. Marion Mercier, "The Confederated Tribes of Grand Ronde Tribal Library," *OLA Quarterly* 12, no. 4 (2006): 8–9; Rayette Sterling, "Tribal Libraries Preserve Native American Heritage," *Alki* 22, no. 3 (December 2006): 24–25.

20. Marjane Ambler, "Releasing Reservations from Isolation: The Tribal Library as Storyteller," *Tribal College Journal of American Indian Higher Education* 6, no. 1 (Summer 1994): 20–23; Holly Koelling, "A Model Collection Process for a Specialized Environment: Recommending Reference Titles for Tribal Community Colleges," *Community & Junior College Libraries* 8, no. 1 (November 1995): 63–68.

21. Loriene Roy and A. Arro Smith, "Supporting, Documenting, and Preserving Tribal Cultural Lifeways: Library Services for Tribal Communities in the United States," *World Libraries* 12, no. 1 (Spring 2002): 55–65.

22. Loriene Roy, "Dream Catchers, *Love Medicine,* and Fancy Dancing: Selecting Native American Studies Material in the Humanities," *The Acquisitions Librarian* 17/18 (1997): 141–57.

23. Juris Dilevko and Lisa Gottlieb, "Working at Tribal College and University Libraries: A Portrait," *Library & Information Science Research* 26, no.1 (Winter 2004): 44–72.

24. Renee Tjoumas, "Native American Literature for Young People: A Survey of Collection Development Methods in Public Libraries," *Library Trends* 41, no. 3 (Winter 1993): 493–523.

25. Breu, "Band and Tribal Libraries," 254.

26. Breu, "Band and Tribal Libraries," 254.

27. Shiraz Durrani and Elizabeth Smallwood, "The Professional Is Political: Redefining the Social Role of Public Libraries," in *Questioning Library Neutrality: Essays from Progressive Librarian,* ed. Alison Lewis (Duluth, Minn.: Library Juice Press, 2008), 119–40.

28. Kateri Akiwenzie-Damm, *My Heart Is a Stray Bullet* (Wiarton, Ont.: Kegedonce Press, 1993).

29. Kateri Akiwenzie-Damm, ed., *Without Reservation: Indigenous Erotica* (Wiarton, Ont.: Kegedonce Press, 2005); Kateri Akiwenzie-Damm, ed., *Skins: Contemporary Indigenous Writing* (Wiarton, Ont.: Kegedonce Press, 2000).

30. Kateri Akiwenzie-Damm, *Standing Ground* [Compact Disc] (Cape Croker Reserve, Ont.: Nishin Productions, 2003).

31. Kuipers, *American Indian Reference Books for Children and Young Adults,* 6.

32. Kay Marie Porterfield and Emory Dean Keoke, "Resources for Selecting Fair and Accurate American Indian Books for Libraries, Schools and Home," 2002, http://www.kporterfield.com/aicttw/excerpts/antibiasbooks.html (accessed 31 December 2009).

33. Donna E. Norton and Saundra E. Norton, "Developing the Library Collection for Native American Studies," *The Acquisitions Librarian* 5, no. 9 (1993): 247–66.

34. Linda Alcoff, "The Problem of Speaking for Others," *Cultural Critique* 20 (Winter 1991–1992): 5–32.

35. Tatiana de la Tierra, "Latina Lesbian Subject Headings: The Power of Naming," in *Radical Cataloging: Essays at the Front,* ed. K. R. Roberto (Jefferson, N.C.: McFarland & Company, 2008): 94–102.

36. Daniel Heath Justice, *Our Fire Survives the Storm: A Cherokee Literary History* (Minneapolis: University of Minnesota Press, 2006), 209.

37. Justice, *Our Fire Survives the Storm,* 212.

38. See Daniel Heath Justice's website for a quick overview: www.danielheathjustice.com (accessed 29 August 2010)

39. Justice, *Our Fire Survives the Storm*; Daniel Heath Justice, *Kynship: Way of the Thorn and Thunder, Book One* (Wiarton, Ont.: Kegedonce Press, 2005); Daniel Heath Justice, *Wyrwood: Way of the Thorn and Thunder, Book Two* (Wiarton, Ont.: Kegedonce Press, 2006); Daniel Heath Justice, *Dreyd: Way of the Thorn and Thunder, Book Three* (Wiarton, Ont.: Kegedonce Press, 2006).

40. Alcoff, "The Problem of Speaking for Others," 5.

41. Lotsee Patterson, "History and Status of Native Americans in Librarianship," *Library Trends* 49, no. 1 (Summer 2000): 182–93.

42. Loriene Roy, "To Support and Model Native American Library Services," *Texas Library Journal* 76, no. 1 (Spring 2000): 32–35.

43. Monique Lloyd, "The Underrepresented Native Student: Diversity in Library Science," *Library Student Journal* (February 2007), http://www.librarystudentjournal.org/index.php/lsj/article/view/39 (accessed 2 September 2010).

44. Alcoff, "The Problem of Speaking for Others," 20.

45. Breu, "Band and Tribal Libraries," 256.

46. Wordcraft Circle of Native Writers and Storytellers, http://www.wordcraftcircle.org/ (accessed 2 September 2010).

47. Janice Acoose et al., *Reasoning Together: The Native Critics Collective* (Norman: University of Oklahoma Press, 2008).

48. Phillip M. White, *American Indian Studies: A Bibliographic Guide* (Englewood, Colo.: Libraries Unlimited, 1995); Kuipers, *American Indian Reference and Resource Books for Children and Young Adults*.

49. Justice, *Our Fire Survives the Storm*, 209.

50. Christopher Shaffer, "Native American Literature in Collection Development," *Collection Building* 26, no. 4 (2007): 128.

51. James Thull, "The Tribal College Librarians Institute: Providing Professional Development and Networking in a Close-Knit Environment," *PNLA Quarterly* 71, no. 1 (Fall 2006): 8–9.

52. The Chickasaw Nation, "Recent Acquisitions," http://www.chickasaw.net/history_culture/index_220.htm (accessed 2 September 2010).

53. Patterson and Taylor, *Directory of Native American Tribal Libraries*, 43.

54. Gabriel Dumont Institute, GDI Curriculum & Publishing, http://www.gdins.org/gdites.shtml (accessed 2 September 2010).

55. Kegedonce Press, "Welcome to Kegedonce Press," http://www.kegedonce.com/ (accessed 2 September 2010).

56. Oyate, http://www.oyate.org/ (accessed 2 September 2010).

57. Pemmican Press, http://www.pemmican.mb.ca/ (accessed 4 September 2010).

58. Sun Tracks, University of Arizona Press, http://www.uapress.arizona.edu/series/series_detail.php?s=13 (accessed 4 September 2010).

59. Sun Tracks.

60. Theytus Books, "About Us," http://www.theytus.com/About-Us (accessed 4 September 2010).

61. Peterson, "Collection Development in California Tribal Libraries," 131.

62. Robert Allen Warrior, *Tribal Secrets: Recovering American Indian Intellectual Traditions* (Minneapolis: University of Minnesota Press, 1995), 87.

63. John R. Burch, "From Time Immemorial," *Library Journal* 127, no. 14 (September 1, 2002): 59–63.

64. Patterson, *Trails*, 97.

65. Shonda Brisco, "*School Library Journal*'s 10 Best Digital Resources for 2009," *School Library Journal* 55, no. 6 (June 2009): 36.

66. Brisco, "*School Library Journal*'s," 36.

67. Cheryl LaGuardia, "The American Indian Experience: An American Mosaic Online Resource," *Library Journal* 134, no. 1 (January 2009): 124.

68. Mary Jane Cedar Face and Deborah Hollens, "A Digital Library to Serve a Region: The Bioregion and First Nations Collections of the Southern Oregon Digital Archives," *Reference & User Services Quarterly* 44, no. 2 (Winter 2004): 117.

69. Cedar Face and Hollens, "A Digital Library," 118.

70. Cedar Face and Hollens, "A Digital Library," 119.

71. Cedar Face and Hollens, "A Digital Library," 120.

72. Anita Scheetz, "Review of *Tiller's Guide to Indian Country*," *Tribal College Journal* 18, no. 2 (Winter 2006): 55.

12

Organizing Information Resources: A Path for Access in Tribal Settings

Rhonda Harris Taylor

In every information setting, whether library, archive, or museum, the librarian, archivist, curator, or other information specialist is called upon to organize information, often in many more ways than cataloging books. Regardless of the nature of the information setting or of the resources to be organized, the task of organizing should not be a confusing or onerous one for the staff. But frequently, and especially in settings with few staff members, organizing is viewed negatively and set aside to be done later, and then still later. What follows are simple steps for taking a path toward better service for the people who use information settings, through effective organizing.

STEPS ON THE PATH

The first step is to remind yourself that the only purpose for the organization of information is the retrieval of that information. Do organize! One quick way to start is by making a list of the categories of information resources that are already in the information setting. Next, prioritize the list in *first*, *second*, and *third* order by the resources that are most *important*, whatever this term means in your own setting. Often, the first items on the ranked list are the resources that are used most frequently, and so they should be organized first.

Second, remember the users! Make a list of all the categories of people who use, or might use, the information setting: children, adults, new readers, individuals who need large print, etc. How do these people prefer to access information? Do they like to browse? Are they comfortable with computer searching? Are they often seeking particular types of information, such as biographies? Every decision about how resources are to be organized must consider both the information needs and the preferences of the users.

The third step is to accept the fact that simple is fine. For instance, there is a long tradition of libraries organizing magazines and newspapers by alphabetizing the titles. This was (and still is) a system that was easy to use, easy to explain, and easy to maintain. Although university libraries might classify all journals and magazines, a simple system, such as alphabetization of titles, is perfectly acceptable for many settings. It is also acceptable for some things in the information setting to be organized in a complex way, while other things are arranged in a simple fashion.

Fourth, do not re-create paths that already exist. Use professional standards that are available. Many of these standards are discussed later in this chapter. At the same time, be willing to balance the requirements of existing professional standards with changes that you can make that will help to meet the needs of *your* users. For instance, standard subject headings and classifications for resources about Native Americans are too often neither as accurate nor as helpful as we would hope. Most widely used subject heading lists and classification schemes reflect a Eurocentric world view, which poses challenges for tribal information settings. For example, more than thirty years ago, Thomas Yen-Ran Yeh discussed "The Treatment of the American Indian in the Library of Congress E-F Schedule."[1] A 1987 article by Tamara Lincoln focused on "Ethno-linguistic Misrepresentations of the Alaskan Native Languages as Mirrored in the Library of Congress System of Cataloging and Classification."[2] A 1994 article by Mary L. Young and Dara Doolittle highlighted the shortcomings of subject headings and other standards for American Indian art resources.[3] In 2001, Rhonda Harris Taylor explored "Native Americans & Issues of Bibliography."[4] In 2002, Nancy Carter examined, for Native American law resources, the ways that "Native American materials are organized and presented to readers," noting shortcomings, and reminding us that "cataloging and classification send powerful—if sometimes implicit—messages to library users."[5]

Fifth, have on-site access to the professional resources that you will need for organizing. Today, important tools for organizing are available for free on the Internet, but it will still be necessary to buy a minimum number of tools for your use. Even if the vast majority of your cataloging is copy cataloging (making use of a cataloging record created by someone else), you will still need access to basic tools for verification, modifications, occasional original cataloging, and training. One method for obtaining basic tools is collaborating with other information settings, such as libraries or archives, in your geographic area—perhaps staff members there would be willing to share older editions that they are replacing. Also, be familiar with how these tools are to be used. Make liberal use of the introductions, glossaries, and internal and external guides to the organization of the tools themselves. A list of essential resources is at the end of this chapter.

Sixth, always plan for the future and new generations. You will organize first to meet current needs, but change will always come. The organizing systems implemented today are the foundations for accommodating the next changes. As you organize, plan for changes, whether those will be automating for the first time, migrating to a new automation system, or adding new functions to your current duties, such as archival responsibilities.

WHILE ON THE PATH

While you are progressing along the path to your organizing goals, take time to consider the audiences who will need to understand the organization of information in your setting. These audiences include staff members who will do the actual organizing (such as catalogers and web designers) as well as staff members (such as reference staff, individuals who do instruction for the patrons, etc.) who must access the resources and help patrons/users locate them. Do not forget that there will always be a need for training the new staff and volunteers who help in your setting. Of course, the all-important audience of the patrons/users is constantly changing, with changing interests and information needs, and new ways must be found to keep them up-to-date on the organization of information resources, including those out there on the web. There are also external audiences, such as agencies that provide funding for grants sought by your organization—it will be important for them to know that you have organized information resources to make them accessible. Finally, all of these audiences need to know not only how resources are currently organized, but also when resources are reorganized in the future.

It will save trouble in the long run if, as you organize, you document (i.e., keep good records) of organizing decisions that you make. This way, important processes are not forgotten, steps do not have to be retaken, and you are planning for the future.

USEFUL TERMS FOR GUIDANCE ON THE PATH

As you continue along the path to organization, three fundamental terms will recur in tools that you will use. This terminology has evolved as the information professions have tried to accommodate a universal reality that Native peoples have always understood: many things are carriers of information and knowledge. Also, these newer terms are capturing older concepts that are already very familiar to those individuals who have worked for quite a while in information settings. The first term is *information package*, which refers to a carrier of recorded information, such as a book, magazine article, DVD, web page, or other information resource. A *bibliographic record* (also sometimes called a *surrogate record* or *metadata record*) is, in general terms, a description of an information package. An example is the information on a catalog card or in the record that appears in the online public access catalog (OPAC). Finally, there is *metadata*, a term currently used for many concepts. Its most simple definition, however, is data about data. A catalog card is actually metadata. Usually, however, metadata is used to refer to a description of an information package that is *encoded*, so that it can be manipulated by a computer, such as a MARC record or a Dublin Core record. More information about these schemes is included at the end of this chapter.

THE EASIEST PATH

Usually the easiest path is one that has been trod by others. When it comes to cataloging, copy cataloging is the easiest path. For over thirty years, thanks to the Library of Congress (LC), many books have carried their own bibliographic (catalog) records on the backs of their title pages, and many information settings have taken advantage of Cataloging-in-Publication (CIP) data for their own cataloging purposes. The format for CIP is a catalog card. The CIP data are provided prior to publication, so they are not always complete and can have errors. An explanation of CIP can be found on the LC website (http://cip.loc .gov/purpose.html), and a history of the program is available at http://www.loc .gov/loc/lcib/0105/cip.html.[6] Besides being useful for copy cataloging, CIP can be used for training staff. One approach to understanding the relationships between a catalog card format (such as CIP) and the MARC or Dublin Core or other formats is to compare one information package's bibliographic record in these various formats. Available on the web is the Library of Congress Z39.50 "Gateway to Library Catalogs" (http://lcweb.loc.gov/z3950/gateway.html#lc).[7] This site allows searching of the Library of Congress Online Catalog (which contains fourteen million records of "books, serials, music, maps, manuscripts, computer files, and visual materials") in either a simple or an advanced search mode.[8] Once a record is located, it can be viewed either in a MARC-tagged format or in the display format that a patron would see in an OPAC. The gateway also provides links to access the online catalogs of other libraries and the National Library Service for the Blind and Physically Handicapped Union Catalog. An alternative approach to the Library of Congress online catalog is the access provided at http://catalog.loc.gov/, with separate links to the Library of Congress Prints & Photographs Online Catalog (PPOC) and the Library of Congress Sound Online Inventory & Catalog (SONIC).[9]

Of course, it is becoming more common for even smaller information sites to be networked together for purposes of sharing bibliographic records electronically. A vital factor in making such collaboration successful is ongoing training for the staff involved, including provision of documentation for processes that are used.

THE WELL-TROD PATH

General Guidance

Whether you are cataloging books for a library setting or describing a collection of papers for an archives, the end results of organizing should be the same. Charles Cutter's "Objects" of a catalog have, for more than a century, offered clear guidance on what final goals to keep in mind when organizing anything:

1. To enable a person to find a book of which either
   a. the author
   b. the title
   c. the subject is known
2. To show what the library has
   a. by a given author
   b. on a given subject
   c. in a given kind of literature
3. To assist in the choice of a book
   a. as to its edition (bibliographically)
   b. as to its character (literary or topical)[10]

In other words, whether books, websites, historic documents, or pottery bowls are being organized, the goals of organizing are to help staff and patrons in (1) identification, (2) gathering together of like items (collocation), (3) evaluation for choosing between options, and (4) location of what is needed.

Basic Steps in Cataloging

When the organizing approach that is being taken is cataloging an information package, the basic steps are as follows:

1. Describing, which means recording characteristics that will help distinguish one item from another item.
   a. Describing the item "in hand."
   b. Establishing access points (headings for names and uniform titles and making references to access points, such as *see* and *see also*).
2. Assigning subject headings, which indicate what the item is *about*.
3. Classifying, which means placing the item in a category with similar items (including assigning a call number, basically an address, for future retrieval).
4. Encoding, which means coding so that a computer can manipulate the data; for example, encoding could be done using MARC coding.
5. Always remembering the users/patrons/clients and their interests and information needs!

Hints for Deciding on the Subject(s) of an Information Package

Basic steps in determining what an information package is *about* will assist in choosing the most appropriate subject heading(s) for that item. Following is a list compiled from advice offered by the *Sears List of Subject Headings* and *Dewey Decimal Classification* (DDC)[11]:

1. Look at the title.
2. Check the table of contents/chapter headings.
3. Look over the preface/introduction/foreword.
4. Scan the text (for nonbook items, examine the container, label, or any accompanying guides, and view or listen to the contents if possible).
5. Check the bibliography and index.
6. Check cataloging of similar information packages.
7. Consult reviews, reference works, and subject experts.

Hints for Classifying (Assigning to a Discipline) an Information Package

These are the basic steps, summarized from an introduction to the DDC, to follow in deciding what classification is needed for an information package[12]:

1. Class in the discipline for which the work is intended so similar works are together. Determine the most appropriate discipline by asking: Where does the patron/user expect to find this information package?
2. Check the index, if using DDC, and follow up in the schedules.
3. Check the schedules.

TREADING OUR OWN PATH

There is a history of Native people using fundamental organization principles to create or modify systems to meet the needs of users. As an example, in *Native Libraries*, Gordon H. Hills discusses a classification system developed by A. Brian Deer in the 1970s.[13] A website that presents the history and an explanation of the system is available at http://www.slais.ubc.ca/courses/libr517/02-03-wt2/projects/deer/development.htm.[14]

Today, the Internet has expanded the opportunities for sharing both resources and knowledge. Professional networking is especially important for those information specialists who are in settings that are geographically isolated or who are the only "organization" persons in their settings. For instance, an April 2004 dialogue on the American Indian Library Association (AILA) listserv offered links to a PDF list of "British Columbia First Nations Subject Headings" for the First Nations Library at the University of British Columbia, at http://www.library

.ubc.ca/xwi7xwa/bcfn.pdf, and an online guide, "American Indian Children's and Young Adult Materials Author Research," at the University of Washington, at http://www.lib.washington.edu/subject/Childrens/AmericanIndian/authors .html.[15] Both resources are still available online. The former is an example of a Native-focused tool for subject heading assignment, and the latter is an example of a guide that organizes information about American Indian authors to assist researchers. Another example of sharing is the Native American Rights Fund's National Indian Law Library, which offers basic and advanced search access to its online catalog, and "[m]ost of the 10,000+ information resources indexed in the catalog can be delivered to patrons for a nominal fee via document delivery or interlibrary loan service."[16] Ultimately, the best, and most informative, path is traveled together.

HELP ALONG THE PATH

The following list of resources is organized alphabetically by categories and then alphabetically by author or title within each category. The items with an asterisk (*) are especially useful for beginners and for training staff. The list deliberately includes resources that meet a wide range of knowledge and skill levels and information needs—there is "something for everyone."

The list includes web resources that can be accessed for free. Though print resources can be purchased, they may also be obtained through interlibrary loan.

As well as print and online resources, the list includes professional associations. Specialized professional associations are particularly helpful in organization of information, offering free resources on the web, sponsoring continuing education opportunities, facilitating networking with colleagues, and publishing resources.

I. List of Resources for the Organization of Information, Including Professional Associations
    A. Glossaries of Vocabulary Used in the Organization of Information
        1. *American Library Association, Association for Library Collections & Technical Services. "Serials Acquisitions Glossary Supplement," 2003, 2005, http://www.ala.org/ala/mgrps/divs/ alcts/resources/collect/serials/acqglossary/index.cfm (accessed 29 January 2011).
        2. University of California, California Digital Library. "Glossary," 2010, http://www.cdlib.org/gateways/technology/glossary.html (accessed 29 January 2011).
        3. *OCLC. "WorldCat Cataloging Partners Glossary," 2010, http:// www.oclc.org/support/documentation/glossary/promptcat/ (accessed 29 January 2011).

4. *Pearce-Moses, Richard. "A Glossary of Archival and Records Terminology," 2005, http://www.archivists.org/glossary/intro.asp (accessed 29 January 2011).

B. General Resources for Cataloging Various Formats of Resources

1. American Library Association. "American Libraries Online," http://www.ala.org/alonline/ (accessed 29 January 2011). Useful reading for organization staff are the recurring columns titled "Internet Librarian" and "Technology in Practice," which can be accessed directly at http://americanlibrariesmagazine.org/columns.

2. American Library Association, Association for Library Collections & Technical Services. "ALCTS: Association for Library Collections & Technical Services," http://www.ala.org/ala/mgrps/divs/alcts/index.cfm (accessed 29 January 2011). "A division of the American Library Association," ALCTS is focused on the "development of principles, standards, and best practices for creating, collecting, organizing, delivering, and preserving information resources in all forms."[17] Visit the website for conferences and events, including webinars, web courses, and e-forums.

3. Baca, Murtha, Patricia Harpring, Elisa Lanzi, Linda McRae, and Ann Baird Whiteside. *Cataloging Cultural Objects: A Guide to Describing Cultural Objects and Their Images*. Chicago: American Library Association, 2006.

4. Also see the related website, Visual Resources Association, "CCO Commons: Cataloging Cultural Objects," 2006, http://www.vra-foundation.org/ccoweb/index.htm (accessed 29 January 2011).

5. Fritz, Deborah A. *Cataloging with AACR2 & MARC21: For Books, Electronic Resources, Sound Recordings, Videorecordings, and Serials*. 2nd ed., 2006 cumulation. Chicago: American Library Association, 2007.

6. *Hoffman, Herbert. *Small Library Cataloging*. 3rd ed. Lanham, Md.: Scarecrow Press, 2002.

7. *Intner, Sheila I., Joanna F. Fountain, and Jean Weihs, eds. *Cataloging Correctly for Kids: An Introduction to the Tools*. 5th ed. Chicago: American Library Association, 2010.

8. Intner, Sheila S., and Jean Weihs. *Standard Cataloging for School and Public Libraries*. 4th ed. Westport, Conn.: Libraries Unlimited, 2007.

9. *Kao, Mary L. *Cataloging and Classification for Library Technicians*. 2nd ed. New York: Haworth Press, 2001.

10. *Kaplan, Allison. *Crash Course in Cataloging for Non-catalogers: A Casual Conversation on Organizing Information*. Westport, Conn.: Libraries Unlimited, 2009.

11. Library of Congress. "Program for Cooperative Cataloging," 2011, http://www.loc.gov/catdir/pcc/ (accessed 29 January 2011). A website for accessing information about the various projects of national and international cooperative cataloging efforts. Includes "Top Five Reasons Why Library Administrators Should Support Participation in the Program for Cooperative Cataloging," by Mark Watson (http://www.loc.gov/catdir/pcc/topfive.html), which provides an on-target rationale for any collaborative organization of information project.

12. McRae, Linda, and Lynda S. White, eds. *ArtMARC Sourcebook: Cataloging Art, Architecture, and Their Visual Images.* Chicago: American Library Association, 1998.

13. Olson, Nancy B., Robert L. Bothmann, and Jessica J. Schomberg. Cataloging of Audiovisual Materials and Other Special Materials: *A Manual Based on AACR2 and Marc 21.* 5th ed. Westport, Conn.: Libraries Unlimited, 2008.

14. *Patterson, Lotsee, et al. *TRAILS: Tribal Library Procedures Manual.* 3rd ed. Chicago: American Library Association, Office for Literacy and Outreach Services; American Library Association, Committee on Rural, Native, and Tribal Libraries of All Kinds, December 2008. The manual is available in full text online at http://www.ala.org/ala/aboutala/offices/olos/toolkits/TRAILS3 .pdf. Consult chapter eight, "Technical Services," and the end of chapter seven on archival services.

15. *Taylor, Arlene G., and David P. Miller. *Introduction to Cataloging and Classification.* 10th ed. Westport, Conn.: Libraries Unlimited, 2006. This is a textbook.

16. *Weber, Mary Beth, and Fay A. Austin. *Cataloging Nonbook, Electronic, Web, and Networked Resources: A How-to-Do-It Manual for Librarians.* 5th ed. New York: Neal-Schuman, 2009.

17. *Weihs, Jean, and Sheila S. Intner. *Beginning Cataloging.* Santa Barbara, Calif.: Libraries Unlimited, 2009. This is a textbook.

C. Archives

1. *Archives Association of British Columbia. "The AABC Archivist's Toolkit," 2010, http://aabc.ca/TK_00_main_page.html (accessed 29 January 2011). This free online resource, "originally intended for small and medium-sized archives in British Columbia, . . . has evolved into much more. . . . [I]t now offers access to a wide range of on-line and published resources for archivists and archives workers at all levels."[18]

2. The Association of Moving Image Archivists. "AMIA: The Association of Moving Image Archivists," http://www.amianet.org/ (accessed 29 January 2011).

3. *First Archivists Circle. "Protocols for Native American Archival Materials," 2007, http://www2.nau.edu/libnap-p/protocols.html (accessed 29 January 2011). The protocols were developed to reflect the *"best professional practices for culturally responsive* care and use of American Indian archival material held by non-tribal organizations."[19]

4. Hensen, Steven L. *Describing Archives: A Content Standard.* Chicago: Society of American Archivists, 2007.

5. The Society of American Archivists. "SAA: Society of American Archivists," http://www.archivists.org/ (accessed 29 January 2011).

6. *Stielow, Frederick J. *Building Digital Archives, Descriptions, and Displays: A How-to-do-it Manual for Archivists and Librarians.* New York: Neal-Schuman, 2003.

7. Theimer, Kate. *Web 2.0 Tools and Strategies for Archives and Local History Collections.* New York: Neal-Schuman, 2010.

8. *Wythe, Deborah, ed. *Museum Archives: An Introduction.* 2nd ed. Chicago: Society of American Archivists, 2004.

D. Authority Work

1. *Furrie, Betty. "Understanding MARC Authority Records: Machine-Readable Cataloging," 2004, http://www.loc.gov/marc/uma/ (accessed 29 January 2011).

2. Library of Congress. "Library of Congress Authorities," 2010, http://authorities.loc.gov/ (accessed 29 January 2011). "Using *Library of Congress Authorities,* you can browse and display authority headings for Subject, Name, Title and Name/Title combinations; and download authority records in MARC format for use in a local library system. This service is offered free of charge."[20]

3. Maxwell, Robert L. *Maxwell's Guide to Authority Work.* Chicago: American Library Association, 2002.

E. Classification

1. Brian Deer Classification Scheme

a) *MacDonnell, Paul, Reiko Tagami, and Paul Washington. "Brian Deer Classification System," The University of British Columbia School of Library, Archival and Information Studies, 2003, http://www.slais.ubc.ca/courses/libr517/02-0-wt2/projects/deer/index.htm (accessed 29 January 2011). This site has a history and explanation of the Brian Deer Classification Scheme.

b) University of British Columbia, First Nations House of Learning,*X̱W17X̱WA Library. "BC First Nations Subject Headings," 2009, http://www.library.ubc.ca/xwi7xwa/bcfn.pdf (accessed 29 January 2011). This web page provides the classification scheme.

2. Dewey Decimal Classification
   a) *Middle Tennessee State University, James E. Walker Library. "Let's Do Dewey," http://frank.mtsu.edu/~vvesper/dewey2.htm#What (accessed 29 January 2011). This is a simple online tutorial, useful for training, covering Dewey and Cuttering.
   b) Mitchell, Joan S., et al., eds. *Dewey Decimal Classification and Relative Index.* 22nd ed. Dublin, Ohio: OCLC, 2003. Obtain the most recent print edition of the four-volume set or the one-volume abridged fourteenth edition, published in 2004.
   c) *Mortimer, Mary. *Learn Dewey Decimal Classification (Edition 22).* Friendswood, Tex.: TotalRecall, 2007.
   d) OCLC. "Dewey Decimal Classification Summaries," 2011, http://www.oclc.org/dewey/resources/summaries/ (29 Jan. 2011).
   e) OCLC. "Dewey Frequently Asked Questions," 2011, http://www.oclc.org/support/questions/dewey/ (29 Jan. 2011).
   f) *OCLC. "Dewey Services," 2011, http://www.oclc.org/fp/ (accessed 29 January 2011). Print or WebDewey, the electronic version, are available from OCLC Forest Press at this website.
   g) *OCLC. "Four Printed Volumes Help Keep Your Collections Organized," 2011, http://www.oclc.org/dewey/versions/ddc-22print/ (accessed 29 January 2011). The site also has links to full text of the "Introduction" (which is the best overview of DDC) and to the "Glossary" in the DDC volumes, as well as "New Features."
   h) OCLC. "Resources for Teachers and Students of the DDC," 2011, http://www.oclc.org/dewey/resources/default.htm (accessed 29 January 2011). This site has a link to "Resources for Public and K-12 Libraries." On that page are links to brief PowerPoint slide shows for kids and adults and a brief biography of Melvil Dewey. The home "Resources" page also has a link to "Resources for Scholars and Classifiers," which provides links to training courses, a tutorial for WebDewey or Abridged WebDewey, and a Dewey blog.
   i) Scott, Mona L. *Dewey Decimal Classification, 22nd Edition: A Study Manual and Number Building Guide.* Westport, Conn.: Libraries Unlimited, 2005.
3. Library of Congress Classification (LCC)
   a) Chan, Lois Mai. *A Guide to the Library of Congress Classification.* 5th ed. Englewood, Colo.: Libraries Unlimited, 1999.
   b) *Dittmann, Helena, Jane Hardy, and Lorraine Musgrave. *Learn Library of Congress Classification.* 2nd ed. Friendswood, Tex.: TotalRecall, 2007.

   c) LC Classification Schedules
- (1) Library of Congress. "Cataloging and Acquisitions Home," http://www.loc.gov/aba/ (accessed 29 January 2011).
- (2) Library of Congress. "Cataloging Distribution Service," http://www.loc.gov/cds/ (accessed 29 January 2011). Obtain the most recent editions of the schedules volumes. Tools to assist in the use of LCC can also be obtained here.
- (3) Library of Congress, "Library of Congress Subject Headings (LCSH) Weekly Lists," http://www.loc.gov/aba/cataloging/subject/weeklylists/ (accessed 29 January 2011). "Weekly lists of new and changed subject headings are posted to this Web site by the Policy and Standards Division as they are approved."[21]
- (2) Library of Congress, Cataloging Policy and Support Office. *Classification and Shelflisting Manual.* Washington, D.C.: Library of Congress, 2008.
- (5) *Library of Congress, Cataloging Policy and Support Office. "Library of Congress Classification Outline," http://lcweb.loc.gov/catdir/cpso/lcco/lcco.html (accessed 29 January 2011). Available online are "the letters and titles of the main classes of the Library of Congress Classification. Click on any class to view an outline of its subclasses."[22]

   4. Superintendent of Documents Classification (SuDoc Numbers)
- a) *Government Printing Office, Federal Depository Library Program. "An Explanation of the Superintendent of Documents Classification System," 2004, http://www.access.gpo.gov/su_docs/fdlp/pubs/explain.html (accessed 30 January 2011).

F. Copyright. Particularly in the era of the Internet, information services staff must be concerned about copyright, because often what is being "organized" belongs to someone else.
- 1. Copyright Clearance Center, Inc. "Copyright Clearance Center (CCC)," http://www.copyright.com/ (accessed 30 January 2011). At this site, "you can search for and obtain permission to use and share content from the world's leading titles in science, technology, medicine, humanities, news, business, finance and more."[23]
- 2. *U.S. Copyright Office. "Copyright," 2011, http://lcweb.loc.gov/copyright/ (accessed 30 January 2011). Useful for the pages "Copyright Basics," also available in Spanish; "Frequently Asked Questions (FAQ)"; and "Taking the Mystery out of Copyright" for students and teachers, a short video for Adobe Flash Player.

G. Crosswalks. Crosswalks are simply bridges between equivalents.
- 1. Resources Available Electronically

a) Library of Congress, Nework Development and MARC Standards Office. "Dublin Core to MARC Crosswalk," 2008, http://www.loc.gov/marc/dccross.html (accessed 30 January 2011).

b) Library of Congress, Network Development and MARC Standards Office. "MARC to Dublin Core Crosswalk," 2008, http://www.loc.gov/marc/marc2dc.html (accessed 30 January 2011).

2. Resources Available in Print Format

a) Fountain, Joanna F. *Subject Headings for School and Public Libraries: An LCSH/Sears Companion.* 3rd ed. Englewood, Colo.: Libraries Unlimited, 2001.

b) Scott, Mona L. *Conversion Tables: Volume 1, LC to Dewey.* 3rd ed. Westport, Conn.: Libraries Unlimited, 2006.

H. Cuttering for Library of Congress Classification and for Dewey Classification

1. *Cotton, Gregory. "Notes on Cutter Numbers and Cuttering," 1999, http://www.uiowa.edu/~libsci/faculty/cotton/122-cutter.htm (accessed 30 January 2011).

2. *Memorial University Libraries, Queen Elizabeth II Library. "Cataloguer's Toolbox: LC Cutter Tables," http://staff.library.mun.ca/staff/toolbox/tables/lccutter.htm (accessed 30 January 2011). Online access to LCC Cutter tables.

3. *University of Illinois at Urbana–Champaign, University Library. "Video Tutorials, Cataloging/Bibliography Records: Understanding a Dewey Call Number," http://www.library.illinois.edu/cam/training/videos.html (accessed 30 January 2011). Click on the link for the video tutorial, which is approximately four minutes long.

I. Description

1. American Library Association, Joint Steering Committee for Revision of AACR. *Anglo-American Cataloguing Rules.* 2nd ed., 2002 revision, 2005 update. Chicago: American Library Association, 2005. Obtain this loose-leaf version of AACR2R from the American Library Association at http://www.ala.org. Use link to "Publications" and then link to "ALA Store" and then search by title.

2. *Gorman, Michael. *The Concise AACR2.* 4th ed. Chicago: American Library Association, 2004.

3. Johnson, Bruce Chr., ed. *Guidelines for Bibliographic Description of Reproductions.* Chicago: American Library Association, Association for Library Collections & Technical Services, Committee on Cataloging Description and Access, 1995.

4. Library of Congress. "Library of Congress Rule Interpretations Updates," http://www.loc.gov/cds/PDFdownloads/lcri/index.html (accessed 30 January 2011).

5. Liheng, Carol, and Winnie S. Chan. *Serials Cataloging Handbook: An Illustrative Guide to the Use of AACR2R and LC Rule Interpretations.* 2nd ed. Chicago: American Library Association, 1998.
6. Maxwell, Robert L. *Maxwell's Handbook for AACR2: Explaining and Illustrating the Anglo-American Cataloguing Rules Through the 2003 Update.* 4th ed. Chicago: American Library Association, 2004.
7. *Mortimer, Mary. *Learn Descriptive Cataloging.* 2nd ed. Friendswood, Tex.: TotalRecall, 2007.
8. Resource Description and Access (RDA)
   a) *American Library Association, Canadian Library Association, and CILIP: Chartered Institute of Library and Information Professionals. "RDA Background," http://www.rdatoolkit.org/background (accessed 30 January 2011). Background information and a simplified explanation of RDA are found here.
   b) American Library Association, Canadian Library Association, and CILIP: Chartered Institute of Library and Information Professionals. "RDA Toolkit: Resource Description & Access," http://www.rdatoolkit.org/ (accessed 30 January 2011). It is expected that there will be a migration from the AACR2 to the forthcoming standard. Information about it is on the official website for RDA.
J. Encoding
   1. Encoded Archival Description (EAD)
      a) Library of Congress, Network Development and MARC Standards Office, and Society of American Archivists. "Encoded Archival Description Version 2002 Official Site," http://www.loc.gov/ead/ (accessed 30 January 2011).
   2. Dublin Core
      a) Dublin Core Metadata Initiative. http://www.dublincore.org/ (accessed 30 January 2011).
   3. HTML (Hypertext Markup Language)
      a) *w3schools.com. "HTML Tutorial," http://www.w3schools.com/html/ (accessed 30 January 2011).
   4. MARC
      a) Byrne, Deborah J. *MARC Manual: Understanding and Using MARC Records.* 2nd ed. Englewood, Colo.: Libraries Unlimited, 1998.
      b) Fritz, Deborah A., and Richard J. Fritz. *MARC21 for Everyone: A Practical Guide.* Chicago: American Library Association, 2003.
      c) *Furrie, Betty. "Understanding MARC Bibliographic: Machine-Readable Cataloging," 2009, http://lcweb.loc.gov/marc/umb (accessed 30 January 2011). "Written by Betty Furrie in conjunction with the Data Base Development Department of

The Follett Software Company. 8th ed. reviewed and edited by the Network Development and MARC Standards Office. The Library of Congress."[24]

d) The Library Corporation. "Cataloger's Reference Shelf," http://www.itsmarc.com/crs/ (accessed 30 January 2011). Based on MARC 21 and other reference resources, the "Cataloger's Reference Shelf" provides free access to MARC data formats and code lists.

e) Library of Congress. "Gateway to Library Catalogs: Z39.50," 2011, http://lcweb.loc.gov/z3950/gateway.html#lc (accessed 30 January 2011). Search the online Library of Congress Catalog as well as those of other libraries and view the records in the MARC format option.

f) Library of Congress, Network Development and MARC Standards Office. "MARC Standards," http://lcweb.loc.gov/marc/ (accessed 30 January 2011). Includes access to "MARC 21 Lite Bibliographic Format, 2008 edition," as a link, as well as links to the latest editions, with updates, of the bibliographic, authority, holdings, classification, and community MARC data formats (MARC 21).

g) Piepenburg, Scott. *Easy MARC: A Simplified Guide to Creating Catalog Records for Library Automation Systems.* 5th ed. San Jose, Calif.: F. & W. Associates, 2007.

K. Ethics (Codes of Ethics). In the organization of information as well as in other aspects of professional practice and in training, codes of ethics can provide guidance.

1. *American Library Association. "Code of Ethics of the American Library Association," 2008, http://www.ala.org/ala/issuesadvocacy/proethics/codeofethics/codeethics.cfm (31 January 2011).

2. American Library Association, Association for Library Collections & Technical Services. "Guidelines for ALCTS Members to Supplement the American Library Association Code of Ethics," 1994, http://www.ala.org/ala/mgrps/divs/alcts/resources/alaethics.cfm (31 January 2011).

3. American Library Association, Association for Library Collections & Technical Services. "Statement on Principles and Standards of Acquisitions Practice," 1994, http://www.ala.org/ala/issuesadvocacy/proethics/explanatory/acquisitios.cfm 31 January 2011).

L. Filing. Even when organization is electronic, attention still must be paid to the order in which things appear and how to have them displayed as results that will be helpful for a user.

1. *American Library Association, Resources and Technical Services Division, Filing Committee. *ALA Filing Rules.* Chicago: American

Library Association, 1980. "These rules apply to the arrangement of bibliographic records of library materials whether displayed in card, book, or online format."[25] Obtain this publication from ALA at http://www.ala.org. Use the link to "Publications" and then to the "ALA Store" and then search for the title.

2. Rather, John C., and Susan C. Biebel. *Library of Congress Filing Rules.* Washington, D.C.: Library of Congress, 1980. Obtain from Library of Congress Cataloging Distribution Service at http://www.loc.gov/cds/products/index.php.

M. Indexing
1. *The American Society for Indexing. "American Society for Indexing," http://www.asindexing.org/i4a/pages/index.cfm?pageid=1 (accessed 2 February 2011). Under the area "About Indexing," this site includes a list of frequently asked questions, such as "What is indexing?" "About Indexing" also has a link to a very useful "Indexing Evaluation Checklist" for evaluating the quality of indexes in books.
2. *Cleveland, Donald B., and Ana D. Cleveland. *Introduction to Indexing and Abstracting.* 3rd ed. Englewood, Colo.: Libraries Unlimited, 2001. This is a textbook.
3. Lancaster, F. Wilfrid. *Indexing and Abstracting in Theory and Practice.* 3rd ed. London: Facet, 2003.

N. Museums
1. American Association of Museums. "American Association of Museums," http://www.aam-us.org/ (accessed 2 February 2011).
2. *Buck, Rebecca A., and Jean Allman Gilmore, eds. *MRM5: The New Museum Registration Methods.* 5th ed. Washington, D.C.: American Association of Museums, 2010.

O. Records Management
1. ARMA International. "The Authority on Managing Records & Information," 2011, http://www.arma.org/ (accessed 2 February 2011).
2. Shepherd, Elizabeth, and Geoffrey Yeo. *Managing Records: A Handbook of Principles and Practice.* London: Facet, 2003.

P. Serials
1. *CONSER. "Conser Cataloging Manual: Module 2, What Is a Serial?" 1993, http://www.itsmarc.com/crs/manl1459.htm (accessed 2 February 2011).
2. Genereux, Cecilia, and Paul D. Moeller. *Notes for Serials Cataloging.* 3rd ed. Santa Barbara, Calif.: ABC-CLIO, 2009.

Q. Standards Relevant to the Organization of Information. These resources provide information about the groups that produce and maintain standards. They also offer access to, and explanations of, many standards used for the organization of information.

1. American National Standards Institute. "ANSI: American National Standards Institute," http://www.ansi.org/ (accessed 2 February 2011).
2. International Federation of Library Associations and Institutions. *International Standard Bibliographic Description(ISBD)*. Preliminary Consolidated Edition. Munich, Germany: K.G. Saur, 2007. A description of the book is found at http://www.ifla.org/en/publications/international-standard-bibliographic description. The PDF full-text version can be found at http://www.ifla.org/VII/s13/pubs/ISBD_consolidated_2007.pdf.
   a) International Federation of Library Associations and Organizations. "Functional Requirements for Bibliographic Records," 2009, http://www.ifla.org/en/publications/functional-requirements-for-bibliographic-records (accessed 3 February 2011). The designation of mandatory International Bibliographic Description elements is now in conformity with the *Functional Requirements for Bibliographic Records*, available in full-text in HTML and PDF at this website.
3. International Organization for Standardization (ISO). "International Organization for Standardization: International Standards for Business, Government and Society," 2011, http://www.iso.ch/iso/en/ISOOnline.frontpage (accessed 3 February 2011).
4. Library of Congress. "Standards at the Library of Congress," 2010, http://lcweb.loc.gov/standards/ (accessed 3 February 2011). This website provides links to information about formats including MARC, MARCXML, EAD (Encoded Archival Description), Z39.50, METS (Metadata Encoding & Transmission Standard), and MIX (NISO Metadata for Images in XML).
5. Library of Congress. "U.S. ISSN Center," 2010, http://www.loc.gov/issn/ (accessed 3 February 2011).
6. National Information Standards Organization. "NISO: How the Information World Connects," http://www.niso.org/ (accessed 3 February 2011).
7. R. R. Bowker LLC. "Bowker," 2011, http://www.bowker.com/bowkerweb/ (accessed 2 February 2011). The website provides links to information about the Digital Object Identifier (DOI) the International Standard Book Number (ISBN).
8. Walch, Victoria Irons, comp. "Standards for Archival Description: A Handbook," 1994, http://www.archivists.org/catalog/stds99/index.html (accessed 3 February 2011). This online version of the book "describes technical standards, conventions, and guidelines used by archivists in describing holdings and repositories. . . . Detailed entries are provided for 86 standards, while another 157 are identified in summary lists."[26]

R. Style Manuals. Many people do not think about style manuals being basic tools for organization of information. In addition to their use for term papers in educational settings, they are also used to help create aids in information settings and for publishing, both internal and external to the information setting. These are the most commonly used style manuals for term papers, manuscripts, etc., but they are not the only ones used.

   1. General

      a) ipl2. "Special Collections Created by ipl2: Citing Electronic Information," 2011, http://www.ipl.org/div/farq/netciteFARQ .html (accessed 3 February 2011). Lists of links to websites offering guidance on citing electronic resources.

      b) *Lipson, Charles. *Cite Right: A Quick Guide to Citation Styles—MLA, APA, Chicago, the Sciences, Professions, and More.* Chicago: University of Chicago, 2006.

      c) *The University of Texas at San Antonio Libraries. "Cite it Right," http://lib.utsa.edu/Instruction/citeitright/ (accessed 3 February 2011).

   2. American Psychological Association (APA)

      a) American Psychological Association."APA Style," http://www.apastyle.org/ (accessed 3 February 2011).

      b) American Psychological Association. "APA Style Help," 2011, http://www.apastyle.org/apa-style-help.aspx (accessed 3 February 2011). The web page of help resources includes links to "Frequently Asked Questions" about APA style, a "Free Tutorial on the Basics of APA Style," a "Learning Resources" section of more guides about using this style, and a blog.

      c) *Houghton, Peggy M., Timothy J. Houghton, and Michael F. Peters. *APA—The Easy Way! A Quick and Simplified Guide to the APA Writing Style.* 2nd ed. Flint, Mich.: Baker College, 2005.

      d) *Publication Manual of the American Psychological Association.* 6th ed. Washington, D.C.: American Psychological Association, 2010.

   3. Chicago

      a) *The Chicago Manual of Style.* 16th ed. Chicago: University of Chicago, 2010. This resource also has a very lengthy section that explains the different parts of the book, such as title page, index, etc.

      b) "The Chicago Manual of Style Online." 2010, http://www .chicagomanualofstyle.org/home.html (accessed 3 February 2011). Frequently asked questions are answered, and there are links to other content, including an online forum and a "Chicago-Style Citation Quick Guide" with examples. The online version of the manual can be purchased at this site.

4. Modern Language Association (MLA)
   a) *Gibaldi, Joseph. *MLA Handbook for Writers of Research Papers*. 7th ed. New York: Modern Language Association of America, 2009.
   b) Gibaldi, Joseph. *MLA Style Manual and Guide to Scholarly Publishing*. 3rd ed. New York: Modern Language Association of America, 2008.
   c) Modern Language Association. "Frequently Asked Questions About the *MLA Style Manual*," 2011, http://www.mla.org/style_faq (accessed 3 February 2011).
   d) *Trimmer, Joseph F. *A Guide to MLA Documentation: With an Appendix on APA Style*. 8th ed. Boston: Wadsworth/Cengage, 2010.
5. Turabian
   a) *Houghton, Peggy M., and Timothy J. Houghton. *Turabian: The Easy Way!* Flint, Mich.: Baker College, 2008.
   b) Turabian, Kate L. *A Manual for Writers of Term Papers, Theses, and Dissertations: Chicago Style for Students and Researchers*. 7th ed. Chicago: University of Chicago Press, 2007.

S. Subject Headings
1. General Subject Heading Lists
   a) Library of Congress Subject Headings (LCSH)
      (1) *Ganendran, Jacki, and Lynn Farkas. *Learn Library of Congress Subject Access*. 2nd ed. Friendswood, Tex.: TotalRecall, 2007.
      (2) Library of Congress. "Library of Congress Subject Headings," http://www.loc.gov/cds/products/product.php?productID=159 (accessed 3 February 2011). Obtain the most recent edition from the Library of Congress Cataloging Distribution Service at the website. The best introduction to LCSH is the section of prefatory pages in the first volume.
      (3) Auxiliary Aids for LCSH
         (a) Library of Congress. "Free-Floating Subdivisions: An Alphabetical Index," http://www.loc.gov/cds/products/product.php?productID=28 (accessed 3 February 2011).
         (b) Library of Congress. "Subject Cataloging Manual: Subject Headings," 2009, http://www.loc.gov/cds/PDFdownloads/shm/SHM_2009-01.pdf (accessed 3 February 2011).
   b) Sears List of Subject Headings
      (1) Lighthall, Lynne. *Sears List of Subject Headings, Canadian Companion*. 6th ed. New York: H. W. Wilson, 2001. In-

formation about this publication is found at http://www
.hwwilson.com/print/searslst_can.cfm.

(2) *Miller, Joseph, and Susan McCarthy, eds. *Sears List of
Subject Headings*. 20th ed. New York: H. W. Wilson, 2010.
The best introduction to *Sears* is the section of prefatory
pages in the book itself. Obtain the most recent edition of
Sears from H. W. Wilson at http://www.hwwilson.com/
print/searslst_20th.cfm. At this site is also posted a link
to a short biography, "Minnie Earl Sears, The Woman
Behind *Sears List*."

(3) *Sears: Lista de Encabezamientos de Materia*. New York:
H.W. Wilson, 2008. Information about the Spanish language edition of *Sears* is at http://www.hwwilson.com/
print/searslst_spanish.cfm.

2. Specialized Subject Heading Lists

a) *American Library Association, Association for Library Collections & Technical Services. "Guidelines for Subject Analysis of Audiovisual Materials," 1992, http://www.ala.org/ala/
mgrps/divs/alcts/resources/org/cat/guidesubjt.cfm (accessed
4 February 2011).

b) American Library Association, Subcommittee on the Revision
of the Guidelines on Subject Access to Individual Works of
Fiction, Drama, Etc. *Guidelines on Subject Access to Individual
Works of Fiction, Drama, Etc.* 2nd ed. Chicago: American Library Association, 2000.

c) Library and Information Association New Zealand Aotearoa
(LIANZA), Te Rōpū Whakahau and the National Library of
New Zealand. "Ngā Ūpoko Tukutuku; Māori Subject Headings," http://mshupoko.natlib.govt.nz/mshupoko/index.htm
(accessed 4 February 2011). To see a more detailed explanation of a subject heading, access the "top terms" from the list
on this web page.

d) *U.S. National Library of Medicine, National Institutes of Health.
"Introduction to MeSH—2004," 2004, http://www.nlm.nih.gov/
mesh/introduction2004.html (accessed 4 February 2011).

(1) *U.S. National Library of Medicine, National Institutes of
Health. "MeSH Browser," 2010, http://www.nlm.nih.gov/
mesh/MBrowser.html (accessed 4 February 2011). Here is
where one can conduct online searching of MeSH.

T. Thesauri. In general terms, thesauri are subject heading lists (with the
subjects called *descriptors*) devoted to one subject area.

1. American Library Association, Association of College and Research Libraries, Rare Books and Manuscripts Section, Biblio-

graphic Standards Committee. "Genre Terms: A Thesaurus for Use in Rare Book and Special Collections Cataloguing," 1991, http://www.rbms.info/committees/bibliographic_standards/controlled_vocabularies/genre/alphabetical_list.htm (accessed 4 February 2011).

2. *Education Resources Information Center. "Search & Browse the Thesaurus," http://eric.ed.gov/ERICWebPortal/thesaurus/thesaurus.jsp?_pageLabel=Thesaurus (accessed 4 February 2011). This site is the search engine for thesauri terms for the online database of ERIC resources, which constitute the "world's largest digital library of education literature."[27] The "help with this page" link provides guidance to using the thesaurus, including a two-minute tutorial on finding the right descriptor.
   a) Education Resources Information Center. "ERIC," http://eric .ed.gov/ (accessed 4 February 2011).

3. Indian and Northern Affairs Canada, Communication Branch, "Words First: An Evolving Terminology Relating to Aboriginal Peoples in Canada," http://www.collectionscanada.gc.ca/webarchives/20071114213423/http://www.ainc-inac.gc.ca/pr/pub/wf/index_e.html (accessed 4 February 2011). The intent of this vocabulary is to "provide writers with background information and guidance on appropriate word usage and style issues."[28]

4. J. Paul Getty Trust, The Getty Research Institute. "Getty Vocabularies," http://www.getty.edu/research/conducting_research/vocabularies/aat/ (accessed 4 February 2011). The Getty vocabularies "contain structured terminology for art, architecture, decorative arts and other material culture, archival materials, visual surrogates, and bibliographic materials. Compliant with international standards, they provide authoritative information for catalogers and researchers, and can be used to enhance access to databases and Web sites."[29] This is where you can access online the Art & Architecture Thesaurus (AAT), The Union List of Artist Names (ULAN), and The Getty Thesaurus of Geographic Names (TGN). Check the link to "Frequently Asked Questions" at the bottom of the page.

5. Library of Congress. "Library of Congress Thesauri," http://www .loc.gov/lexico/servlet/lexico/ (accessed 4 February 2011). This web page links to two thesauri that are searchable by public users. One is the Legislative Indexing Vocabulary (LIV), "a thesaurus developed by the Congressional Research Service for use with legislative and public policy material."[30] The second is Thesaurus for Graphic Materials II: Genre and Physical Characteristic Terms (TGM II), "a tool for indexing visual materials by subject

and genre/format. The thesaurus includes more than 7,000 subject terms to index topics shown or reflected in pictures, and 650 genre/format terms to index types of photographs, prints, design drawings, ephemera and other categories."[31]

6. Native American Rights Fund, National Indian Law Library. "Thesaurus Project," http://www.narf.org/nill/catalog/the.htm (accessed 4 February 2011). This page provides information about the fourth edition of the thesaurus of the National Indian Law Library (NILL), which may be requested from the NILL.

6. U.S. Department of Agriculture, National Agricultural Library. "Thesaurus and Glossary Home," 2011, http://agclass.nal.usda.gov/agt/agt.shtml (accessed 4 February 2011). This thesaurus and the glossary of agricultural terms may be searched and browsed online in English or Spanish.

   a) U.S. Department of Agriculture, The National Agricultural Library, http://agricola.nal.usda.gov/ (accessed 4 February 2011).

U. Web Pages and Digitization

1. Lynch, Patrick J., and Sarah Horton. *Web Style Guide: Basic Design Principles for Creating Web Sites.* 3rd ed. Yale University, 2001. A free online version (can also be purchased as a book) of a guide that "explains established design principles and covers all aspects of web design—from planning to production to maintenance" and is appropriate for both "beginning and advanced designers."[32]

2. OCLC, Office of Research. "PURL [Persistent Uniform Resource Locator]," http://purl.oclc.org/ (accessed 4 February 2011).

V. Web Pages and Digitization and Accessibility

1. U.S. General Services Administration, IT Accessibility and the Workforce. "Section508.gov: Opening Doors to IT," http://www.section508.gov/index.cfm?FuseAction=Content&ID=3 (accessed 4 February 2011). Section 508 of the 1998 amendment of the Rehabilitation Act requires "federal agencies to make their electronic and information technology accessible to people with disabilities."[33] The detailed standards for compliance that are available on the website are useful for any setting that is addressing accessibility.

2. W3C, Web Accessibility Initiative. "Web Accessibility Initiative (W3C)," http://www.w3.org/WAI (accessed 4 February 2011). The Web Accessibility Initiative (WAI) "develops . . . guidelines widely regarded as the international standard for Web accessibility; support materials to help understand and implement Web accessibility; resources, through international collaboration."[34]

II. Catalogs of Libraries and Other Information Settings

  A. Dowling, Thomas. "LIBWEB: Library Servers via WWW," http://lists
     .webjunction.org/libweb/ (accessed 4 February 2011). Dowling pro-
     vides a source with links to library web pages, including international
     libraries with their catalogs.

  B. Library of Congress. "Gateway to Library Catalogs: Z3950," http://
     lcweb.loc.gov/z3950/gateway.html#lc (accessed 4 February 2011).

  C. Library of Congress. "SONIC—Sound Online Inventory and Catalog,"
     http://www.loc.gov/rr/record/Soniccont.html (accessed 4 February
     2011). "In addition to 78s, 45s and copyright cassettes, the database
     includes many broadcast and archival recordings."[35]

  D. Library of Congress, Prints & Photographs Reading Room. "Prints
     & Photographs Online Catalog," http://www.loc.gov/pictures (ac-
     cessed 4 February 2011). "The Prints and Photographs Online Catalog
     (PPOC) contains catalog records and digital images representing a
     rich cross-section of still pictures held by the Prints & Photographs
     Division and, in some cases, other units of the Library of Congress."[36]

  E. Smithsonian Institution, National Museum of the American Indian
     (NMAI). "Collections Search," 2011, http://www.nmai.si.edu/searchcol-
     lections/home.aspx (accessed 4 February 2011). The current "search the
     collection" option "includes a representative sample of NMAI's object
     and historic photo collections. Each item is accompanied by basic,
     standardized information."[37] Search by "peoples/cultures," "artists/indi-
     viduals," "places," and "object specifics" as well as "advanced search."[38]

III. Selected Publishers of Commonly Used Resources for the Organization of
    Information

  A. American Library Association. "ALA: American Library Association,"
     2011, http://www.ala.org (accessed 4 February 2011). To browse titles,
     click on the image for the "ALA Online Store" and then click on the
     links to "Books/Professional" and to "Cataloging and Classification."

  B. Libraries Unlimited, an Imprint of ABC-CLIO. "Welcome to Librar-
     ies Unlimited," 2011, http://www.lu.com/ (accessed 4 February 2011).

  C. Library of Congress, Cataloging Distribution Service. "Cataloging Dis-
     tribution Service," http://www.loc.gov/cds/ (accessed 4 February 2011).

  D. Rowman & Littlefield Publishing Group. "The Scarecrow Press, Inc.,"
     http://www.scarecrowpress.com/ (accessed 4 February 2011).

  E. Taylor & Francis. "Book Search," http://www.taylorandfrancis.com/
     books/ (accessed 4 February 2011).

IV. Directory of Supplies and Services for Libraries and Other Information
    Settings

  A. Librarian's Yellow Pages. "Librarian's Yellow Pages," http://www
     .librariansyellowpages.com/ (accessed 4 February 2011).[39] This source
     offers "searchable access to thousands of library products and services."

NOTES

1. Thomas Yen-Ran Yeh, "The Treatment of the American Indian in the Library of Congress E-F Schedule," *Library Resources & Technical Services* 15, no. 2 (Spring 1971): 122–28.

2. Tamara Lincoln, "Ethno-linguistic Misrepresentations of the Alaskan Native Languages as Mirrored in the Library of Congress System of Cataloging and Classification," *Cataloging & Classification Quarterly* 7, no. 3, (Spring 1987): 69–89.

3. Mary L. Young and Dara L. Doolittle, "The Halt of Stereotyping: When Does the American Indian Enter the Mainstream?" *The Reference Librarian* no. 47 (1994): 109–19.

4. Rhonda Harris Taylor, "Claiming the Bones Again: Native Americans & Issues of Bibliography," *Social Epistemology* 15, no. 1 (January 1, 2001): 21–26.

5. Nancy Carol Carter, "American Indians and Law Libraries: Acknowledging the Third Sovereign," *Law Library Journal* 94, no. 1 (Winter 2002): 7–26.

6. Library of Congress, "The Cataloging in Publication Program," http://cip.loc.gov/cip/ (accessed 28 January 2011); "Cataloging in Publication Celebrates 30th Birthday," *The Library of Congress Information Bulletin*, 60, no. 5 (May 2001), http://www.loc.gov/loc/lcib/0105/cip.html (accessed 28 January 2011).

7. Library of Congress, "Gateway to Library Catalogs: Z39.50," http://lcweb.loc.gov/z3950/gateway.html#lc (accessed 28 January 2011).

8. Library of Congress, "Z39.50 Gateway to Library of Congress Online Catalog, Simple Search," http://www.loc.gov/cgi-bin/zgate?ACTION=INIT&FORM_HOST_PORT=/prod/www/data/z3950/locils2.html,z3950.loc.gov,7090&CI=232608 (accessed 18 July 2010).

9. Library of Congress, "Library of Congress Online Catalog," http://catalog.loc.gov/ (accessed 28 January 2011).

10. Charles A. Cutter, *Rules for a Dictionary Catalog*, 4th ed., rewritten (Washington, D.C.: Government Printing Office, 1904).

11. Joseph Miller, ed., *Sears List of Subject Headings*, 17th ed. (New York: H. W. Wilson, 2000); Melvil Dewey, *Dewey Decimal Classification and Relative Index*, 21st ed., ed. Joan S. Mitchell (Albany, N.Y.: Forest Press, 1996), 1: xxxv.

12. *Dewey Decimal Classification*, 1: xxxv–xxxvi.

13. Gordon H. Hills, *Native Libraries: Cross-Cultural Conditions in the Circumpolar Countries* (Lanham, Md.: Scarecrow, 1997): 137–40.

14. Paul MacDonell, Reiko Tagami, and Paul Washington, "Brian Deer Classification System," The University of British Columbia School of Library, Archival and Information Studies, 2003, http://www.slais.ubc.ca/courses/libr517/02-03-wt2/projects/deer/index.htm (accessed 28 January 20110).

15. XWI7XWA Library, First Nations House of Learning, University of British Columbia, Vancouver, "BC First Nations Subject Headings," 2009, http://www.library.ubc.ca/xwi7xwa/bcfn.pdf (accessed 28 January 2011); Samantha Harris, "American Indian Children's & Young Adult Literature: Author Research," University Libraries, University of Washington, 2008, http://www.lib.washington.edu/subject/Childrens/AmericanIndian/authors.html (accessed 28 January 2011).

16. Native American Rights Fund, "National Indian Law Library: Justice Through Knowledge," http://narf.org/nill/catalog/catalog.htm (accessed 28 January 2011).

17. American Library Association, Association for Library Collections & Technical Services (ALCTS), "About ALCTS," http://www.ala.org/ala/mgrps/divs/alcts/about/index.cfm (accessed 18 July 2010).

18. Archives Association of British Columbia, "History of the AABC Archivist's Toolkit," http://aabc.ca/TK_00_main_page.html (accessed 29 January 2011).

19. First Archivists Circle, "Protocols for Native American Archival Materials: Introduction," http://www2.nau.edu/libnap-p/protocols.html (accessed 29 January 2011).

20. Library of Congress, "Library of Congress Authorities," http://authorities.loc.gov/ (accessed 29 January 2011).

21. Library of Congress, "Library of Congress Subject Headings (LCSH) Weekly Lists," http://www.loc.gov/aba/cataloging/subject/weeklylists/ (accessed 29 January 2011).

22. Library of Congress, "Library of Congress Classification Outline," http://www.loc.gov/catdir/cpso/lcco/ (accessed 29 January 2011).

23. Copyright Clearance Center, "Get Permission," http://www.copyright.com/viewPage.do?pageCode=gp1(accessed 30 January 2011).

24. Bettie Furrie, "Understanding MARC Bibliographic: Machine-Readable Cataloging," 2009, http://lcweb.loc.gov/marc/umb (accessed 30 January 2011).

25. Victoria Irons Walch, comp., "Standards for Archival Description: A Handbook," 1994, http://www.archivists.org/catalog/stds99/chapter10.html (accessed 2 February 2011).

26. Walch, "Standards for Archival Description," (3 Feb. 2011).

27. Education Resources Information Center, http://www.eric.ed.gov/ (accessed 19 July 2010).

28. Indian and Northern Affairs Canada, Communication Branch, "Words First: An Evolving Terminology Relating to Aboriginal Peoples in Canada," 2004, http://www.collectionscanada.gc.ca/webarchives/20071114213423/http://www.ainc-inac.gc.ca/pr/pub/wf/index_e.html (accessed 4 February 2011).

29. J. Paul Getty Trust, the Getty Research Institute, "Getty Vocabularies," http://www.getty.edu/research/tools/vocabularies/index.html (accessed 4 February 2011).

30. Library of Congress, "Library of Congress Thesauri," http://www.loc.gov/lexico/servlet/lexico/ (accessed 4 February 2011).

31. Library of Congress, "Library of Congress Thesauri."

32. Patrick J. Lynch and Sarah Horton, "Web Style Guide: Basic Design Principles for Creating Web Sites," 2009, http://www.webstyleguide.com/ (accessed 4 February 2011).

33. U.S. General Services Administration, IT Accessibility and the Workforce, "Laws: Section 508 Laws," http://www.section508.gov/index.cfm?fuseAction=Laws (accessed 4 February 2011).

34. W3C, Web Accessibility Initiative, "Web Accessibility Initiative (W3C)," http://www.w3.org/WAI (accessed 4 February 2011).

35. Library of Congress,"SONIC—Sound Online Inventory and Catalog," http://www.loc.gov/rr/record/Soniccont.html (accessed 4 February 2011).

36. Library of Congress, Prints & Photographs Reading Room, Prints & Photographs Online Catalog, "About PPOC," http://www.loc.gov/pictures/about/ (accessed 4 February 2011).

37. Smithsonian Institution, National Museum of the American Indian, "Collections Search," 2011, http://www.nmai.si.edu/searchcollections/home.aspx (accessed 4 February 2011).

38. Smithsonian Institution, National Museum of the American Indian,"Collections Search."

39. Librarian's Yellow Pages, "Welcome to LYPOnline!" http://www.librariansyellowpages.com/ (accessed 4 February 2011).

13

Empowering Indigenous Students in the Learning Library[1]

Victoria Beatty

THE LIBRARY THROUGH INDIGENOUS EYES

When I moved to the Navajo Nation in 2004 as the new instruction librarian at Diné College, I began learning the importance of introductions. In addition to needing a good answer to the question, "Who are you, and what are you doing here?" I soon learned that I needed to have an equally good answer to the question, "What is the library, and why is it here?"

I stood in classrooms and faced students whose folded arms and challenging stares created a palpable impression that they viewed libraries as irrelevant at best and as representatives of cruelly colonizing educational systems at worst. Many of the students' parents remembered well the taste of lye soap from boarding school days.

I struggled with this at first, especially since the Diné word for "library" is *Naaltsoos Baahooghan*, or "house of papers," a term that is also used for the post office! What could be more emblematic of the alien forces of colonization than paper itself, let alone the many tomes on Diné culture written by non-Navajo authors? But my initial discomfiture melted away as I pondered the library's position in the center of campus. The main campus of Diné College is built in a circle like the traditional hogan, with campus buildings placed according to their metaphorical functions.[2] Like the First House made of dawn, evening light, and cloud and rain, the campus is a microcosm that is both a haven and a gathering place for intellectual and spiritual sustenance.[3] By siting the library in the place of the fire, the founders of Diné College demonstrated that they did not see it as a deep freeze or glorified root cellar, but rather as the living, everyday gathering place of conversation, storytelling, thinking, and planning—the site where traditions stay alive through daily use.

David P. McAllester has written in *Hogans: Navajo Houses and House Songs* that, "in Diné philosophy, the material world is the result and also the manifestation of the power of sacred words. The words, in turn, proceed from thought, and behind thought lies knowledge."[4] When introducing the library to students, I tell them that all human knowledge is an ongoing, never-ending conversation, whether it happens face to face, through audio or visual recordings, through the electronic word, or through words inscribed on paper or other media. For many student research projects, the library may only be able to take a student halfway, and he or she will have to interview elders in the community to complete the project. Medicine men, singers, tribal judges, and other culture keepers use the library as a resource to compare their own practices and beliefs with historical records of earlier practices. There are many ways of conducting research, some of which lead into the library and others that lead out into the world.

INFORMATION LITERACY THROUGH INDIGENOUS EYES

Soon after I arrived at Diné College, I began to realize that "information literacy" might encompass much more than the technological, library-centric model that was familiar to me. My students ran the gamut from tech-savvy urban Indians to those who followed traditional lifeways, moving between sheep camps that lacked water, telephones, and certainly computers. Many lived in both worlds, busily texting their friends and updating their MySpace pages on the library computers before rushing home to care for the family flock of sheep.

I began to view information literacy as a set of tools of the mind, ranging from knowing how to track a lost animal or how to recognize toxic plants, to knowing how to locate scholarly articles in an online database or how to sift trustworthy websites from spurious ones.[5] I thought about how my students and I were regularly negotiating many overlapping cultures, each with its own set of rules and norms and survival strategies.[6] My Diné students, who gracefully stepped from oral ceremony to written college exam, from sheep slaughtering to scripting a computer program, from oral to print to digital, and from ceremony to library to MySpace, made me more aware of how I moved among the sometimes mutually exclusive worlds of libraries, academic scholarship, and musical performance or storytelling.

Wrestling with my own dominant cultural assumptions as I absorbed new ways of looking at the world, I began to realize how many of the portable strategies and practices that enable us to succeed in our various worlds are transmitted orally or learned informally. The Haida sculptor Bill Reid has written eloquently of the natural way that young people of Haida Gwaii would have been educated on their home beach, the center of village activity: "A thousand trips up and down the beach would probably have been sufficient to make each of them a universal man or woman, [with] a working knowledge of all the techniques . . . by which the Haida coped with their environment, as well as complete knowledge of the language and legends of their kind."[7]

So I began presenting the library to my students as a comfortable home away from home, with abundant opportunities for informal learning. As their guide to knowledge that could be gained from electronic digital resources, research of all kinds, and library and archival collections, I would help them to hone a set of "tools of the mind" that would be useful not just in the academic world but also in the twenty-first-century information economy.

CONNECTING WITH STUDENTS

Studies have shown that when people are seeking information, they prefer to turn to a relative or friend.[8] Cheryl Metoyer's study of gatekeepers in ethnolinguistic communities quoted one gatekeeper who noted that many of the people she helped did not feel comfortable in the library: "The library might become important and powerful if it became part of the real life of the community."[9] So I began introducing myself to students as their "personal librarian."

"Some people have personal trainers," I would tell each class. "Some people have personal shoppers. Well, I'd like for you to think of me as your personal librarian and your guide to the world of information. I don't expect you to remember everything that we cover in today's session. But when you start working on your papers and research projects, you'll want to go back to some of these great resources that we're going to look at today. If you get stuck, please don't hesitate to call or e-mail me, or stop by my office, and I'll be happy to work with you individually on your specific project."

Students began to seek me out, in person or by e-mail or telephone, for an individual consultation at their point of need. I also noticed that some of them were not students whom I had met before; they had heard about the "personal librarian" from their friends. Even the faculty members began introducing me to their classes as "our personal librarian."

Tanya Gorman Keith, former vice president of academic and student affairs at Diné College, has written that "learning is a shared responsibility between teacher and student, according to the Diné paradigm."[10] Interdependent student–faculty relationships encourage informal interaction and opportunities for instructors to offer guidance and advice, thus promoting wholeness. Winona Wheeler has also described Cree education as "a reciprocal and interactive teaching relationship between student and teacher."[11]

As I worked to become a better teacher and to make the library a part of the real life of our community, I took heart from Parker Palmer's observation that "[g]ood teachers join self, subject, and students in the fabric of life because they teach from an integral and undivided self; they manifest in their own lives, and evoke in their students, a 'capacity for connectedness.'"[12]

A CULTURALLY RELEVANT APPROACH TO RESEARCH

As I sought ways to make my information literacy instruction more relevant to students, two books were especially helpful, introducing a number of approaches to creating indigenous educational models. *Indigenous Educational Models for Contemporary Practice: In Our Mother's Voice*, edited by Maenette Kape'ahiokalani Padeken Ah Nee-Benham and Joanne Elizabeth Cooper, emphasizes the centrality of community and relationships as it fruitfully introduces a number of educational models and discussions of student-centered learning.[13] Gregory Cajete's seminal book, *Look to the Mountain: An Ecology of Indigenous Education*, also presents a number of models that were of tremendous value to me.[14] Several chapters of this book are available online through the Northwest Indian College Oksale Program's Virtual Library.[15]

The curriculum at Diné College is built upon the Diné educational philosophy, and this offered a perfect framework for teaching students about information literacy and research in a way that aligned with their other courses.[16] Although this model may seem complex and arbitrary to outsiders, for the Diné people there are so many stories and other layers of meaning associated with the sacred mountains and the cardinal directions that the system serves as a powerful memory palace. It is not very much of a stretch to map the five Information Literacy Competency Standards for Higher Education developed by the Association of College and Research Libraries onto the four principles of the Diné paradigm.[17]

By creating a culturally relevant scaffolding for teaching these concepts, I hoped to help students make an easier transition to the information literacy expectations they would encounter when transferring to other colleges and universities. But I also emphasized the value of these portable "tools of the mind" for everyday information needs, such as researching medical information for family members experiencing health problems or researching repair records before purchasing vehicles or major appliances.

A DINÉ RESEARCH MODEL

Referring to the Diné paradigm has helped students understand the recursive nature of the research process. I am indebted to Anthony Lee Sr., a Diné College faculty member and president of the Diné Medicine Men's Association, for introducing the idea of applying the Diné paradigm to the research process.

One evening, when I was taking his class in Navajo culture, Lee drew a tripartite model of the research process on the board, explaining that this model had been proposed to him as an aid for his dissertation research and that it exemplified the dominant, Western tradition: (1) overview, (2) in-depth research, and (3) application of research. This reminded me of the research model introduced by Carol Collier Kuhlthau in 1989. She has described the process as holistic, because

ARE YOU INFORMATION LITERATE?*

Nitsáhákees: An Information Literate person *thinks* about what information is needed:

- determines the extent of information needed
- formulates questions based on information needs
- identifies potential sources of information

Nahat'á: An Information Literate person *plans* how to get needed information:

- develops successful search strategies
- accesses sources of information in all formats effectively and efficiently
- selects and interprets the needed information

Iiná: An Information Literate person uses information for *real-life* problem solving and decision making:

- organizes and applies information gathered in order to achieve a specific goal
- benefits the community by effectively communicating the new information to others

Siihasin: An Information Literate person analyzes information critically for *assurance* of its value, and through *reflection* gains fresh insights:

- evaluates information to determine its reliability, validity, accuracy, authority, timeliness, and point of view or bias
- discovers additional information and selectively incorporates information into his or her knowledge base and value system
- understands the social, economic, and legal issues concerning the use of information
- accesses and uses information ethically and legally
- incubates fresh insights based upon reflection, feedback, and discovery of additional information

Adapted from American Library Association, Association of College & Research Libraries, "Information Literacy Competency Standards for Higher Education," 2000, http://www.ala.org/ala/mgrps/divs/acrl/standards/informationliteracycompetency.cfm (accessed 6 September 2010).

it incorporates students' emotional states, and she has noted that some studies "revealed a more recursive rather than strictly linear process."[18] Nevertheless, she created her model as a linear sequence.

It is interesting to contrast a linear research model such as Kuhlthau's Information Search Process with a circular model such as the one proposed for digital libraries by Andreas Paepcke.[19] On the surface, they do not appear that dissimilar. Kuhlthau's model outlined six activities: (1) initiation, (2) selection, (3) exploration, (4) formulation, (5) collection, and (6) presentation. Models like this one seem to have an implicit final step: (7) you're done!

In Paepcke's circular model, the five search activities were (1) resource discovery and selection, (2) retrieving information from relevant sources, (3) interpreting what was retrieved; (4) managing the filtered-out information locally, and (5) sharing results with others. However, Paepcke arranged his activities in a circular model and stipulated that "these activities are not necessarily sequential, but are repeated and interleaved."[20]

Janel Hinrichsen of the Diné College Center for Diné Teacher Education introduced me to another, highly relevant circular model, the Action Research Model. A simple version of the cycle includes four steps: (1) plan, (2) act, (3) observe, and (4) reflect. A more detailed version specifies five steps in each cycle: (1) diagnosing, (2) action planning, (3) taking action, (4) evaluating, and (5) specifying learning.[21]

Keeping these models in mind, it is easy to see how the Diné paradigm offers a perfect template for explaining the research process to Navajo students. Figure 13.1 organizes the process into four activities.

Figure 13.1   Diné Research Model

Moving clockwise around the circle, *Nitsáhákees* (Thinking) is associated with choosing a broad subject area for research (thinking about what information is needed, formulating questions, and identifying potential sources of information). *Nahat'á* (Planning) is associated with focusing the topic and starting research (developing search strategies, accessing information sources, and interpreting and selecting information). *Iiná* (Living According to a Pattern) is associated with writing and presenting the paper or research project (organizing and applying information for decision making and communicating new information to benefit the community). *Siihasin* (Confidence, Security, Assurance) is associated with getting feedback (sharing and evaluating information, discovering additional information, using information ethically, and incubating fresh insights).

Students who usually blame themselves when they discover that doing research is not quick and easy find it reassuring to learn that even expert researchers travel around the circle many times before finishing a project. Indeed, a three-dimensional view of the model might resemble a spiral. It is also helpful to forewarn students about the typical moods and feelings associated with different stages of the process.[22] *Nitsáhákees*, associated with task initiation and topic selection in Kuhlthau's model, is characterized by uncertainty and then optimism as the topic is selected. *Nahat'á*, associated with Kuhlthau's stages of prefocus exploration and focus formulation, is marked by initial confusion and then emerging confidence as a focus emerges. *Iiná*, associated with Kuhlthau's stages of collection and presentation, is a time of deepening interest and involvement, culminating in an awareness of new understanding that may be used to help others or put to use in some way. *Siihasin* is not represented in Kuhlthau's model, but is included in the more recent models by Paepcke, Loertscher, and others. As Paepcke noted, researchers must be able to

> move freely in the circle space to get their work done. In general, users will be involved in multiple tasks at the same time. They will need to move back and forth among these tasks, and among the five areas of activity. They need to find, analyze, and understand information of varying genres. They need to re-organize the information to use it in multiple contexts, and to manipulate it in collaboration with colleagues of different backgrounds and focus of interest.[23]

Applying the Diné paradigm to the learning cycle, Gorman Keith has written, "The cycle continues as the learner gains more knowledge. . . . Persistence is measured by returning to *nitsáhákees* [thinking] until the vision is realized."[24]

CRITICAL THINKING FOR DECOLONIZATION

Introducing students to colonization and decolonization as analytical frameworks is an exciting way to get them interested in critical thinking. I like to show them *For Indigenous Eyes Only: A Decolonization Handbook* by Waziyatawin Angela Wilson and Michael Yellow Bird.[25] Michael Yellow Bird's chapter advocating tribal critical thinking centers introduces the idea of critical thinking as "intelligently subversive activity," noting that "people who are ignorant are easier to control, mislead, and oppress than those who are well informed, intellectually skilled, and constantly challenging themselves to discern the 'truths' that make up and guide their existence."[26] Challenging students with Yellow Bird's list of the types of people who may find critical thinking too rigorous and threatening really captures their attention and awakens their inner warriors.[27]

Students also showed great interest in an exhibit we created of books featuring Native American authors/artists, including themes of American Indian decoloni-zation, sovereignty, constitutional history, and representation.[28] The books flew off the display table, as many students chose to write research papers based on these ideas. Dane Ward, associate dean for information assets at Illinois State University, has pointed out that students learn best when they find a reason for caring. In a manifesto calling for more student-centered approaches that apply information literacy skills for a "revolutionary" purpose, he wrote:

> Will we step out of our comfort zone within academia to engage and meet the world where its problems really exist? . . . In part, our difficulty in gaining rapid and wide-spread acceptance of information literacy results from our attempt to fit this revolu-tionary idea within a traditional teaching paradigm, which diminishes it.[29]

In this era of media consolidation and "spin," the educated citizenry necessary for the survival of democratic societies must work harder to read the world rigor-ously, between the lines and beyond the hype. For the indigenous citizens of the world, struggling to protect the sovereignty of their nations, this is an absolutely crucial survival skill, when viewed through the lens of history.

COMING FULL CIRCLE

Recently I had one of those on-the-beach learning experiences described by Bill Reid when I had the rare privilege of witnessing some of my students passing on their library "tools of the mind" to younger students.[30] It was College Career Day, and small groups of middle school students were touring the library, each led by a Diné College student guide. Although my initial impulse was to step in and take over, I hovered at the fringe of the first group and listened with growing wonder as the fully empowered student guide introduced the younger students to his li-brary, extolling its virtues, physical and virtual, with quiet pride. "Let me just log on to this computer," he told them enthusiastically, "so I can show you some of the great databases we have," and he went on to demonstrate a sample search as the younger students clustered around whispering "Cool!" to one another. At first I suspected that that particular guide must have been an exceptional student, but as many more groups toured the library over the course of the day, I discovered that every single student guide was similarly knowledgeable and enthusiastic.

I can't take any special credit, because I had only passed on what I had learned from people like Gregory Cajete and Michael Yellow Bird and especially Cheryl Metoyer, who reminded me to find the beauty in my work, to "stop the 'uglification'" of colonization, and to say to my students, "'Hey look at this—really look at this and listen . . . we have beautiful and wonderful gifts to share with you.'"[31]

Lewis Hyde has written that "it is only when the gift has worked in us, only when we have come up to its level, as it were, that we can give it away again. . . . The transformation is not accomplished until we have the power to give the gift on our own terms."[32] Metoyer has also reminded us that "if something is of beauty, giving it away only increases its beauty."[33] Let us keep the gift moving as we continue to walk in beauty in our richly gifted learning libraries.

NOTES

1. An earlier version of this chapter was published as Victoria Beatty, "Much to Teach, Much to Learn: Teaching Information Literacy Cross-Culturally; Mucho para enseñar, mucho para aprender: enseñanza intercultural del desarrollo de habilidades informativas," in *Proceedings: Transborder Library Forum 2007, Bridging the Digital Divide: Crossing All Borders,* ed. Jeanette M. Mueller-Alexander and Rosa González, 2007, 49–68, http://www.asu.edu/lib/foro/FORO_2007_Proceedings.pdf.

2. "About DC," 2006, https://www.dinecollege.edu/ics/About_DC.jnz (accessed 31 December 2006).

3. Maureen T. Schwarz, *Molded in the Image of Changing Woman* (Tucson: University of Arizona Press, 1997).

4. David P. McAllester and Susan W. McAllester, *Hogans: Navajo Houses and House Songs* (Middletown, Conn.: Wesleyan University Press, 1980), 20.

5. Julie Cruikshank, *The Social Life of Stories: Narrative and Knowledge in the Yukon Territory* (Lincoln: University of Nebraska Press, 1998), 102.

6. Cruikshank, *Social Life of Stories,* 122.

7. William Reid, "The Raw Material of Chaos," in *Solitary Raven: The Selected Writings of Bill Reid* (Seattle: University of Washington Press, 2000), 226.

8. Steven Bell, "Gaining the Trust of Students," *ACRLog: Blogging by and for Academic and Research Librarians,* 5 September 2006, http://acrlblog.org/2006/09/05/gaining-the-trust-of-students/ (accessed 3 March 2011).

9. Cheryl Metoyer-Duran, "The Information and Referral Process in Culturally Diverse Communities," *RQ* 32, no. 3 (1993): 369.

10. Tanya Gorman Keith, "Sihasin, Meaning of Graduation to Navajo College Students at Northern Arizona University: An Interpretive Case Study" (PhD diss., Northern Arizona University, 2004).

11. Winona Wheeler, "Reflections on the Social Relations of Indigenous Oral Histories," in *Walking a Tightrope: Aboriginal People and Their Representations,* ed. Ute Litschke and David T. McNab (Waterloo, Ont.: Wilfrid Laurier University Press, 2005), 198.

12. Parker J. Palmer. *The Courage to Teach; Exploring the Inner Landscape of a Teacher's Life* (San Francisco: Jossey-Bass, 1998).

13. Maenette Kape'ahiokalani Ah-Nee-Benham and Joanne Elizabeth Cooper, eds., *Indigenous Educational Models for Contemporary Practice: In Our Mother's Voice* (Mahwah, N.J.: Lawrence Erlbaum Associates Publishers, 2000).

14. Gregory Cajete, *Look to the Mountain: An Ecology of Indigenous Education* (Durango, Colo.: Kivaki, 1994).

15. NWIC OKSALE Program Virtual Library, "Educational Resources: Cajete's Education Model," http://www.ischool.utexas.edu/~vlibrary/edres/index.html (accessed 3 March 2011).

16. James K. McNeley, "The Pattern Which Connects Navajo and Western Knowledge," *Journal of Navajo Education* 12, no. 1 (1994): 3–14.

17. American Library Association, Association of College & Research Libraries, "Information Literacy Competency Standards for Higher Education," 2000, http://www.ala.org/ala/mgrps/divs/acrl/standards/informationliteracycompetency.cfm (accessed 6 September 2010).

18. Carol Collier Kuhlthau, "Information Search Process: A Summary of Research and Implications for School Library Media Programs," *School Library Media Quarterly* 18, no. 5 (1989), http://www.ala.org/ala/mgrps/divs/aasl/aaslpubsandjournals/slmrb/editorschoiceb/infopower/slctkuhlthau2.cfm (accessed 6 September 2010).

19. Kuhlthau, "Information Search Process"; Andreas Paepcke, "Digital Libraries: Searching Is Not Enough; What We Learned On-Site," *D Lib Magazine* (May 1996), http://www.dlib.org/dlib/may96/stanford/05paepcke.html (accessed 6 September 2010).

20. Paepcke, "Digital Libraries."

21. Rory O'Brien, "Um Exame da Abordagem Metodológica da Pesquisa Ação [An Overview of the Methodological Approach of Action Research]," in *Teoria e Prática da Pesquisa Ação [Theory and Practice of Action Research]*, ed. Roberto Richardson (João Pessoa, Brazil: Universidade Federal da Paraíba [English version], 2001), http://www.web.ca/~robrien/papers/arfinal.html (accessed 7 September 2010).

22. Kuhlthau, "Information Search Process."

23. Paepcke, "Digital Libraries."

24. Gorman Keith, "Sihasin," 99.

25. Waziyatawin A. Wilson and Michael Yellow Bird, eds., *For Indigenous Eyes Only: A Decolonization Handbook* (Santa Fe, N.Mex.: School of American Research, 2005).

26. Michael Yellow Bird, "Tribal Critical Thinking Centers," in *For Indigenous Eyes Only*, ed. Wilson and Yellow Bird, 16.

27. Yellow Bird, "Tribal Critical Thinking Centers," 11.

28. Victoria Beatty, "Silenced Voices: In Hidden, Silenced, Banned, Burned . . . and Beautiful: The Diné College Libraries Present an Exhibit in Observance of Banned Books Week and the September Project," September 2007, http://library.dinecollege.edu/spotlight/bannedbooks/voices.html (accessed 7 September 2010).

29. Dane Ward, "The Future of Information Literacy: Transforming the World," *College & Research Libraries News* 62, no. 9 (October 2001): 922.

30. Cruikshank, *The Social Life of Stories*, 122; Reid, *Solitary Raven*, 226.

31. Cheryl A. Metoyer, "The Beauty of It All," *Easy Access* 30, no. 4 (December 2004), http://northwestarchivistsinc.wildapricot.org/resources/Documents/EAvol30issue4_Dec2004.pdf (accessed 8 September 2010).

32. Lewis Hyde, *The Gift: Imagination and the Erotic Life of Property* (New York: Vintage, 1979), 47.

33. Metoyer, "The Beauty of It All."

14

Weaving Partnerships with the American Indian Peoples in Your Community to Develop Cultural Programming

Loriene Roy

Native peoples are of interest around the world. This is illustrated through museum exhibits, film, and the popularity of indigenous writers. In some locations, teaching and celebrating Native cultures occur annually. In the United States, the arrival of November brings National American Indian Heritage Month and the reminder of Native cultures through the national celebration of Thanksgiving. Libraries have responded to this interest through building collections and offering programs including book discussions, displays, exhibits, film screenings, and speaker series.

In some states, legislation recommends or even requires study of and collaboration with tribal nations. Wisconsin Educational Act 31 requires K–12 educators to teach not only the history but also the culture and treaty rights of Wisconsin tribes.[1] The state of Montana recognizes in its constitution "the distinct and unique cultural heritage of American Indians and is committed in its educational goals to the preservation of their cultural integrity."[2] The constitutional amendment of 1999 came to be known as Indian Education for All and states that:

1. Every Montanan, whether Indian or non-Indian, be encouraged to learn about the distinct and unique heritage of American Indians in a culturally responsive manner; and
2. Every educational agency and all educational personnel will work cooperatively with Montana tribes or those tribes that are in close proximity, when providing instruction or when implementing an educational goal or adopting a rule related to the education of each Montana citizen, to include information specific to the cultural heritage and contemporary contributions of American Indians, with particular emphasis on Montana Indian tribal groups and governments.[3]

This chapter focuses on understanding how to work with Native peoples to develop new services and expand existing ones. Content is organized into five sections: (1) learning about Native communities, (2) indigenous ways of knowing and making connections, (3) initiating and maintaining connections, (4) challenging your motive(s) in providing these services, and (5) resources for cultural programming.

LEARNING ABOUT NATIVE COMMUNITIES

Whether or not librarians are aware of the demographic mix of their user communities, Native people likely live in their service areas. This is true even if the library is not located on tribal lands: largely as a result of twentieth-century urban relocation initiatives, two-thirds of the 4.3 million U.S. American Indian/Alaska Native population lives off reservation homelands.[4]

There are multiple strategies for learning about the Native peoples living in and near your communities. Sir James Henare spoke of the potential benefit of collaborations between Maori, the indigenous peoples of Aotearoa/New Zealand, and Pakeha, citizens of Aotearoa/New Zealand of European descent:

> Each ethnic group has something to give the other and something to learn from each other. Barriers are being created unnecessarily by the hypersensitivity of the Maori and the insensitivity of the Pakeha to Maori aspirations. But with good will, greater understanding, and better knowledge of each other's values and culture, these barriers can be demolished.[5]

While this chapter sketches out a process for learning about indigenous peoples, it is important to note that true understanding evolves from face-to-face contact: "A culture cannot be learned from a textbook. True understanding and appreciation are possible only from first-hand experience."[6] Native educators and leaders have warned against the overreliance on print resources in trying to develop deep understanding of indigenous peoples. The Alaska Native Knowledge Network advises community educators to "get acquainted with your new community through first-hand experience rather than through books, and be careful about over-generalization of insights gained from prior readings."[7] The elders she interviewed for her thesis reminded Manulani Aluli Meyer to "practice culture, experience culture, live culture. . . . It is a reminder of the most important aspect of a Hawaiian knowledge structure: experience . . . *experience, practice and repetition* are fundamental to knowing something."[8]

Devon Mihesuah observed: "The problem with many books and articles about Indians is not with what is included but with what is omitted. There are many works on tribal histories and cultures that are fine examples of library and archival research, but the search usually ends there."[9] So, with these caveats, you might start your search with sources in print, primarily because they are readily available and might provide you with a foundation. From these sources, extend your search and contacts as you follow a path of deeper understanding of yourself and of indigenous peoples.

Start exploring some of the key events in Native history that have impacted contemporary Indian life, especially specific events related to the tribe you are studying. These topics might include treaty rights, the boarding or residential school experience, or military service within Native communities.

Read the stories of contemporary Indian people. Great figures in history are covered in many publications, and there are an increasing number of recent biographies and autobiographies. You might consider reading picture books or books written for youth, as these titles are often well illustrated and may include supplementary features such as maps and glossaries. The American Indian Library Association's Youth Literature Awards, given every other year since 2008, will help you follow well-received titles. Do not overlook the expanding cadre of Native poets and fiction writers. American authors include Louise Erdrich, Sherman Alexie, Joy Harjo, Luci Tapahonso, Joseph Bruchac, Linda Powers, Heid Erdrich, Sherwin Bitsui, Allison Coke Hedge, Lurline Wailana McGregor, Lise Erdrich, Cynthia Leitich Smith, Leslie Marmon Silko, and Tim Tingle.

To begin your understanding of specific tribal peoples, start with demographics. Gather a general overview of the U.S. American Indian and Alaskan Native population through the U.S. Census.[10] In fact, the Census uses the acronym AIAN to refer to these populations. Factfinder will provide general overview statistics but also lead you to Census information by tribe and even reservation. You will find, for example, data on the number of Native-language speakers, households run by single parents, and educational levels. Note, especially, the "We the People: American Indian and Alaska Natives in the United States" brochure and the "American Indians and Alaska Natives in the United States Wall Map."[11] A next step in your process of gathering formal information is to peruse the Tribal Community Resource feature of The American Indian Experience, an online resource produced by ABC-CLIO Greenwood.[12] You will find a clickable map that leads to narrative essays on more than five hundred tribes.

Once you have read about key issues, figures, and writers in the broad landscape of indigenous studies and have examined demographics and narrative surveys of your tribal communities, narrow your search for research and locally developed materials. Find out if a researcher has worked with your tribal communities. If so, are their materials available as dissertations or other publications? What material on the tribe is located in your local historical society?

Create a checklist of topics related to the cultures you are studying and match this list with possible sources for local information. What are some local cultural expressions? Are the tribal communities near you known for a type of artwork such as beading, basketry, or pottery? Are they known for a specific type of traditional food? You might find answers to your questions on a tribal community website, in a course offered at a community college, at a social gathering such as a powwow, or at an event sponsored by an urban Indian center. Public schools might have a Native American parent committee; schools enrolling ten or more Native students can apply for a per capita grant from the U.S. Department of Education. One contingency of the grant is that there must be a parent committee.[13]

Remember that learning about a tribal community is a lifelong activity even for Native people themselves. Angela Cavender Wilson wrote of the effort and impact of documenting her Dakota grandmother's stories: "[I]t becomes apparent to me that the learning of these stories is a lifelong process and, likewise, the rewards of that process last a lifetime."[14]

When studying aspects of a particular tribal community, the question of individual membership within a tribe might arise. Questions about American Indian identity are complex, as Mihesuah explains:

> Because of assimilation, acculturation, and intermarriage with nonIndians, American Indians have a variety of references to describe themselves: full-blood, traditional, mixed-blood, cross-blood, half-breed, progressive, enrolled, unenrolled, re-Indianized, multiheritage, bicultural, post-Indian, or simply, "I'm _____ (tribal affiliation)."[15]

Tribal communities define their membership, whether it is based on biological connections, relationships, or other factors.

In addition to tribal affiliation, many North American Indigenous cultures convey a connection with land, often expressed through recognizing orientations. Gregory Cajete describes this recognition with the "seven basic orientations: the four cardinal directions, north, south, east, west, the center, usually the community, itself or village, or the center of the territory, and then the Above and the Below, the below representing the earth and the above, the celestial or universe."[16] Each of the cardinal directions is associated with a specific color and a strength or source of learning. In designing a curriculum for ethnoscience, Cajete assigns these attributes to the seven orientations: center (balance; holistic thinking), east (insight; philosophy), west (social well-being; social psychology), south (good fortune; health and wholeness), north (dreaming; mythology), below (earth; ecology), and above (spirit; quest for the Universal).[17]

Also remember that Native people demonstrate a range of cultural connectiveness. This is a time to start challenging your assumptions. Not all American Indians live on reservations or tribal homelands, speak their Native languages, have indigenous names, lead traditional lifestyles, observe traditional religious practices, or conform to the general population's mental image of what Indians should look like. Urban Indians, for example, are often forgotten because their lifestyles might be similar to many non-Indian people in the same setting.

INDIGENOUS WAYS OF KNOWING
AND MAKING CONNECTIONS

Western models of understanding are linear and follow what is accepted as the scientific method. This process supports quantification of experiences; posing of hypotheses or testable questions; and a building-block approach wherein results cumulate, resulting in a body of accepted knowledge. Value is attributed to publications that typically follow a formulaic presentation, starting with a literature review, introducing the question, describing the research methodology used, presenting results, adding an analysis or discussion of results, and concluding with a call for further research.

Librarians preparing for community-based work often conduct literature reviews as a step toward conducting a needs assessment. A literature review identifies published accounts, usually in professional literature. A needs assessment usually involves creating one or more data collection instruments, interviewing key leaders, and possibly organizing focus groups of community representatives. Librarians pose questions to members of their user community, generally asking for their answers about present or potential services and relating these offerings to declared audience needs. Such an approach is logical and consistent, but is most likely not the best way to establish a relationship with tribal members. Because needs assessment is based on asking questions, this process falls into the domain of human subjects research and as such is governed by policies set by host institutions.

The scientific method and, by extension, needs assessment are tools of practice that frame thinking. These approaches to engaging with communities might feel familiar to librarians, but, like most research conducted on indigenous topics, too often "the prevailing discourse on community needs assessment conceptualizes community analysis as something that is done *to* the community in question, rather than *with* the community in any meaningful way."[18] And though these approaches are often deemed the only valid ways to conduct study, they have also been associated with misdirection of Native peoples. Linda Tuhiwai Smith wrote the most influential book on conducting research with Native peoples, *Decolonizing Methodologies: Research and Indigenous Peoples*, in which she warned that, to many indigenous peoples, "research is a dirty word."[19]

Librarians and researchers interested in working with tribal communities on studies then have three general options. One is to request tribal permission to follow the human subjects research approach. A number of documents are available that serve to educate researchers on the process and etiquette of working with Native respondents. Mihesuah provided a copy of "Suggested Guidelines for Institutions with Researchers Who Conduct Research on American Indians." These ten statements include the following:

1. Only the tribe's elected political and religious leadership should review and approve the research proposal.
2. Researchers should remain sensitive to the economic, social, physical, psychological, religious, and general welfare of the individuals and cultures being studied.
3. If you are preparing a grant application that deals with Indians, give yourself months, if not a year, to allow the subjects to thoroughly understand every aspect of what you will be doing.

4. Use caution when using cameras and tape-recorders.
5. Fair and appropriate return should be given to informants.
6. The anticipated consequences of the research should be communicated to individuals and groups that will be affected.
7. Every attempt should be made to cooperate with the current host society.
8. Physical anthropologists, archaeologists, and other researchers wishing to desecrate Indian burials in order to study Indian remains and funerary objects should obtain permission to do so from tribes.
9. Results of the study should be reviewed by the tribes' elected representatives and religious leaders.
10. The researcher must follow the guidelines for each new project.[20]

A second approach to gathering information with and from tribes is to adopt a different methodology that demonstrates a blend of professional knowledge with community knowledge. Even the rather strict formats of the scientific method and needs assessment are flexible enough to incorporate collaborative approaches. These approaches demonstrate the following:

> Happily, insights from the fields of collaborative ethnography and action research can provide a framework for an alternative discourse of community needs assessment based on authentic partnership and commitment to social change. Instead of the library assessing the community, subject verb object, progressive librarians can use their creativity and compassion to invent a new, more egalitarian grammar of needs assessment.[21]

More recently, indigenous researchers have proposed new models of study based on indigenous protocol or rules of conduct, indigenous views of the world, and indigenous knowledge systems. When speaking of the difference between Native and non-Native thinking and beliefs, one often finds the term "worldview" used. Mihesuah defines worldview as "a person's value system and how one interprets events and history. There is, of course, no one Indian world view."[22] Indigenous ways of knowing refer not only to the process of learning and understanding, but also to the content, context, and cultural protocol.

When compared with Western approaches, "[m]ethods of Indigenous knowledge generation and application are participatory, communal and experiential, and reflective of local geography."[23] Shawn Wilson refers to research following an indigenous paradigm as ceremony: "The research that we do as Indigenous people is a ceremony that allows us a raised level of consciousness and insight into our world."[24]

Indigenous ways of gathering information are not necessarily complicated. Elizabeth Rockefeller-MacArthur lists some of the Native sources of information, ranging from the stories in oral traditions to inscriptions on stone, bark, and wood, to areas of study we now refer to as ethnoastronomy and ethnobotany.[25] Too often Native knowledge has been classified as myth or folklore. To the people who live and tell them, stories are living aspects of indigenous life as they arise when needed or appropriate and change over time. At its simplest, then, the indigenous knowledge cycle considers the basic unit a story instead of a question. Stories are then integrated into knowledge, resulting in wisdom.[26] One Native researcher explained, "Sometimes when you go into doing research, you don't want to come with a set of questions. Especially with an Elder. So you enter into conversation."[27] Desiring to learn about Native culture is natural and can be fulfilling, but it should follow a process that is respectful.

INITIATING AND MAINTAINING CONNECTIONS

Once you have prepared yourself with some background information, how do you approach tribal communities and start your contact? Wilson describes Tafoya's model of communicating with Native peoples as one that calls on respect, reciprocity, and responsibility.[28] Indigenous communities have philosophies that describe how individuals can work together to attain group and individual fulfillment. One model is that of the Hawaiian notion of "giftedness," a belief that is based on the following:

> *Aloha*: asking, receiving, living and sharing the breath of life
> *Lohe*: obedience, recognizing and sharing one's passion
> *Na'auao*: intuitiveness; intelligence; feeling and thinking
> *Ho'opili*: development and maintenance of relations
> *Ha'aha'a*: ability to tap ancestral memory; humility
> *Kuka'o*: self-reliance
> *Kina'ole*: perfectibility
> *Kela, Imi pono*: excellence[29]

You might need to make your first contact through an intermediary and in a social setting. Wilson describes the importance of an intermediary and the work this person performs:

> One important Indigenous research practice is the use of family, relations or friends as intermediaries in order to garner contact with participants. . . In addition to being a culturally appropriate way of approaching potential participants, the use of an intermediary gives the participant an opportunity to ask candid questions about the nature of the research and the motives behind it. It is inappropriate in many Indigenous cultures to directly turn down a request for assistance: the use of an intermediary provides a way for subjects to decline to participate.[30]

All cultures have ways to do things. There is no one, simple recipe to follow that will bring two peoples together happily and productively. Tribal community protocol might follow an etiquette that helps order the public side of interactions. Do not arrive to meet your tribal members with a clipboard. This immediately places the librarian in the role of researcher, someone who takes information out of the community.

Tribes may have their own protocol for allowing you to meet with members to gather data, and some may even not allow such contacts. Protocol is not in place to make visitors uncomfortable, but rather reflects traditions. Following protocol does not mean that one is subservient to tribal performance requirements. Instead, it "indicates respect for the local people."[31] Theodore Jojola provides this explanation for a relationship between Native and non-Native people at important cultural events: "American Indian communities have been hospitable to non-Indians during public ceremonies, but only on the condition that visitors leave only 'footprints.' Tribal members are prohibited from divulging information about tribal customs and religion to outsiders, especially anthropologists. In some communities, photography is prohibited. In others, some sites are restricted from public access and view."[32]

Protocol may be posted at the entry to tribal homelands. It might be found on tribal websites informing prospective writers or researchers how to conduct their work. It may be imparted, according to tradition, orally. And protocol may exist in published documents, such as those developed by the Alaska Native Knowledge Network.[33] Some detailed protocol might explain behavior at particular events or settings. In certain special cases, such as moving into a *marae* or longhouse in New Zealand/Aotearoa, Native and non-Native visitors might be asked to prepare by reading literature and/or attending an orientation to the protocol.[34]

Protocol comes to bear in answering questions such as the following:

1. How do we refer to or name Native peoples?
   One of the most common questions asked by non-Native people of Indian people is: What do I call you? A related question is: How do I refer to your people? A good rule of thumb is to ask the individual what he or she prefers. A view held by many contemporary Native peoples is that the phrase "Native American" is used by outsiders. It was a preferred phrase for a time and thought by many to be a way to show respect and to be in agreement with the phrases we use for other people of color in the United States, specifically African Americans and Mexican Americans. "Native American" does have the tone of respect, but in some ways it is a stiff courtesy. This phrase can also be confused to imply that a person is Native born American and, thus, affiliated with a cultural community that immigrated to the United States. Today, it is more common to hear Native peoples in the United States refer to themselves as American Indian, Native, or indigenous. Elders still may simply use the word "Indian." American Indian people may also use slang phrases, such as Ndn, with each other or in electronic communication. Canadian indigenous peoples prefer to be referred to as First Nations or Aboriginal peoples. Indigenous people in Hawaii prefer to be referred to as Native Hawaiians. In general, it is best to be very specific when referring to a tribal group or individual's affiliation.

2. How do we introduce ourselves?

   Often when Native people are gathered, someone will remind the group to identify themselves, and the introductions naturally then follow the protocol of each person identifying himself or herself by tribal affiliation. These introductions are evident in formal gatherings both inside the United States and outside of its borders. Protocol in Australia, for example, means that most speakers at conferences or other public events acknowledge the traditional owners of the land. Native peoples might use a reference to homeland areas in their introductions: "Place matters."[35]

   Native peoples might introduce themselves by their homeland connections, which might be defined by the river, rock, and mountain they grew up near. The Navajo introduce themselves with their genealogy, starting with the clan names of both their maternal and paternal sides, their born to and born from connections. Take, for example, my lengthy self-introduction:

   I am Anishinabe, a word that means Spontaneous People in our language, Anishinabemowin. We are also called Ojibwe. You may know us as Chippewa. In Canada we are called Salteaux. If I were in Minnesota, I would also mention that I am enrolled on the White Earth Reservation and am a member of the Minnesota Chippewa Tribe. I sometimes indicate that my father was Mississippi Band and my mother is Pembina Band. My father was makwa or bear clan, so I am also bear clan.

   The proper response to such a formal introduction would be to listen politely and, when the time arrived, to also introduce oneself according to one's tradition. Use questioning tactfully. Paul Chaat Smith describes how he has felt in response to what many might consider the most basic of questions:

   For most of my life I could be paralyzed with either one of two questions. The questions, though rarely asked with malice, were devastatingly personal ones masked as personal conversation. The questions were "Where are you from?" and "How much Indian are you."[36]

3. How do we say thank you?

   Protocol sometimes also means that you bring something to exchange to indicate that you appreciate the time that people spend with you. In some tribal cultures, this is a gift of a sacred herb such as loose-cut tobacco, money, or food. Leave recording equipment in the car, because you need to follow tribal etiquette and also, increasingly, tribal research protocol to capture images through photographs or video or voice through audio recordings. If you have visited or worked with a Pueblo community, you will remember that protocol for visitors is usually posted on a billboard near the Pueblo. A common aspect of such protocol is that photography is not permitted.

4. How do we treat older people?

 Elders are usually given positions of honor and respect at indigenous gatherings. Meyer described the method she followed in conducting interviews with twenty Hawaiian elders in writing her doctoral thesis: "Because the study needed to be grounded in a Hawaiian process, each interview began with a prayer and food was brought as gifts."[37]

5. How do we welcome guests?

 Native peoples often consider hospitality a reflection of their own honor and protocol. "This again is how things should be, starting and finishing with a prayer and sharing of food."[38]

6. How do we determine when something must be done?

 Learn that your sense of time and the tribe's sense of time may be different. This is especially true where grant money is concerned. Grant-funded projects often require reporting according to a schedule, spending money over a specified period of time, and showing results on cue. Have you heard of Indian Time? Things happen when they are supposed to happen. Pollyanna Nordstrand mentions several other reasons why you need to give tribal members sufficient time to consider any request to meet: "Some tribes may require the tribal council to review and approve a plan; the council may meet infrequently. The most appropriate person to review may be difficult to reach. Travel may be difficult to coordinate at certain times of the year due to weather or ceremonies."[39]

7. Am I allowed to witness religious events?

 Non-Native observers of Native culture are often curious about private or sacred information. Paula Gunn Allen described how her university students were "voraciously interested in the exotic aspects of Indian ways— and they usually mean by that traditional spiritual practices, understandings, and beliefs." Yet she warned that "telling the old stories, revealing the old ways, can only lead to disaster."[40]

8. What might I expect to happen at a formal meeting?

 I often advise my students that they might find several notable differences in gatherings of Native people. First, there will be elements of spirituality. Most meetings open with a prayer or blessing. A nontribal member's role during prayer or blessing is just to be respectful and follow instructions, such as the request to stand during the blessing. Some tribal members disclose personal information even during professional gatherings. For example, they might admit that they have been challenged by addictions or that their family is facing certain difficulties. Again, others should just listen and be respectful of this disclosure without adding commentary or asking questions. Finally, there is apt to be a lot of laughter and, if the Native people like someone, they are apt to tease him or her. A person who is teased should know that this is a gift and demonstration of friendship.

Not everyone knows that Native peoples live and survive today. We are more apt to see references to Indian people of the past through the popular media. This approach can perpetuate stereotypes.[41] There are a number of selection criteria guidelines that will help librarians identify resources not only for their patrons but also to help them acquire information about the Native communities they serve. Such guidelines are similar to those we use in evaluating any item we might consider adding to a library collection, but they will usually pay special note to authorship/authority, language, and imagery, especially illustrations.[42]

Continuing contact with tribal members requires an ongoing assessment of the relationship. Nordstrand draws a distinction between consultation and collaboration with tribal communities. A consultation is based on stating goals relating to a specific project and is often delineated in written statements of agreement. Nordstrand includes a quotation from Felton Bricker Sr., who describes how the limits of consultation can lead to miscommunication between tribes and cultural centers: "We have seen a problem with museums 'consulting.' Frequently we will get a telephone call from a museum—whether we agree or disagree with what the museum is doing, they consider this as a 'consultation.'"[43]

Through a collaboration, staff at information settings can work with tribal communities to establish a relationship for continuing and ongoing work together: "[A] collaboration is a mutually beneficial process and begins by identifying how the desired outcomes will be accomplished for all involved."[44] To Hawaiians, "relationship/interdependence offered [them] opportunities to practice reciprocity, exhibit balance, develop harmony with land and generosity with others."[45]

Nordstrand acknowledges the potential impact of the local tribal administration: "The realities of tribal politics cannot be ignored."[46] In general, it is always wise to identify the individual who is authorized by the tribe to serve as the current designated tribal representative and inform him or her about your ideas. You can also confirm with this designee the process for continuing collaborations.

CHALLENGING YOUR MOTIVE(S)

Working with Native people is not a tourist industry. If you want to work with Native communities, then you need to commit to long-term contact. Being a Native person is not a selective exercise. It is not something someone chooses to do out of convenience, fun, or exploration; it is not part of a phase of finding oneself. It is not a persona that someone dons because he or she feels attached to a certain period of history or feels a kinship with indigenous people because of their interesting, oppressed, or romantic pasts. Being Indian means living with all aspects of the culture, from religious and artistic expression to health challenges and the struggle for economic independence. It is living through politics and prejudices. Acknowledging this allows a reader to value a quotation about Indian identity from one of Sherman Alexie's lesser-known novels, *Reservation Blues*. In speaking about wannabees, people who are not Native but like to claim some aspect of indigenous culture, a character in the book observes: "I've always had a theory that you ain't really Indian unless, at some point in your life, you didn't want to be Indian."[47] The only real Indians are those who do not wannabe sometime in their lives.

Continuing contact with a tribal community is a way to say that you like them no matter what. You will be back, no matter if you get paid or if no one showed up at your first program. You will just be back.

We all hope to make a difference in the world. The fact is that American Indian populations have often been the beneficiaries of services by well-meaning people. Sometimes these well-meaning people have believed that they know best. Paul Chaat Smith describes this scenario of well-meaning intent and resultant outcomes:

> And yet, U.S. history teaches us that some of the most catastrophic forces visited upon Indians—boarding schools, allotment, relocation—were created by our most enlightened and progressive friends. Good intentions aren't enough; our circumstances require more critical thinking and less passion, guilt, and victimization.[48]

It is best to enter into agreements with Native people with a humble spirit and to realize that you are very likely an interim step in the community's self-determination. Good intentions sometime mean that nonindigenous people are making the decisions in efforts for, but not with, indigenous peoples. Karen Swisher has summarized the current views on these probable situations: "A time characterized by the statement, *People come among us and tell us that they know what is best for us*, literal or implied, is long gone."[49]

Wilson identified some questions that researchers should ask as they reflect about their work with indigenous peoples. These questions illustrate how this work is based on building relationships:

> How can I relate respectfully to the other participants involved in this research so that together we can form a stronger relationship with the idea that we will share? . . . What am I contributing or giving back to the relationship? Is the sharing, growth and learning that is taking place reciprocal?[50]

In a book on Natives and academics, Swisher wrote that there are now enough Native people with doctorates and specialities in the field of education for them to be able to take the lead. She called on non-Native educators to step back: "If non-Indian educators have been involved in Indian education because they believe in Indian people and want them to be empowered, they must now demonstrate that belief by stepping aside."[51] The same cannot yet be said for our field: there are not yet enough Native librarians to fill all positions. Our common goal, though, should be to work toward that day.

Challenging our motives also relates to our expectations of what we will learn from interactions with Native people. Working in tribal librarianship should not be a path to finding some genealogical thread.

RESOURCES FOR CULTURAL PROGRAMMING
WITH A FOCUS ON INDIGENOUS CULTURES

The following list of resources provides supportive background on preparing programs on American Indian topics for your library. It is divided into four categories, starting with curricular material developed by museums, tribal schools, Native educators, or a public school system. *We Shall Remain* is the largest American experience television series ever produced. Content related to the five-part Public Broadcasting Service, the *We Shall Remain* website provides historical information as well as short films produced by Native peoples today. "If I Can Read, I Can Do Anything" is a national reading club for Native children, and the project website includes several library programming ideas. The final three sources include cultural guidelines, an authors' visit planning book, and a link to the ProgrammingLibrarian.org website hosted by the American Library Association.

I.   Curricular Material and Study Guides
   A. University of Alaska Fairbanks, Alaska Native Knowledge Network. "Lessons & Units," http://ankn.uaf.edu/curriculum/units/index.html (accessed 15 September 2010).
   B. *Four Directions,* http://www.4directions.org (accessed 15 September 2010)
   C Heard Museum. *Native American Fine Arts Resource Guide,* http://www.heard.org/education/curriculummaterials.html (accessed 15 September 2010).
   D. Living Traditions Writers Group. "Study Plans for *When the Spirits Dance*; *As Long as the Rivers Flow*; *The Gathering Tree*," http://www.firstnationswriter.com/ accessed (15 September 2010).
   E. National Museum of the American Indian. "Education," http://www.nmai.si.edu/subpage.cfm?subpage=education&second=dc&third=general (accessed 15 September 2010).
II. Resources available through *We Shall Remain*
   F. Loew, Patty. *We Shall Remain: An Event Kit for Libraries.* Boston: WGBH, 2008. http://www.pbs.org/wgbh/amex/weshallremain/libraries (accessed 15 September 2010).
   G. *ReelNative,* http://www.pbs.org/wgbh/amex/weshallremain/reel_native (accessed 15 September 2010).
   H. *We Shall Remain: Teacher's Guide,* http://www.pbs.org/wgbh/amex/weshallremain/beyond_broadcast/teach_and_learn (accessed 15 September 2010).
III. Programming Ideas
   I. "If I Can Read, I Can Do Anything," http://sentra.ischool.utexas.edu/~ifican/activities/index.php (accessed 15 September 2010).

IV. Planning Resources
    J. Assembly of Alaska Native Educators. *Guidelines for Cross-Cultural Orientation Programs.* Fairbanks: University of Alaska Fairbanks, Alaska Native Knowledge Network, 2003.
    K. Assembly of Alaska Native Educators. *Guidelines for Respecting Cultural Knowledge.* Fairbanks: University of Alaska Fairbanks, Alaska Native Knowledge Network, 2000.
    L. George, Jane Graham. *Author Program Handbook: A Beginner's Guide to Planning and Hosting Literary Programs for Adults in Minnesota's Libraries.* St. Paul: Minnesota Book Awards, 2008. www.thefriends .org/_downloads/Author%20program%20handbook.doc (accessed 15 September 2010).
    M. American Library Association."Programming Librarian," http:// www.programminglibrarian.org/ *(accessed 15 September 2010).*

NOTES

1. Milwaukee Public Museum, "Indian Country Wisconsin," http://www.mpm.edu/wirp/ (accessed 10 September 2010).
2. Linda McCulloch, Montana Office of Public Instruction, "Indian Education for All. MCA 20-1-501," http://www.montanatribes.org/files/IEFA-Law.pdf (accessed 10 September 2010).
3. Montana, Indian Education for All (April 29, 1999), House Bill 528, MCA 20-1-501, http://data.opi.mt.gov/bills/billhtml/HB0528.htm (accessed 17 July 2010).
4. U.S. Bureau of the Census, *The American Indian and Alaska Native Population: 2000,* http://www.census.gov/prod/2002pubs/c2kbr01-15.pdf (accessed 12 September 2010); Stella U. Ogunwole, *We the People: American Indians and Alaska Natives in the United States* (Washington, D.C.: U.S. Bureau of the Census, 2006), http://www.census .gov/prod/2006pubs/censr-28.pdf (accessed 12 September 2010), 14.
5. Hiwi Tauroa and Pat Tauroa, *Te Marae: A Guide to Customs & Protocol* (Auckland, New Zealand/Aotearoa: Reed, 1986), 8.
6. Tauroa and Tauroa, *Te Marae,* 13.
7. Assembly of Alaska Native Educators, "Guidelines for Culturally Responsive Principals & Teachers," in *Guidelines for Cross-Cultural Orientation Programs* (Fairbanks: University of Alaska Fairbanks, Alaska Native Knowledge Network, 2003), 9–10.
8. Manulani Aluli Meyer, *Ho'oulu: Our Time of Becoming: Hawaiian Epistemology and Early Writings* (Honolulu, Hawaii: 'Ai Pōhaku Press, 2004), 159, 185.
9. Devon A. Mihesuah, ed., *Natives and Academics: Researching and Writing about American Indians* (Lincoln: University of Nebraska Press, 1998), 4.
10. U.S. Bureau of the Census, "American Indian and Alaska Native (AIAN) Data and Links," http://factfinder.census.gov/home/aian/index.html (accessed 14 September 2010).
11. U.S. Bureau of the Census, "The American Indians and Alaska Natives in the United States Wall Map," http://www.census.gov/geo/www/maps/aian_wall_map/aian_wall_map.htm (accessed 14 September 2010).

12. ABC-CLIO Greenwood, "The American Indian Experience," http://aie.greenwood .com (accessed 17 July 2010).

13. No Child Left Behind Act of 2001, P.L. 107-110, U.S. 115 Stat. 1425, Sec. VII, Pt. A, Subpt. 1; U.S. Department of Education, "Elementary & Secondary Education, Subpart 1—Formula Grants to Local Educational Agencies," January 8, 2002, http://www2.ed.gov/ policy/elsec/leg/esea02/pg99.html (accessed 17 July 2010).

14. Angela Cavender Wilson, "Grandmother to Granddaughter: Generations of Oral History in Dakota Family," in *Natives and Academics*, ed. Mihesuah, 35.

15. Devon A. Mihesuah, "American Indian Identities: Issues of Individual Choice and Development," in *Contemporary Native American Cultural Issues*, ed. Duane Champagne (Walnut Creek, Calif.: Altamira Press, 1999), 13.

16. Gregory A. Cajete, *Igniting the Sparkle: An Indigenous Science Education Model* (Skyland, N.C.: Kivaki Press, 1999), 116–17.

17. Cajete, *Igniting the Sparkle*, 117–19.

18. Marcel A. Q. LaFlamme, "Towards a Progressive Discourse on Community Needs Assessment: Perspectives from Collaborative Ethnography and Action Research," *Progressive Librarian* 29 (Summer 2007): 57.

19. Linda Tuhiwai Smith, *Decolonizing Methodologies: Research and Indigenous Peoples* (London: Zed Books; Dunedin, New Zealand/Aotearoa: University of Otago Press, 1999), 1.

20. "Appendix B: Suggested Guidelines for Institutions with Researchers Who Conduct Research on American Indians," in *American Indians: Stereotypes & Realities,* by Devon A. Mihesuah (Atlanta, Ga.: Clarity Press, 1996), 125–27.

21. LaFlamme, "Towards a Progressive Discourse," 61.

22. Mihesuah, "American Indian Identities," 32.

23. Janet Smylie et al., "Knowledge Translation and Indigenous Knowledge," *Circumpolar Health 2003*, 141, http://ijch.fi/issues/63suppl2/ICCH12_Smylie.pdf (accessed 15 September 2010).

24. Shawn Wilson, *Research Is Ceremony: Indigenous Research Methods* (Halifax, N.C.; Winnipeg, Man.: Fernwood, 2008), 11.

25. Elizabeth Rockefeller-MacArthur, *American Indian Library Services in Perspective* (Jefferson, N.C.: London: McFarland, 1998).

26. Smylie, "Knowledge Translation and Indigenous Knowledge," 141.

27. Wilson, *Research Is Ceremony*, 113.

28. Wilson, *Research Is Ceremony*, 99.

29. D. E. Martin, "Towards an Understanding of the Native Hawaiian Concept and Manifestation of Giftedness" (PhD diss., University of Georgia, 1996), cited in Meyer, *Ho'oulu*, 87.

30. Wilson, *Research Is Ceremony*, 129–30.

31. Tauroa and Tauroa, *Te Marae*, 147.

32. Theodore S. Jojola, "On Revision and Revisionism: American Indian Representations in New Mexico," in *Natives and Academics*, ed. Mihesuah, 175–76.

33. University of Alaska Fairbanks, Alaska Native Knowledge Network, http://www .ankn.uaf.edu/ (accessed 15 September 2010).

34. Tauroa and Tauroa, *Te Marae*, 13.

35. Meyer, *Ho'oulu*, 143.

36. Paul Chaat Smith, *Everything You Know about Indians Is Wrong* (Minneapolis: University of Minnesota Press, 2009), 167.

37. Meyer, *Ho'oulu*, 187.

38. Wilson, *Research Is Ceremony*, 83.

39. Pollyanna Nordstrand, "The Voice of the Museum: Developing Displays," in *Caring for American Indian Objects: A Practical and Cultural Guide*, ed. Sherelyn Ogden (St. Paul: Minnesota Historical Society Press, 2004), 13.

40. Paula Gunn Allen, "Special Problems in Teaching Leslie Marmon Silko's *Ceremony*," in *Natives and Academics*, ed. Mihesuah, 59, 62.

41. Mihesuah, *American Indians: Stereotypes & Realities*.

42. Doris Seale and Beverly Slapin, eds., *A Broken Flute: The Native Experience in Books for Children* (Walnut Creek, Calif.: Altamira Press; Berkeley: Oyate, 2005); Naomi Caldwell, Gabriella Kaye, and Lisa A. Mitten, "'I' Is for Inclusion: The Portrayal of Native Americans in Books for Young People," 2007, http://www.ailanet.org/publications/I%20 IS%20FOR%20INCLUSION-rev%2010-07.pdf (accessed 15 September 2010).

43. Ogden, *Caring for American Indian Objects*, 97.

44. Nordstrand, "The Voice of the Museum," 13.

45. Meyer, *Ho'oulu*, 167.

46. Nordstrand, "The Voice of the Museum," 13.

47. Sherman Alexie, *Reservation Blues* (New York: Atlantic Monthly Press, 1995), 169.

48. Smith, *Everything You Know about Indians Is Wrong*, 187.

49. Karen Gayton Swisher, "Why Indian People Should Be the Ones to Write about Indian Education," in *Natives and Academics*, ed. Mihesuah, 197.

50. Wilson, *Research Is Ceremony*, 77.

51. Swisher, "Why Indian People Should Be the Ones to Write about Indian Education," 192.

15

Recommendations and Implications for Services to and with Indigenous Elders

Loriene Roy

The changes the elders experienced then, were many: from cedar canoes to power-driven purse seiners; from horse and buggies, to model-T Fords, to contemporary automobiles, to man on the moon; from potlatches to baseball; from respect for elders to undisciplined youth; from food gathering, to farming, to supermarkets; from abundant fishing, duck hunting, oyster and clam digging to a near loss of seafood and game; from secondhand clothes made over on sewing machines, to clothing bought at K-Mart; from basket-making to knitting and sewing; from a life spent gathering abundant wildlife to migrant labor in canneries, logging camps and hop fields; from a fisherman's life to the life of farmers and machine operators.[1]

Kūpuna means elder. In old Hawai'i, *kūpuna* were respected as keepers of Hawai'i's wisdom and knowledge. Still today, younger Hawaiians are told: *Nānā i ke kumu*, "look to the source."[2]

The Ojibwe say that the elders have walked down a long road and gathered a great deal of knowledge on their journey, and for this reason we should always respect them.[3]

Before education as we know it today came, it's the elders—the women especially—that were the teachers of the culture. Talking about education, the teachers of the culture, holders of the culture. Everything. They start you off at birth, and they continue on, and then you take over.[4]

WHO IS AN ELDER?

Elders, *kaumatua, kupuna, kahuna*. Indigenous communities around the world have traditionally honored and respected the place of older members. This chapter focuses on services for individuals who are considered tribal elders.

Elder is a position of respect and denotes that the individual is not only of greater than average age but also possesses skills or cultural knowledge. Some younger people are respected as junior elders and some older tribal members have not earned the respectful title of elder. The Assembly of Alaska Native Educators notes "that the identification of 'Elders' as culture-bearers is not simply a matter of chronological age, but a function of the respect accorded to individuals in each community who exemplify the values and lifeways of the local culture and who possess the wisdom and willingness to pass their knowledge on to future generations."[5] The Maori point out that the attainment of elder status might not come at any particular age; their elders—*nga kaumatua*—might be experts in particular cultural expressions such as *whakapapa* (genealogy), *whai korero* (oration), *waiata* (singing), and/or *karanga* (welcome calls).[6]

According to the Alaska Native Knowledge Network, a community that is culturally supported is one that "provides respected Elders with a place of honor in community functions."[7] Communities know who their elders are.

HOW MIGHT LIBRARIES WORK WITH ELDERS?

Librarians, archivists, and museum staff might seek advice on working with indigenous elders. Protocol documents developed for educational and cultural heritage institutions acknowledge the role of elders. Even national library policies can be interpreted to support library services for indigenous elders: the Library Bill of Rights asserts that "a person's right to use a library should not be denied or abridged because of origin, age, background, or views."[8]

The Alaska Native Knowledge Network produced a series of guideline documents, including "Guidelines for Strengthening Indigenous Languages," "Alaska Standards for Culturally Responsive Schools," "Guidelines for Cross-Cultural Orientation Programs," and "Guidelines for Respecting Cultural Knowledge."[9] Each of these documents specifically acknowledges that elders are "the primary source of language expertise and cultural knowledge."[10] The "Culturally Responsive Guidelines for Alaska Public Libraries" defines a culturally responsive library staff as one that "utilizes the expertise of Elders and culturally knowledgeable leaders in multiple ways."[11] The International Federation of Library Associations and Institutions (IFLA) has issued a "Statement on Indigenous Traditional Knowledge," recommending that libraries and archives involve Elders and communities in the production of resources and teaching children to understand and appreciate traditional knowledge background and sense identity that is associated with indigenous knowledge systems.[12]

Article 22 of the United Nations Declaration on the Rights of Indigenous Peoples includes elders in the list of potentially vulnerable community members and calls on member states to be attentive to their "rights and special needs."[13]

WHAT SERVICES MIGHT A LIBRARY OFFER ELDERS?

Given the call—and moral and cultural responsibilities—to work with elders, what face might these services take? Libraries can consider elders' needs in the design of traditional services, including collection development and instruction. Interviews with elders are unique additions to collections. Given elders' needs for wellness and long-term living support, libraries should collect health-related consumer information. Libraries can provide elders and their families with instruction on how to locate relevant information within the library, in supporting health agencies, and through reputable electronic resources. Libraries can provide exhibit space or newsletters to highlight elders who successfully manage lifestyles built on traditional diets and food gathering and processing. Information on diabetes prevention and living with diabetes is especially needed.

Libraries can also serve as training sites, helping to equip tribal elders with new tools for lifelong learning. The Tigua tribe at Ysleta del Sur in Socorro, Texas, received financial support through SeniorNet to establish the Tigua/IBM technology center. Elders who complete the computer fundamentals and introduction to the Internet courses receive completion certificates and are recognized in the *Tribal Empowerment Chronicle*, a local newsletter. Because some elders may consider use of computers the realm of younger tribal members, training at a comfortable pace and in a trusted environment can help challenge their thinking about technology in a provocative yet gentle way. As reported in the tribal newsletter, "At the tribal elder center, computers were a subject that no one really talked about. Most people were too afraid to even touch them for the fear of breaking them, and not understanding how to use them."[14] The tribal website notes that the United States Department of the Interior recognized the center as one of the top economic development accomplishments in Indian country for 2008.[15]

Tribal libraries are excellent venues for social engagement in which elders can gather with each other and with community members. Tribal community libraries can collaborate with elders in language preservation efforts, local history documentation, and genealogy research. Libraries and other cultural centers are trusted spaces for intergenerational activities. Tribal school libraries can include elders in sharing cultural knowledge with tribal youth. The Santa Clara Pueblo (New Mexico) Community Library has an ongoing Grandparent Grandchild

Reading Program, in which elders read to preschool children in a Headstart program.[16] Elders can assist other community members in interpreting the past: "When a tribal museum or cultural center acquires an object, it can be a focal point for elders to pass knowledge to young people and share information with each other."[17] Kathryn Beaulieu, director of the Red Lake Tribal Library and Archives, confirmed the relationships among elders, cultural objects, and community members: "Objects assist in having memories flourish. Elders see objects, and then stories flow from them, and younger Indians learn."[18]

Technology training naturally is a forum for interchange between the younger and older members of a library's community. The librarian at the award-winning Ft. Washakie Library, a joint use public library/school library in Wyoming, described how a student brought her grandmother to the library to demonstrate how to use a computer.[19]

Libraries can serve as an essential partner in community-wide elder services. They can partner with other tribal service agencies that connect elders with transfer-of-knowledge initiatives. Tribal libraries and their services should be included in tribal education planning, grant writing, and other economic development efforts. Tribal librarians should have a direct line of communication to tribal councils. This includes advertising and reporting on services offered and collaborating with elders' councils and other social service agencies such as Indian Health Service, chapter or meeting houses, elder services/centers, tribal archives, and community centers.

Libraries serving urban Indian populations should likewise promote services available to elders and support efforts to connect urban tribal members with their tribal homelands. Libraries should explore the potential for technology to assist in making these connections. And through their services to all community members, libraries are establishing good relationships with future elders.

SHARED AUTHORITY: ROLES FOR
ELDERS IN TRIBAL HERITAGE CENTERS

Information professionals should provide elders with a role in planning and delivering library services. Though such shared authority might be unheard of in majority library settings, this approach reflects traditional indigenous education and is the model to which information settings in Indian country must strive. The role of elders can also be more formalized: the Minister's Advisory Committee on Library Services for Aboriginal People recommends that public libraries include elders as ex-officio members on library boards.[20]

Librarians and information professionals can call on elders to help incorporate cultural protocol into library policies and services. Elders can serve as co-instructors when cultural topics are presented. Elders are often asked to perform services such as giving blessings or welcomes. For example, at gatherings in Australia, librarians often contract with local tribal members to provide a "welcome to country," especially if international indigenous guests are attending. In Norway, a Sami elder provided a blessing at the launch of the South Sami bookmobile.[21] The Alaska Native Knowledge Network recommends using flexibility in scheduling and extending invitations far in advance of events.[22] Elders should receive compensation for their efforts, usually in the form of a gift.

CONCLUSION

Tribal libraries can serve as national models for providing services for older patrons. One such innovative, tribally based project was launched at a tribal college library with funding from a 2009 Native American Library Services Enhancement Grant through the Institute of Museum and Library Services (IMLS).[23] This program is one illustration of the value tribal communities place on the presence of elders and their commitment to providing exemplary, customized services.

The Little Priest Tribal College in Nebraska has a full-time staff position specifically designated as the Library Aide to Elders. The job description for this position outlines the aide's role:

> With a collaborative approach, the Library Aide to Elders helps to initiate, develop, deliver, and evaluate both in-house and outreach public library programming for senior citizens, elders, and homebound individuals on the Winnebago Reservation. Specifically, the Library Aide to Elders would
>
> 1. Initiate, develop, deliver and evaluate both in-house and outreach public library programming for elders on the Winnebago Reservation;
>
> 2. At least 60 percent of this individual's work time will be spent providing library-related outreach services and computer training skills to the Winnebago Elder community. Such tasks specifically include those outlined in number one, above, but may also include
>
> a. Transportation for elders to and from library for computer training/assistance.
>
> 3. Provide basic computer training to senior citizens interested in learning to use computers, including assisting them in writing their personal histories with a computer.[24]

NOTES

1. Ann Nugent, "Introduction," in *Lummi Elders Speak*, ed. Ann Nugent (Blaine, Wash.: Pelican Press, 1999), 6.

2. M. J. Harden, *Voices of Wisdom: Hawaiian Elders Speak* (Kula, Hawaii: AKA Press, 1999), 10.

3. Elizabeth M. Tornes, "Editor's Introduction," in *Memories of Lac du Flambeau Elders*, ed. Elizabeth M. Tornes (Madison, Wisc.: Center for the Study of Upper Midwestern Cultures, 2004), 1.

4. Kimberly L. Lawson, *Precious Fragments: First Nations Materials in Archives, Libraries, and Museums* (master's thesis, University of British Columbia, 2004), 57.

5. Assembly of Alaska Native Educators, *Guidelines for Respecting Cultural Knowledge* (Fairbanks: University of Alaska Fairbanks, Alaska Native Knowledge Network, 2000), 3.

6. Hiwi Tauroa and Pat Tauroa, *Te Marae: A Guide to Customs & Protocol* (Auckland, New Zealand/Aotearoa: Reed, 1986), 40.

7. Assembly of Alaska Native Educators, *Alaska Standards for Culturally Responsive Schools* (Fairbanks: University of Alaska Fairbanks, Alaska Native Knowledge Network, 1998), 21.

8. American Library Association, "Library Bill of Rights," http://www.ala.org/ala/issuesadvocacy/intfreedom/librarybill/index.cfm (accessed 10 September 2010).

9. Assembly of Alaska Native Educators, *Guidelines for Strengthening Indigenous Languages* (Fairbanks: University of Alaska Fairbanks, Alaska Native Knowledge Network, 2001); *Alaska Standards for Culturally Responsive Schools*; Assembly of Alaska Native Educators, *Guidelines for Cross-Cultural Orientation Programs* (Fairbanks: University of Alaska Fairbanks, Alaska Native Knowledge Network, 2003); *Guidelines for Respecting Cultural Knowledge.*

10. *Guidelines for Strengthening Indigenous Languages*, 3.

11. Alaska Library Association, "Culturally Responsive Guidelines for Alaska Public Libraries," http://www.akla.org/culturally-responsive.html (accessed 7 September 2010).

12. International Federation of Library Associations, "IFLA Statement on Indigenous Traditional Knowledge," http://ifla.queenslibrary.org/III/eb/sitk03.html (accessed 10 September 2010).

13. United Nations, General Assembly, "United Nations Declaration on the Rights of Indigenous Peoples. Resolution 61/295," September 13, 2007, http://www.un.org/esa/socdev/unpfii/en/drip.html (accessed 10 September 2010).

14. Ysleta del Sur Pueblo, "Tigua/IBM Technology Center Introduces Elders to Computers," *Tribal Empowerment Chronicle* 1 (January 2009): 3.

15. "IBM Technology Center Highlighted by DOI, April 22, 2009," http://www.ysletadelsurpueblo.org/news_detail.sstg?id=21 (accessed 10 September 2010).

16. "Santa Clara Pueblo Community Library," http://www.santaclarapueblo.org/library/ (accessed 10 September 2010).

17. Joseph D. Horse Capture, "Foreword: Our Obligation to Our Past," in *Caring for American Indian Objects: A Practical and Cultural Guide*, ed. Sherelyn Ogden (St. Paul: Minnesota Historical Society Press, 2004), v.

18. Kathryn Beaulieu, in *Caring for American Indian Objects*, 3.

19. "It Took a Community to Build This Library," *Wyoming Library Roundup* 49, no. 4 (Fall 2007): 4–6.

20. The Minister's Advisory Committee on Library Services for Aboriginal People, *Information Is for Everyone: Final Report of the Minister's Advisory Committee on Library Services for Aboriginal People*, October 2001, http://www.lib.sk.ca/Default.aspx?DN=14df7615-b452-4268-b043-8da272a83bdd (accessed 10 September 2010).

21. Johan Koren, "Editorial: Library Services and Indigenous Identity," *World Libraries* 12, no. 1 (Spring 2002): 5.

22. *Guidelines for Respecting Cultural Knowledge*, 11.

23. Institute of Museum and Library Services, "Awarded Grants Search Results," http://imls.gov/results.asp (accessed 9 September 2010).

24. "Little Priest Tribal College, Job Announcement, November 5, 2009," http://74.125.47.132/search?q=cache:zCPQjKMZ8xgJ:www.lptc.bia.edu/images/job_announcements/Library%2520Aide%2520to%2520Elders%2520Nov2009.doc+tribal+library+services+for+elders&cd=34&hl=en&ct=clnk&gl=us&client=firefox-a (accessed 24 December 2009).

III

TRIBAL ARCHIVES: COLLECTIONS AND FUNCTIONS

16

Where Are the Records?

Shayne Del Cohen

WHERE ARE THE RECORDS?

This chapter covers what tribes collect and what constitutes a record worthy of collecting. First of all, what *are* the records? Technically, records are documents that ultimately become "archives." The Society of American Archivists defines *archives* as

> [m]aterials created or received by a person, family, or organization, public or private, in the conduct of their affairs and preserved because of the enduring value contained in the information they contain or as evidence of the functions and responsibilities of their creator, especially those materials maintained using the principles of provenance, original order, and collective control.[1]

In contrast, permanent records are defined as

> [m]aterials created or received by a person, family, or organization, public or private, in the conduct of their affairs that are preserved because of the enduring value contained in the information they contain or as evidence of the functions and responsibilities of their creator.[2]

A "record" connotes documents rather than artifacts or published materials, although collections of archival records may contain artifacts and books.[3] Archival records may be in any format, including text on paper or in electronic formats, photographs, motion pictures, videos, or sound recordings. The phrase "archival records" is sometimes used as an expanded form of archives to distinguish the holdings from the program.[4]

There are many kinds of records: administrative, architectural, business, corporate, electronic, emergency-operating, engineering, essential, housekeeping, municipal, organizational, program, rights and interests, and vital records, to name a few.

There are also categories for records such as active, current, frozen, inactive, noncurrent, noncustodial, nonrecords, semiactive, semicurrent, special, and nontextual. Records are everywhere, and should you choose to accept this assignment, it will become a lifetime work and a perennial treasure hunt, to say nothing of a constant source of joy and frustration.

Records generally have four values that can be used to quickly evaluate an item: administrative, fiscal, legal, and historical.

Generally, the *administrative value* of a record decreases quickly, for example, a memo calling a meeting. It is good for setting one's schedule, assembling the materials that might be needed, and for a period of time afterward to recount one's schedule. But after a year, this is no longer a needed document for administrative purposes.

Records exhibiting *fiscal value*, such as a bill, will have a longer period of value. For instance, a lamp purchased as part of a grant will generate a bill as well as a receipt. These records hold fiscal value in administering the grant/contract budget, auditing an inventory list, determining insurance coverage, and/or determining the value of the business or operation. Fiscal records are generally kept for three years past the time of an accepted audit.

Records holding *legal value* are those that document a variety of rights, including the right to exist, to hold or use property, and/or to transact business. Records holding legal value also document the actions and intent of the generating entity. Thus constitutions, by-laws, resolutions, minutes, etc., have legal, permanent value.

The *historical value* of a record is mostly a personal call. Records that show or narrate information that does not exist elsewhere are obviously historical.

Because so many groups have been oral cultures, language, stories, and songs also are very critical records. They contain knowledge of this continent, from flora to fauna, from weather patterns to the course of rivers, from the manifestations of unique culture to the essentials for survival within a particular geography. They document the *history* of a tribe; they often serve as the basis for *legal* and *fiscal* assertion of rights, restitution, or reimbursement.

Documents generated during the Indian Claims Commission epoch (1946–1978), for instance, provided the basis for successful navigation of the four criteria required to get through the resultant process required for tribes to receive monetary compensation for actions taken against them, in five categories of claims, such as land grabs and treaty violations.[5] Tribes needed documents to provide

1. proof of tribal existence/cohesiveness prior to European contact,
2. proof of uncontested control of an area,
3. documentation of adverse federal action within that area/damage to the tribe, and
4. evaluation of the fiscal value of such damage.[6]

Because it was the intruders/defendants who had generated most of the historical paper documentation, it became incumbent on tribes to "research" their oral traditions to provide counter-information for the prosecution of their claims.

WHAT DO (SHOULD) TRIBES COLLECT?

Again, an archival principle is that if you, your family, your organization, or your business did not create a record, it is not your responsibility to maintain it. However, we live in a paper or digital document world, so collecting items that address an oral tradition is important. Often articles produced by non-Indians were biased or did not contain pertinent information. Those "collecting" must be sure to provide counter or additional information for such items. This is particularly true of newspaper clippings and manuscripts.

Tribes as cultural entities, particularly those that resent being put in an anthropological box, need to collect information from the past, but also to document the present as a statement that culture is fluid and to provide succeeding generations with the guidance of their ancestors "straight" from the ancestors themselves.

Tribes as governmental entities generate a high volume of records, for which they need to set up a records management policy and protocol to manage the paper onslaught and maintain a high quality of governance. Minimal requirements are found in federal, state, and local statutes.

Tribes as corporate entities have a fiduciary responsibility to maintain records that create and nurture integrity in the market and workplace.

So where are these records? They are everywhere. And today, they come in many formats: photographs, videos, DVDs, and other physical objects. They are in obvious repositories as well as under beds and in outbuildings all across the continent and the world.

A tribe trying to define what it is going to collect first needs to inventory what it has within the community, then the immediate area and the region, and then expand its search nationally. In the technology age, with the benefit of search engines, this task has become quite a bit easier as more and more institutions and their records come online. If another institution has a document digitized and accessible, the tribe may not have to "collect" it but merely create an electronic link.

Locating "collectibles" involves a constant public relations program as well as "training" tribal members how to perform basic steps. The essential step is to begin to assemble a "cast of characters," a chronology of given and place names of people who interacted with the tribe and/or the geographic sites involved in the tribe's evolution. One cannot simply Google the tribe's current name or town. It is necessary to know the names of prominent tribal members since first European contact, along with the military figures, agents, clerics, doctors, teachers, and others who conducted some sort of activity in Indian Country, who would have generated paper documents. In more modern times, it takes a review of almost every federal agency, many of which no longer exist, to glean some amazing collections.

In conclusion, this chapter has introduced definitions from the archival profession and has attempted to place them in the context of the unique needs of tribal archivists. With the increasing number of resources available in electronic format, the need for well-trained archivists working in Indian country will only increase in the future.

NOTES

1. Richard Pearce-Moses, comp., *A Glossary of Archival and Records Terminology*, s.v., "Archives," http://webcache.googleusercontent.com/search?q=cache:B8VksT3TFMIJ:www.archivists.org/glossary/term_details.asp%3FDefinitionKey%3D156+%22materials+created+or+received+by+a+person,+family,+or+organization%22&cd=1&hl=en&ct=clnk&gl=us&client=firefox-a (accessed 18 July 2010).

2. Pearce-Moses, *Glossary of Archival and Records Terminology*, "Permanent Records."

3. Pearce-Moses, *Glossary of Archival and Records Terminology*, "Record."

4. Pearce-Moses, *Glossary of Archival and Records Terminology*, "Archival Records."

5. Bruce E. Johansen and Barry M. Pritzker, eds., "Indian Claims Commission," in *Encyclopedia of American Indian History* (Westport, Conn.: ABC-CLIO, Inc., 2007); *The American Indian Experience*, Greenwood Publishing Group, http://aie.greenwood.com//doc.aspx?fileID=AMINDH1C&chapterID=AMINDH1C-8224&path=encyclopedias/greenwood/ (accessed 18 July 2010).

6. James S. Olson, Mark Baxter, Jason M. Tetzloff, and Darren Pierson, "Compensation," in *Encyclopedia of American Indian Civil Rights* (Westport, Conn.: Greenwood Press, 1997); *The American Indian Experience*, Greenwood Publishing Group, http://aie.greenwood.com//doc.aspx?fileID=GR9338&chapterID=GR9338-949&path=encyclopedias/greenwood// (accessed 18 July 2010).

17

Tribal Archives in Preserving Our Language, Memory, and Lifeways

Amy Ziegler

"A tribal archives is an organized way to supplement oral traditions and the other ways that groups remember by gathering, preserving, and making recorded information available."[1] Tribal archives present specific challenges related to legal issues, collecting, privacy concerns, and processing. Policies need to be determined to establish priorities and balance preservation and access.

LEGAL ISSUES RELATED TO COLLECTING

Archives hold a wealth of information providing insight into the identity of peoples. The increase in usage of and access to tribal archives is evidence that individuals are more aware of these resources, especially when seeking information regarding their genealogy. Documents can even hold many different interpretations, including varying oral accounts of key events in history such as battles. In addition to documenting family histories, archival materials can also be used to reassert tribal rights. People researching tribal issues must be aware that relevant information may be held in institutions outside of tribal lands. William T. Hagan describes the impact of this scenario: "To be an Indian is having non-Indians control the documents from which other non-Indians write their version of your history."[2]

The Maori in New Zealand frequently have used archives to access their heritage.[3] They have taken the lead in issues related to cultural and intellectual property rights of indigenous peoples. In 1993, the Mataatua Declaration on Cultural and Intellectual Property Rights, signed in New Zealand, declared "that indigenous peoples of the world have the right to self determination and in exercising that right must be recognized as the exclusive owners of the cultural and intellectual property."[4] The declaration asserts that materials must be offered back to the original owners. Even with the return of materials, indigenous peoples need to take an active role in gathering as complete a history of the written record as can be obtained, especially when so much of it has been destroyed.

Tribes in the United States are seeking ownership of cultural materials in a similar fashion. There is a process to obtain material culture and place it back in the hands of the tribe. The Native American Graves Protection and Repatriation Act (NAGPRA) "provides a process for museums and Federal agencies to return certain Native American cultural items to lineal descendents, and culturally affiliated Indian tribes and Native Hawaiian organizations."[5] Lawrence Hart, executive director of the Cheyenne Cultural Center in Clinton, Oklahoma, who is familiar with the reparation process, stated, "Most of the elders will tell you the spirits of those who are there in those museums and universities are wandering. Those spirits will continue to wander until they are buried."[6] Grants are available through the U.S. secretary of the interior to ease the workload involved in repatriation.

The development of a records management program will protect the legal rights of the tribe. The program will help the administration have better control over the management of its information, providing easier access when legal complexities arise. For instance, there may be challenges to its jurisdiction, which can be proved in the records. Not only will the records be kept, but a records management program distinguishes the essential records from nonessential records and allows individuals to find the information they need when they need it. Archivists should keep up to date on legal issues that affect the tribe. What has the tribal government declared? What are some of the "hot issues" in the media to which the tribe must respond? An archivist's inability to follow professional legal standards, such as allowing the destruction of vital records, can be damaging for an institution. The records management program can help the archives project a positive image and retain a positive reputation.

WHAT AND HOW TO COLLECT

The archives provides a wealth of original source material concerning a tribe's history. This is especially important when so much of the written history of the tribe may be inaccurate. Errors may occur when nontribal members interpret documentation differently or do not understand cultural events. Thus, tribal members can write their own history from accurate documents from the tribe's perspective.[7]

What should a tribal archives collect? Tribal government records, personal papers, and organizational papers form the foundation for a tribal archives. For instance, records can represent all branches of the government organization, chiefs' papers, tribal members' papers, festival papers, or pageant papers. Records from the tribal government are acquired from the records management program. The program focuses on records throughout their life cycle from creation to disposition, which ultimately ends in either preservation in the archives or destruction. Materials that are created throughout the daily course of business affairs can end up in the archives. The material in the archives is not only from a specific point in time, but is also a continuous collection that reveals the evolving identity of the tribe. Thus archives are not just "old stuff" or material from the "old days."

A variety of formats capture tribal history and culture. Formats may include personal papers, membership rolls, financial documents, legal records, oral histories, artifacts, newspaper clippings, audio recordings, video recordings, scrapbooks, maps, oversize material, ephemera, and photographs. From these materials individuals gain an understanding of tribal heritage. Different formats covering the same topic can provide individuals with different perspectives. For example, a stomp dance recorded in a photograph, audio recording, and a transcript provides varied interpretations of the same event.

Library-related material in an archives also aids researchers. For instance, serials, reference texts, and noncirculating monographs support research. Secondary sources about the tribe may provide different interpretations or a basic starting point to learn more about a specific event. The tribe's newspaper could also be found in the archives on microfilm or in the original format.

Which donations should an archives accept, and which should it reject? One of the most intellectually engaging acts includes the work of appraisal. F. Gerald Ham evaluates the perceptive task of selection in *Selecting and Appraising Archives and Manuscripts*. Ham discusses the finality of selecting records. Only those selected will remain for future researchers to access. Individuals may want to keep all the records, but a selection must be made to accommodate space.[8] It can be difficult to imagine which materials will be of importance to researchers in the future. However, with thoughtful selection, the relevant materials will remain.

Where will items be stored? Will the program exist in the tribal government offices, in a separate library and archives, or in a tribal college? The location of the archives shapes the direction and emphasis of the archives program. Inside the government offices, an emphasis on records management emerges. In a tribal college, the university records become central.

In all locations, collection material should be well protected with regard to the environment and security. The environment of the archives should be monitored for temperature, relative humidity, and lighting. Preventative measures include protection from theft and following fire safety procedures. The community must be convinced that the site is secure, so that they trust the materials will be protected.

Private collections may find their way into the archives, which reveals the importance of donor relations. Archivists must be able to promote the archives program. It may be difficult to convince members of the tribe to donate materials. Archivists should work on building trust with those in the community by explaining how the archives benefits the tribe. Keep files to document all interaction with donors. It may be years before the donor actually donates material, and keeping abreast of the relationship is essential.

Through positive social interactions, an archival program will hopefully excel in reference services, outreach, and donor relations. For example, establishing excellent customer service in the reference department can lead to donations and positive feedback from the public, which can only aid in advocacy. Mary Jo Pugh argues in *Providing Reference Services for Archives and Manuscripts* that reference archivists are a prominent connection to advocacy. The formation of carefully cultivated relationships will allow an institution to grow and flourish. Without adequate promotion, the acquisition of new records may be limited.[9]

DEEDS OF GIFT

A deed of gift is the legal instrument that transfers ownership of the materials to the archives. The elements of a deed of gift include the name of the donor and recipient, the title and a description of the materials donated, transfer of ownership, access to the collection, transfer of copyright, separations, and signatures.[10] It may be helpful to write down an explanation of the deed of gift to donors, because it may seem confusing at first glance.

The deed of gift specifies the donor's specific requests for access to the records. Will all or a portion of the material be restricted? Individuals may find some of the material embarrassing and may be uncomfortable with the subject matter becoming available to the public. As a result, the restriction may have a time limit, such as opening the records ten years after the donor's death. The deed of gift should outline the requests of the donor with regard to unwanted material. It should specify whether materials are to be destroyed or returned to the donor.

SENSITIVITIES

Work with the community to determine who has access to what. Staff members should be sensitive to the tribe's desires. Archives should be careful to draw clearly defined guidelines for restricted material. The tribal government may have input on materials that should be classified.

Archivists should ensure that they are following the cultural beliefs of the tribe, because they do not want to lose the trust of the community or exploit them. Continued communication between the archives and the tribe ensures a greater understanding among staff members of what is ethically acceptable.

PRIVACY

Some of the material may be restricted to protect the privacy of individuals. Constructing privacy policies will allow the archives to have a formalized procedure for routine requests.

The archives wants to protect the donor's privacy, but at the same time allow records to be used for research. Sometimes the line between access and privacy can get blurry. Complicated issues can arise with regard to privacy. Related to the question of ownership is whether to provide patrons with access to material in the collection that belongs to a third party not identified in the deed of gift.

ESOTERIC KNOWLEDGE

A process should be established to determine whether information may be made public or not. Some information may only be available to men and some only to women. Archivists should consult with tribal elders regarding which information is sacred.

ARRANGEMENT AND DESCRIPTION

Community members may assist in identifying cultural objects. According to standard archival practice, arrangement of the collection adheres to the philosophy of *respect des fonds*. The arrangement of holdings remains unique to archives because of the need to maintain the authenticity of the records information. It is a grouping and not an item-level description. Original order must be maintained. If there is no recognizable order, then the archivist must organize the material.

Through preparing written finding aids for the collection, the archivist gives users insight into the collection's provenance.

SELF-ASSESSMENT AND PRIORITIES

What are the institution's priorities? These should be established from the outset of the program, answering questions such as whether the focus should be more on records management or on oral histories. The policy that is set regarding collection development will guide the archives into a direction for donations or which records to seek. In addition, it is important to set priorities, because many programs will lack funding for developing comprehensive collections.

It is important to work with the community to decide on priorities. The archivist should also initiate a continuous evaluation of collection use. From there, staff can take stock of where they want to take the program. These usage data can help make decisions on what areas need to be focused on in collection building, which collections should be processed first, and which materials are most needed by the community immediately.

CONCLUSION

Archives exist to preserve the cultural heritage of tribes. Archivists accomplish their tasks through the development of policies leading to the proper handling and storage of materials. Through providing outreach, archivists not only collect materials but also let individuals know they exist and that the archives program is for everyone to use.

NOTES

1. John A. Fleckner, *Native American Archives: An Introduction* (Chicago: The Society of American Archivists, 1984), 1.

2. William T. Hagan, "Archival Captive—The American Indian," *The American Archivist* 41, no. 2 (April 1978): 135–46.

3. Evelyn Wareham, "'Our Own Identity, Our Own Taonga, Our Own Self Coming Back': Indigenous Voices in New Zealand Record-Keeping," *Archivaria* 52 (Fall 2001): 27.

4. Alaska Native Knowledge Network, "Mataatua Declaration on Cultural and Intellectual Property Rights," June 1993, http://www.ankn.uaf.edu/IKS/mataatua.html (accessed 17 January 2011).

5. U.S. Department of the Interior, National Park Service, "National NAGPRA," http://www.cr.nps.gov/nagpra/ (accessed 17 January 2011).

6. "Tribal Leader Works to Repatriate Tribal Remains," *The Oklahoman*, 2 April 2006.

7. Hagan, "Archival Captive."

8. F. Gerald Ham, *Selecting and Appraising Archives and Manuscripts* (Chicago: The Society of American Archivists, 1993).

9. Mary Jo Pugh, *Providing Reference Services for Archives and Manuscripts* (Chicago: The Society of American Archivists, 1992).

10. Christine Weideman, "Deeds of Gift: What Donors Should Know," http://www.archivists.org/publications/deed_of_gift.asp (accessed 17 January 2011).

18

The Record Road: Growing Perspectives on Tribal Archives[1]

Loriene Roy and Daniel Alonzo

INTRODUCTION

Tribal archives are an essential resource for documenting cultural history. This chapter explores the archival functions of a tribal repository and addresses special concerns tribal archivists may face in managing these unique institutions. In addition, we highlight funding sources and several notable archival collections.

Tribal archives are growing in number, sparking new initiatives for training and collaboration among those tribes that house archives and with other repositories of information. As more and more documentation becomes available in electronic form, more archivists feel the pressure to contribute material to digitization efforts, making unique content available to wider audiences.

Although tribal records and manuscript materials are held in many locations, including museums, major libraries such as the Library of Congress, and university archives and special collections, our focus is on archives on tribal lands.

DEFINING THE TRIBAL ARCHIVES

As John Fleckner recounted in his 1984 book on tribal archives, an archive has two meanings. A tribal archive is both the records created by a tribe that are retained permanently for their enduring historical value and the physical repository that houses these materials.[2] When comparing indigenous and nonindigenous perspectives on the world, archives both as documents and institutions are viewed more holistically by indigenous peoples: "[A]rchives did not reside in a building but lived, on a daily basis, among, interconnected with, and interpreted by the community, its people, the land, and an overarching spirit."[3] In Australia, Aboriginally governed archives are called "keeping places": "a kind of archives or cultural repository in which to preserve and promote objects and records created by and for Aboriginal people so that they might have some measure of control over their own identities, as well as be able to educate and interact with their community and beyond."[4]

Physical locations of tribal archives vary as well. Tribal archives may be housed in tribal government offices, separate archival facilities, cultural centers or museums, multipurpose community information centers, or tribal public or college libraries. Collections of material on tribal peoples are also found at universities and even at tribal schools. Rita-Sophia Mogyorosi has described the emergence of the tribal information center: "Increasingly, Aboriginal organizations appear to be moving towards the development of holistic, all-encompassing, cultural centers that may contain museums, archives, libraries, community gathering and sharing places, and so on, linking the tangible to the intangible, memory and history to people and the land."[5] In Canada, tribal libraries, archives, or museums may be more frequently referred to as cultural education centers or resource centers.[6] Joan Berman, special collections librarian at Humboldt State University and library consultant with the Yurok (California) Tribe, summed up the unique status of archives on tribal land: "What is unusual about tribal libraries . . . is the mix of library and archival materials and the mix of library and archives principles needed to manage the unique collections."[7]

Tribal archives facilities might also serve as public spaces that expand the traditional warehouse model of the collection to one that provides opportunities to share and learn. Thus, archives might host exhibits and training, sponsor and create publications, and provide room for gatherings focused on Native language recovery and cultural programming.

THE FUNCTIONS AND CONTENT OF TRIBAL ARCHIVES

Tribal archives serve multiple purposes. They help tribal communities

- to preserve documents on their own heritage, such as letters, photographs, diaries, and records of their organizations;
- to keep languages and oral traditions alive by making and storing sound recordings of interviews with elders;
- to keep records of government decisions at all levels of governance; and
- to ensure preservation of documents telling the Aboriginal side of treaty and other negotiations.[8]

Over the past thirty to forty years, we have seen a great interest on the part of tribes in establishing and expanding archival collections and services as these communities have emerged from federal policies advocating assimilation and even termination.[9] This is evidenced by the pervasive presence of tribal archival collections, the growing number of new tribal collections, and new initiatives in training and collaboration. Over a third (thirty-six) of the ninety-seven libraries listed in the 1995 *Directory of Native American Tribal Libraries* reported housing an archives collection.[10] The 2005 "Tribal Archive, Library, and Museum Directory" lists 169 institutions, including libraries, museums, archives, tribal college libraries, tribal cultural organizations, and nontribal organizations.[11] Although twenty-eight of the institutions are coded as archives, it is obvious from the descriptions of goals, current projects, and/or challenges that many of the institutions house materials that would be found in archives such as photographs and audiotapes. Mogyorosi points out that prior to the establishment of tribally controlled archives, much Aboriginal archival material in Canada was not housed in archives but instead was collected by museums, due to the Western view of these records as ethnographic.[12]

Establishing an archives of the records for a tribal government is an important step in preserving the culture of the tribe. Brooke M. Black posits three reasons for tribes to have archives. First, "the primary reason for tribes to maintain their own archives is to gain control over their own material and more importantly their own history." The second reason is "to control documents that can be used in cases against the federal and state governments." The third reason is "to give them [the tribe] a place to hold, organize, and use material that they obtain from other institutions."[13]

Tribal government records are used to support and document tribes' status as sovereign nations. A proper and thorough records management program is instrumental if the tribal government is to retain its most valuable records, which may both protect and serve the tribe in the event of legal action. For example, the Native American Graves Protection and Repatriation Act (NAGPRA) provides for the return or repatriation of certain sacred items from federal agencies and selected local or state institutions that receive federal funding.[14] In order to repatriate objects, tribes must have documentary proof of what is theirs. Once a tribe recovers an artifact, naturally the paperwork involved would also be retained in the tribe's archives.

Repatriation is only one type of legal matter that may face tribes. Mogyorosi described the rationale behind the development of tribal archives in Canada: "With a focus on such evidentiary proof and the need for expert witnesses (such as archaeologists, historians, anthropologists, the tangible documentation found in Euro-Canadian archives, etc.), it is hardly surprising that Aboriginal people have sought out, created, and ended up with volumes of Euro-Canadian-style documentation, and have thus recognized the need or have had to establish Euro-Canadian-style repositories to manage these records accordingly."[15] For matters such as land and water rights, disputes in the local industry or economy, and tribal enrollment and membership, tribal government records may only tell part of the story.

Tribal archives collect a greater scope of materials beyond the records of the tribal governments. These include genealogical materials, such as tribal membership rolls; financial and legal records of individual tribal members and institutions; and documents that support legal claims. Tribal archives facilities may house other primary source materials, including language recordings, traditional art and decorative art expressions, photographs, oral history interviews, recordings of performing arts and ceremonies on audio- and videotape; and realia, or three-dimensional cultural objects, such as wampum (shell) belts, botanical specimens, birch bark scrolls, and ceremonial objects including drums. The archives often house print library resources such as published tribal histories, tribally produced publications, ethnographic reports, periodicals, and vertical files of miscellaneous material such as newspaper clippings. As Richard Pearce-Moses points out, the most important tribal records may be held outside of the tribe in other tribal collections, in federal archives, or even in private collections.[16] Tribal archivists need to identify these cultural materials and arrange to secure copies.

Based on work with her family history and assisting Aboriginal peoples in accessing content in archives, Lynette Russell found that archivists play a special mediating role between people and records: "Therefore, while I do not believe that the material housed in archives and libraries in general is Indigenous knowledge per se, such material can become Indigenous through reclamation processes which can be facilitated by libraries and archives and which, I believe, will bring the two parties closer together."[17]

Placing cultural content within archival collections is a way of acknowledging their status as containers of cultural knowledge and serves to negate "marginisation of Aboriginal peoples and their different recording, remembering, and archiving traditions, which have often been viewed as inferior to Euro-Canadian traditions and even irrelevant to an understanding of the key features of the past, if not misunderstood outright."[18] Tribal cultural records and materials themselves "were better accepted [by non-tribal archival centers] as ethnographic, aesthetic, highly suspect, and certainly poor evidence of history."[19]

TRIBAL ARCHIVES ESSENTIALS AND CONCERNS

Like other archives, tribal archives are concerned with collecting and acquiring materials, arranging and describing the collections, preserving the collections, and providing access to the material through reference and other public services. When considering applying archival standards of practice, tribal archivists must ask: "To what extent will non-Aboriginal archiving methods hinder the proper handling and remembering required by traditional and community records?"[20] Archival principles of provenance might be at odds with indigenous thinking: "[T]he provenance recorded in museum catalogue records for First Nations materials—particularly the oldest objects—often lacks association with First Nations families, clans or individuals."[21] The most important attribute of tribal documents might be their context. Expert voices in indigenous archival practice support "integration of management of archival, library and museum collections or networking institutions as a way to address problems of fragmentation" of related cultural material into different repositories.[22]

In addition to these professional skills, tribal archivists also need to acquire local cultural competence and knowledge of issues related to intellectual and cultural property rights. Tribal archivists, therefore, may have critical needs for training in local community traditions and continuing education in tribal issues.

There are several options to receive specific training and continuing education in tribal archives. Workshops may be available through grant-funded opportunities. The National Historical Publications and Records Commission (NHPRC) awarded a $65,000 grant to the Society of American Archivists for the two-year "Strengthening Tribal Archives Programs," which provided training for fifteen tribal archivists in 2005 and 2006.[23] In 2004, the Museums Association of Montana received a grant from the National Endowment for the Humanities for a workshop, "Preferred Practices for Historical Repositories."[24]

For over twenty years, the Society of California Archivists has held the Western Archives Institute, a two-week summer program cosponsored with the California State Archives.[25] The curriculum, developed through funding from the NHPRC, covers basic management issues in tribal archives along with the more specialized topics on appraisal, photographic care, and grant writing. The National Museum of the American Indian (NMAI) has hosted Native Museum Practices Workshops as recently as 2007.[26]

Similarly, in May 2002, the federal Institute of Museum and Library Services (IMLS) sponsored a national conference entitled "Preserving Our Language, Memory, and Lifeways," which provided a review of basic archival practice. That meeting has grown in organization and stature to become the national conference on tribal archives, libraries, and museums. Archival topics presented at the 2008 national conference included "Developing an Archives in the Library Setting"; the 2009 event included an all-day "Basic(s) of Archives" preconference, with programs on records control and tribal and university archives collaborations.[27] Other organizations interested in tribal archives include the Association of Canadian Archivists Special Interest Section on Aboriginal Archives and the Society of American Archivists Native American Archives Round Table.

Along with basic archival training, there are special concerns for tribal archivists. The staff may need to modify archival practices for a tribal setting. For instance, one challenge of working with a tribe can be the difficulty of convincing community members and tribal offices to deposit their materials in the archives. This reticence may be due in part to tribal members' mistrust of institutions, especially those with perceived rigid guidelines and policies. Tribal archivists may need to work diligently on long-term strategies to earn trust from community members. One way of doing this is to acknowledge shared ownership of cultural material.

Through continuing training and involvement in collaborative projects, tribal archivists are learning to apply information technologies such as Encoded Archival Description (EAD). EAD standardizes the way finding aids are created, thus facilitating transferability of search records from one institution to the next. Digitization technologies serve to preserve images and also make them more widely available. With all of the advantages that technology brings, it may also be an intrusive presence in tribal communities. Technological applications cause additional hesitancy when non-Native staff are involved in handling cultural material and in displaying it both to the community and beyond. This hesitancy is to the result of two concerns: technology may erode cultural knowledge, and the presence of technology is a reminder of the mistreatment of community members and cultural objects by earlier generations of anthropologists and museum personnel.

Archivists therefore need to become sensitive to local protocol or cultural guidelines. Kimberly Lawson provides this definition for protocol:

> First Nations have knowledge which is freely shared; knowledge which is shared and used under specific conditions; and knowledge which is maintained but rarely shared. The complex protocols guiding sharing and use of knowledge are compared to but do not equate directly to western concepts such as copyright and public domain.[28]

Such guidelines may determine who has access to what. That is, whether Native or non-Native archives patrons have access to similar records, and even whether all tribal members have access to the same archival records. For example, restrictions may be placed on maps to safeguard the location of sacred and burial sites and prevent their being seen or even looted by nontribal members. Within a tribe, material may be restricted by gender, with some information available only to men and other information available only to women. Some documents may be restricted to observe cultural beliefs, such as a prohibition against displaying portrait photographs during a mourning period. Archivists working with collections that include tribal cultural material that has already been deposited should also consider opening discussions about access to these materials. As Paula Gunn Allen reminds us, "telling the old stories, revealing the old ways, can only lead to disaster."[29] In this case, the disaster may be the loss of trust between the archives and the tribal community.

Lawson reminds us that records that are not cataloged or not well described are also inaccessible.[30] She summarizes indigenous concepts that impact archival processes and description of indigenous cultural heritage: "memory, spirituality, protection of authenticity and trustworthiness, cultural concepts of truthfulness, individual and collective ownership, cultural survival, cultural concepts of privacy and openness, political conflicts, and conflicting juridical systems."[31]

Perhaps the best alternative is to use technology to forge working relationships with tribal people. Archives involved in digitizing images or artifacts might invite community members to help identify and interpret cultural materials. Similarly, archivists may ask tribal members for assistance in choosing indexing terms. Tribal names may be more appropriately listed in the tribe's language as well as in English. The best use of an archival website might be to post access policies and thus work toward establishing goodwill. The Yurok Tribe in California described its initial plan for its website to include a biographical "elder of the month" feature, providing elder community members with virtual space to narrate content on tribal history and/or culture.[32] Other archives may improve delivery of information to the tribal community by delivering imaged documents and/or images directly to tribal offices, schools, or tribal homes.

Tribal archivists should acknowledge Donald L. Fixico's advice: "The sensitivity of tribal knowledge, especially that of ceremonials, should compel scholars to publicly acknowledge a code of ethics and responsibilities to avoid exploiting American Indians."[33] Tribal archivists will need to determine who will sanction work with cultural materials. This may best be accomplished by establishing an archives subcommittee with community member representatives who will aid in communication with tribal elected officials and religious personnel.

Thomas Gates, head of the Yurok Tribe's Cultural Department, reminds us that the technological applications in tribal archives do not replace traditional means of cultural learning: "It is important to remember that the functions of the archive should never replace the traditional methods of transmission of cultural practices. Rather, the tribal culture must be lived, as it has been for thousands of years, and passed down from elders to their grandchildren in their language, traditions, and ceremonies."[34]

FUNDING

Though tribal archives are dependent on tribal financial support for day-to-day operating expenditures, tribes sometimes jumpstart archives development by securing grant funding. Two agencies that provide funding for archives development or collaborative projects are the federal IMLS and the National Park Service.

Tribes may apply to the IMLS for grants supporting libraries, museums, or collaborations including libraries, museums, and/or other qualifying institutions.[35] Tribal cultural centers may receive IMLS funding through state library agencies or by applying directly to the IMLS in the form of a grant application. National Leadership Grants for libraries are awarded for several types of projects, including those involving community engagement, digital collections and tools, and informal learning. IMLS administers separate grant programs for Native American library services and Native Hawaiian library services. The two Native American Library Grants are the noncompetitive Basic Grants, which are awarded to tribes that have long-range plans for their libraries and submit complete applications and end-of-year evaluation reports, and the competitive Enhancement Grants for up to $150,000 for a two-year funding period. Tribal museums may apply for a

series of museum grants. Because grant programs change over time, it is important to review the IMLS website (imls.gov) for details including announcements
of past grant recipients.

Tribes have been awarded IMLS funding to support archival initiatives. The
Yurok Tribe in California used funding from two Enhancement Grants for "the
refinement of the archives policies, the development of an Yurok educational
packet for public inquiries, the purchase of computers for Yurok schools and
tribal offices, and the creation of an archive and Cultural Department Web
site."[36] Montana State University and the Museum of the Rockies created a digital
database of 1,500 images of Plains Indian peoples from original materials held at
universities and tribal colleges. In addition to digitizing images, project partners
created a relational database and developed training workshops.[37] In 2009, the
Jamestown S'Klallam Tribe in Washington State received nearly $150,000 to
extend a new online tribal archive to digitize tribal records as well as privately
owned materials about tribal history.[38]

The National Park Service also manages the Historic Preservation Fund Grants
for Indian Tribes and Alaska Natives. Grants supported the Chickaloon Village's
(Alaska) production of a multimedia local history curriculum, videotaping of beading classes for deposit in the Fort Mojave Indian Tribe (California), and the Pueblo
of Pojoaque's (New Mexico) use of a global positioning system (GPS) to map the
boundaries of two historic sites.[39] Grants awarded in 2009 included one to the
Sun'ag Tribe of Kodiak to document and archive its Alutiiq dancing and one to the
Red Cliff Band of Lake Superior Chippewa to start an electronic archive.[40]

The NHPRC funds the development of archives and records programs, sur-
veying or copying tribal records in other repositories, microfilming of historical
documents, and developing and delivering training events such as workshops,
and oral history.

SELECTED ARCHIVAL COLLECTIONS

Details about tribal archives were once difficult to locate on the Internet, although
this has started to change as tribes reach out to members living at a distance. This
final section illustrates the range of tribal material available and the innovative
services that archives are providing.

The Tamástslikt Cultural Institute has a pleasant presence on the Internet.[41]
The institute, which means "interpret" in the Walla Walla language, opened its
doors in August 1998. It is owned by the Confederated Tribes of the Umatilla Indian Reservation in Oregon and was constructed as part of a tribal resort complex
that also includes a casino, hotel, golf course, and recreational vehicle park. The
Tamástslikt website describes the holdings of the archives and encourages use by
listing what the center has to offer to facilitate research. The descriptions of the
archival holdings, however, only describe the format of materials (e.g., photo-

graphs and reports). Perhaps tribal custom, in the interest of privacy, only allows for a general account of the collection. Or perhaps the holdings are too large to describe in one paragraph.

Although the Fond du Lac Cultural Center website is not as aesthetically pleasing, it provides more digitized archival content than does the Tamástslikt website.[42] For instance, it includes scanned images of selected historical documents, consisting of six pages of land allotments and photographs from the private collections of tribal members. Inscriptions on the photographs were also scanned and appear on the website, along with requests for community members to identify those depicted in the images. The inclusion of the photographs illustrates that tribal archives can use technology to create social spaces for community dialogue.

Three noteworthy archival collections document the boarding school experiences of Native youth and young adults.

Haskell Indian Nations University (HINU) (originally the U.S. Industrial Training School) in Lawrence, Kansas, was founded in 1884. HINU is now an institution of higher education granting two- and four-year degrees. Notable materials in the HINU Cultural Center and Archives collection include HINU historical information as well as a rare photographic collection. The Frank Rinehart and Adolph Muhr photograph collections contain 800 portraits of over 500 American Indian delegates attending the Trans-Mississippi Exposition and Indian Congress held in Omaha, Nebraska, in 1898. The HINU archivists developed a database for the photographs that is searchable by tribal and individual names.[43]

Hampton Normal and Agricultural Institute was founded in Virginia to provide education to former slaves. In 1878, Hampton began to admit American Indian students, enrolling more than 1,300 students from over sixty tribal groups by 1923. More than eight million items are housed in the archives, including thousands of photographs, prints, and glass lantern slides, along with student records, artwork, and three-dimensional objects.[44]

The Carlisle Indian Industrial School operated from 1879 to 1918. Digitized maps of the campus, including an annotated map that serves as a self-guided walking tour. The website provides bibliographies of primary (e.g., Carlisle school newspapers and magazines) and secondary sources, tribal enrollment tally, scanned photographs, and biographical material on Jim Thorpe, Indian athlete. Barbara Landis, the archivist, will provide upon request electronic copies of the *Indian Helper*, the school paper, through an electronic distribution list.[45]

SUMMARY

Tribal archives are essential resources for documenting cultural history. Those in tribal archives must contend with the challenges of working with a variety of formats, of description and arrangement, and of continual professional education and training. Tribal archives are starting to utilize technologies to document holdings and provide access; services must be balanced with the community's desire to protect cultural knowledge. Tribal archives show remarkable potential. Mogyorosi's 2008 master's thesis was based on responses to a questionnaire she received from thirteen archivists working with tribal content in Australia, Canada, and the United States. She concluded by projecting that "the future of Aboriginal archives and archiving in BC [British Columbia], and indeed the world, lies in innovation and adaptability—the ability of Aboriginal people to take Euro-Canadian and Aboriginal archival methods and make them their own, push boundaries, and adapt and shift. . . . Perhaps this is the future of 'archives' created by and for Aboriginal people—places to gather, learn, share knowledge, and heal, and where perhaps Aboriginal holistic worldviews can be rejuvenated, understood, and once again lived."[46]

NOTES

1. An earlier version of this chapter was published as Loriene Roy and Daniel L. Alonzo, "Perspectives on Tribal Archives," *The Electronic Library* 21, no. 5 (2003): 422–27.

2. John Fleckner, *Native American Archives: An Introduction* (Chicago: Society of American Archivists, 1984).

3. Rita-Sophia Mogyorosi, "Coming Full Circle?: Aboriginal Archives in British Columbia in Canadian and International Perspective" (master's thesis, University of Manitoba/University of Winnipeg, 2008), http://mspace.lib.umanitoba.ca/bitstream/1993/3118/1/Mogyorosi%20-%20Thesis.pdf (accessed 9 September 2010), 1.

4. Mogyorosi, "Coming Full Circle?" 116.

5. Mogyorosi, "Coming Full Circle?" 73.

6. Kimberly L. Lawson, "Precious Fragments: First Nations Materials in Archives, Libraries and Museums" (master's thesis, University of British Columbia, 2004), 69.

7. "The Yurok Archive: Collecting, Protecting the Paper Record of a Native People," *Cantu Ota* 53 (12 January 2002), http://www.turtletrack.org/Issues02/Co01122002/CO_01122002_Yurok.htm (accessed 9 September 2010).

8. Association of Canadian Archivists, Public Awareness Committee, *Aboriginal Archives Guide;* Canadian Church Historical Society Occasional Paper no. 8, 2007, http://www.archivists.ca/sites/default/files/Attachments/Outreach_attachments/Aboriginal_Archives_English_WEB.pdf 34 (accessed 9 September 2010).

9. Mogyorosi, "Coming Full Circle?" 4.

10. Lotsee Patterson and Rhonda Taylor, *Directory of Native American Tribal Libraries* (Norman: The University of Oklahoma, School of Library and Information Studies, 1995).

11. The University of Arizona, Arizona State Museum, "Tribal Archive, Library, and Museum Directory," 2005, http://www.statemuseum.arizona.edu/frame/index.php?doc=/aip/leadershipgrant/directory/tlam_directory_03_2005.pdf (accessed 9 September 2010).

12. Mogyorosi, "Coming Full Circle?" 7.

13. Brooke M. Black, "Freeing the 'Archival Captive': A Closer Look at [Native American Indian] Tribal Archives," *Provenance.ca for Librarians, Archivists & Professional Pre-*

servers-Creators of Information 7 (2005), http://www.provenance.ca/2005-vol7/libraries-archives/native-american-archives-2005-black.html (accessed 9 September 2010).

14. Native American Graves Protection and Repatriation Act, 25 U.S.C. 3001–3013, http://www.nps.gov/history/nagpra/ (accessed 9 September 2010).

15. Mogyorosi, "Coming Full Circle?" 40.

16. Richard Pearce-Moses, "Tribal Archives Workshop Given at Ak-Chin," *Labriola National American Indian Data Center* 5, no. 3 (1997), http://www.asu.edu/lib/archives/fall97.htm#TRIBALARCHIVES (accessed 9 September 2010).

17. Lynette Russell, "Indigenous Knowledge and Archives: Accessing Hidden History and Understandings," *Australian Academic & Research Libraries* 36, no. 2 (June 2005), http://www.accessmylibrary.com/article-1G1-140922648/indigenous-knowledge-and-archives.html (accessed 9 September 2010).

18. Mogyorosi, "Coming Full Circle?" 6.

19. Mogyorosi, "Coming Full Circle?" 8.

20. Mogyorosi, "Coming Full Circle?" 73.

21. Lawson, "Precious Fragments," 66.

22. Lawson, "Precious Fragments," 181.

23. Briana Bob, "Strengthening Tribal Archives Programs," *TribalNEWS*, September 2005, http://tribune.colvilletribes.com/archives/2005/september2005/tribalnews.htm (accessed 27 December 2009); National Historical Publications and Records Commission, *Newsletter* 32, no. 4 (Summer 2005), http://74.125.47.132/search?q=cache:4Lxy9QA8TQIJ:www.archives.gov/nhprc/annotation/2005/summer.pdf+%22Strengthening+Tribal+Archives%22&cd=7&hl=en&ct=clnk&gl=us&client=firefox-a (accessed 9 September 2010).

24. "Preferred Practices Workshop to be Held at MAM Conference," *The Montana Archivist* 5, no.1 (Winter 2004): 1.

25. California State Archives, "2010 Western Archives Institute," http://www.sos.ca.gov/archives/wai/ (accessed 9 September 2010).

26. National Museum of the American Indian, "Past Workshops and Participants," http://www.nmai.si.edu/subpage.cfm?subpage=collaboration&second=training&third=workshops (accessed 9 September 2010).

27. "Tribal Archives, Libraries, and Museums 2009 National Conference," http://www.tribalconference.org (accessed 9 September 2010).

28. Lawson, "Precious Fragments," 132.

29. Paula Gunn Allen, "Special Problems in Teaching Leslie Marmon Silko's *Ceremony*," in *Natives and Academics: Research and Writing About American Indians*, ed. Devon A. Mihesuah (Lincoln: London: University of Nebraska Press, 1998), 62.

30. Lawson, "Precious Fragments," 145.

31. Lawson, "Precious Fragments," 226.

32. "The Yurok Archive."

33. Donald L. Fixico, "Ethics and Responsibilities in Writing American Indian History," in *Natives and Academics*, ed. Mihesuah, 84.

34. "The Yurok Archive."

35. United States, Institute of Museum and Library Services, http://www.imls.gov (accessed 9 September 2010).

36. "The Yurok Archive."

37. Institute of Museum and Library Services, "Status of Technology and Digitization in the Nation's Museums and Libraries 2002 Report," http://74.125.47.132/

188 Chapter 18

Web+Delivers+Digital+Picture+of+Native+American+History%22&cd=2&hl=en&ct=cl
nk&gl=us&client=firefox-a (accessed 9 September 2010).

38. Institute of Museum and Library Services, "Awarded Grants Search Results," http://
imls.gov/results.asp (accessed 9 September 2010).

39. U.S. Department of the Interior, National Park Service, "Fiscal Year 2001 Historic
Preservation Fund Grants to Indian Tribes and Alaskan Natives and Native Hawaiian
Organizations," http://www.nps.gov/hps/HPG/Tribal/downloads/Grants/FY01.pdf (accessed 9 September 2010).

40. U.S. Department of the Interior, National Park Service, "Fiscal Year 2009
Historic Preservation Fund Grants to Indian Tribes and Alaskan Natives and Native Hawaiian Organizations," http://www.nps.gov/hps/HPG/Tribal/downloads/
Grants/2009TribalGrantsReport.pdf (accessed 9 September 2010).

41. Tamástslikt Cultural Institute, http://www.tamastslikt.org/ (accessed 9 September
2010).

42. Fond du Lac Cultural Center & Museum, http://www.fdlrez.com/Museum/documents.htm (accessed 9 September 2010).

43. Haskell Indian Nations University, http://www.haskell.edu/index.html (accessed 9
September 2010).

44. Hampton University Archives, http://museum.hamptonu.edu/university_archives
.cfm (accessed 9 September 2010)

45. "Carlisle Indian Industrial School History," http://home.epix.net/~landis/histry
.html (accessed 9 September 2010).

46. Mogyorosi, "Coming Full Circle?" 5, 73.

IV

WORKING IN TRIBAL LIBRARIES AND ARCHIVES

19

Your Tribal Library and Strategic Planning: Vision, Mission, Service Responses, Goals, Objectives, and Output Measures

Loriene Roy

How do you explain to others why your tribal library exists? Planning is based on understanding the what, when, where, why, who, and how of your library. Since 1980, the Public Library Association (PLA), a division of the American Library Association, has engaged in providing national training and resources on strategic planning for its members. This is a process of developing a mission statement and aligning one's goals and objectives for a five-year cycle according to one or more service responses. These service responses describe the role of the library and the services it provides, using phrases such as "Stimulate Imagination: Reading, Viewing, and Listening for Pleasure," and "Success in School: Homework Help."[1]

The library then measures its success in meeting these service responses through ratios called output measures, such as stock turnover rate and program attendance per capita. All of these planning documents—vision statement, mission statement, service roles, goals, objectives, and output measures—are designed with input from library staff, institutional administrators, and the patrons that libraries serve.

Following the PLA model, the first step in framing your decision making is to prepare your library's vision statement. Vision statements are usually concise and inspirational. The library vision is aligned with and supports the vision of the library's larger institution, whether it is a school, university/college, or the tribal government. Following is the vision statement for a tribal college. Note that the statement balances two contexts: education and the Blackfeet traditional view of the world. The focus is on the impact of the vision on an audience that not only includes tribal members but also embraces a world community.

The Blackfeet Community College vision statement reads as follows:

It is the vision of the Blackfeet Community College to strengthen and enrich our Blackfeet Nation and universal community through quality education integrating the *Ni-tsi-ta-pi* World of Knowledge.[2]

A library vision statement could be crafted to support the college's vision. For example, a library vision statement built on the previous college vision statement might read:

The library at Blackfeet Community College is a supportive partner in the college's vision for tribal education and does so through developing library services reflective of Blackfeet indigenous culture and beliefs.

This hypothetical example illustrates how a library's vision statement extends and supports the vision of the greater institution.

MISSION STATEMENT

The vision provides the framework for the other planning documents. When viewed hierarchically, the next more specific or narrower task is to then adopt a mission. Carlyle Edwards describes a library's mission statement as "short, concise, positive, clearly defined."[3] Mission statements may indicate the historical beginnings of the library and place it in its organizational environment. Let us look at examples from two tribal colleges and a tribal community library. The first example comes from the Blackfeet Community College:

Finally, and most importantly, it is the mission of the Blackfeet Community College to serve as a living memorial to the Blackfeet Tribe, in preserving the traditions and culture of a proud and progressive people.[4]

The second mission statement is from Diné College on the Navajo Nation:

The mission of Diné College is to apply the *Sá'ah Naagháí Bik'eh Hózhóón* principles to advance quality student learning through *Nitsáhákees* (Thinking), *Nahatá* (Planning), *Iiná* (Living) and *Siih Hasin* (Assuring).[5]

Examine, also, the mission of a tribal public or community library, which identifies the community served and the library's responsibility for access, education, recreation, culture, and preservation:

Laguna Public Library is committed to serving the people of Laguna Pueblo as well as its surrounding communities by providing access to quality information and resources that enhance and contribute to individual knowledge, enlightenment, and enjoyment through library materials and emerging technologies.

Laguna Public Library recognizes their responsibility to provide a place for cultural learning and preservation of the Laguna People; as well as creating a pleasant and safe environment for children to discover the joy of reading and the value of libraries.[6]

SERVICE RESPONSES OR ROLES

Over time, public libraries have served multiple roles in their communities. They have been referred to as the children's door to learning, the students' auxiliary, the community center, and the people's university. Since 1980, public libraries have been advised to work with their communities to prioritize their service, set goals and objectives related to these roles, and evaluate how they perform in these roles. PLA identifies a number of service roles that can provide guidance to tribal libraries,[7] including "Connect to the Online World: Public Internet Access," "Create Young Readers: Early Literacy," and "Discover Your Roots: Genealogy and Local History." Tribal libraries may also identify unique service roles or derivations of the national roles, such as "Celebrate Cultural Diversity: Awareness of the Cultures of Your Tribe and that of Others" and "Learn to Read and Write in English and Your Native Language: Children's, Youth, Adult, and Family Literacy." Once your tribal library selects one or more service roles over the next five-year cycle, it will then identify goals and objectives to meet those service responses.

GOALS AND OBJECTIVES

The mission statement is visionary and indicates the ultimate impact of the tribal library. Goals are long-range guidelines that suggest how the library will interpret its mission over time. Goals are still abstract and indicate a desired future.

Objectives are measurable steps the library staff will take to accomplish the goals. A library's objectives are short term. Take, for example, the Miami Tribe of Oklahoma's goal and objectives for an oral history project of tribal members. By including calendar dates, the librarian can assess whether or not he or she achieved any particular objective by the projected completion date:

Miami Tribe of Oklahoma: Goals for an Oral History Project
The goal of this proposal is to better provide library services to the tribal community. This involves four objectives to achieve over the next twelve months and by the end of the current fiscal year.
(1) Tape twenty-five oral history interviews covering topics not collected previously, such as how the tribes worked together to fight political opposition.
(2) Conduct inventories of the resources held at all library sites, comparing the inventory against the online catalog and the accession records.
(3) Upgrade the catalog software to allow better usage and accessibility.
(4) Purchase and add 1,000 new items to each library to include books, videos, newspapers, and audio recordings.[8]

OUTPUT MEASURES

Finally, you will select one or more ways to measure whether you are meeting your objectives and goals on your way to living your service role. Each service role lends itself to being measured with certain data. For example, you might need to count the number of visits your patrons make to your library to attend cultural programs. The old standby of library evaluation, circulation of library materials, can still be used, divided by the number of library card holders, to determine circulation per capita.

This process of vision-mission-service-responses-goals-objectives sets your library on the road to determining the activities or tasks you need to perform day by day. Tribal libraries also have the unique opportunity to infuse their services with tribal history and values.

NOTES

1. June Garcia and Sandra Nelson, "The PLA Service Responses: Selecting and Implementing the Right Mix for Your Library" (paper presented at the Spring Symposium of the Public Library Association, Nashville, Tenn., April 2009), http://www.ala.org/ala/mgrps/divs/pla/plaevents/plaspringsymposium/Service%20Responses.pdf (accessed 19 January 2011).

2. "Blackfeet Community College: Vision Statement," http://www.bfcc.org/About_BCC/Vision.html (accessed 19 January 2011). The website also provides a link to content on core values, specifically tribal values, which are:

Tsi-ksi-ka-ta-pi-wa-tsin: Blackfeet Way of Knowing. Blackfeet culture/spirituality in philosophy, thought, and action.

Nin-na-wa-tsin: Being a Leader. Professionalism, integrity, and responsibility in human interaction.

Ini-yimm: Respect. Respect for one's self, all other people, all other ideas, and each thing in the natural world.

Ni-ta-pi-pa-ta-pi-tsin: Living in a Good Way. Being honest in all thoughts and actions.

Li-yi-kah-kii-ma-tsin: Trying Hard. Commitment, dedication, sincerity in the pursuit of all our goals.

Aoh-kan-otah-tomo: Accepting Everyone. Embracing the unique talents and contributions of each individual.

Li-ta-mii-pa-ta-pi-yoip: Happy Living. Humor, laughter, and enjoyment of life.

3. Carlyle Edwards, "Why Write a Long-Range Plan? Most Companies Don't!" *Texas Libraries* 51, no. 3 (Fall 1990): 83–87.

4. "Blackfeet Community College: Mission Statement," http://www.bfcc.org (accessed 19 January 2011).

5. "Diné College," http://www.dinecollege.edu/ (accessed 19 January 2011).

6. Janice Kowemy, e-mail message to author, 30 August 2008.

7. Sandra Nelson, *Strategic Planning for Results* (Chicago: American Library Association, 2008).

8. This example was drawn from "Miami Tribe of Oklahoma Library/Archives 'Libraries: Lost and Found' Project Abstract," http://www.imls.gov/applicants/samples/Miami%20Tribe%20Libraries%20Lost%20and%20Found.pdf (accessed 19 January 2011).

20

Gaining Local Tribal Support for Library Development: Twenty-One Steps for Success

Cheryl A. Metoyer

During a conference session entitled "Everything You Need to Know About Being a Tribal Librarian, But Were Afraid to Ask" at the 2002 national conference, "Preserving Our Language, Memory, and Lifeways: Tribal Archives, Libraries, and Museums," participants posed several notable questions. This chapter reflects on them while synthesizing the ensuing discussion. The theme common to those questions and discussion was, "How does a tribal librarian (Native or non-Native) gain support for library development in American Indian tribal communities?"

To answer this question, the formal presentation addressed fundamental management principles and practices, including the value of effective listening, collaboration versus conflict models, the development of a vision statement, and coping with common organizational obstructions. These practices and principles were related to tribal communities, which by their very nature offer unique opportunities and challenges for library development. Emerging from the presentation was a set of twenty-one steps that could lead to success. Those steps are discussed below.

One: Approach the development process as a gift. Library development represents an opportunity to serve the community. This view is more conducive to effectiveness than an attitude that characterizes the process as a major problem to be solved. "Community" and "service" are the operative words that should provide the rationale for the existence of tribal libraries. Being grounded in serving the community is a traditional tribal value that transcends professional rhetoric. To be part of a tribal community means to serve that community—to give of oneself for the good of the group.

Two: Cultivate and express gratitude. Make a point of formally and informally thanking those who provide assistance. "Thank-you" notes, informal e-mail messages, telephone calls, and formal celebrations can accomplish this. The point is to express your sincere gratitude frequently and consistently to all those who assist—this means not only to decision makers.

Three: Know your community. In addition to having current facts about the community, knowing includes respecting community members and connecting with tribal council members in a personal way. Though e-mail and telephone calls may be expedient, there is no true substitute for face-to-face conversations. This type of interpersonal exchange more readily permits one to see matters from other perspectives.

Four: Wake up. It is vital that one be aware of local issues and alert to their potential impact on library development. The purpose is to understand where the library fits within the larger scheme of the tribe's mission, priorities, and dreams. Be cognizant of how the community's story is evolving and the library's role in that story.

Five: Generate a vision. A vision focuses on long-term aspirations and the future the library and tribe want to develop; a mission statement, on the other hand, explains what the library is trying to do today. Questions that help to construct a vision include the following:

- What is a library?
- What is a tribal library?
- Why should this community have a library, here and now?
- What is its purpose?
- Whom will it serve?
- What are the consequences of not having a library?
- How will the library be supported and sustained?

Six: Articulate the vision. Develop the ability to speak from the heart about the community's vision of the library. This speaking should be honest and reflective of the passion and interest you have for the library.

Seven: Stay focused. Because communities are organic and dynamic, it is tempting to jump to other projects. However, if the library is to be an effective organization, it is important to concentrate consistently on realizing the vision.

Eight: Identify a support base. Elicit the assistance of community members from all age groups. The guiding principle is that the library belongs to the entire community, not only to children or students. It is critical to gain the support of tribal elders. In many communities, elders' councils have been powerful forces in providing library support.

Nine: Seek an apprentice. Foster an apprenticeship program that allows you to teach a community member as you yourself learn from the community. It may be helpful to instruct and guide someone who shares an interest in the library and is willing to learn by example. The questions and concerns that an apprentice raises can help you ascertain the strengths and weaknesses within your development strategy.

Ten: Collaborate. Try not to engage in competition as a means of achieving your goals. Recognizing that there are instances when this may be difficult, the objective is to find ways to work with, not against, other tribal agencies. A cooperative stance and a reputation for collaboration will go far in creating advocates for the library.

Eleven: Listen to the voices of opposition. If there are concerns about proposed development plans, it is necessary to consider the source and reasons behind the opposition. Careful listening, with an ear to learning and not automatically dismissing negative positions, may reveal ways to negotiate differences.

Twelve: Trust in the collective wisdom of the community. If your personal view or goals for the library are at odds with the community's priorities, it is best to wait and abide by the community's decision. Though you have expert knowledge, it may be more constructive to offer that knowledge for consideration, without playing the role of the expert. Recognize that some community members may perceive changes as risky. These cautionary voices are often legitimately concerned about the lack of stability that change often signifies. In tribal communities, history suggests that there is indeed just cause for concern about changes that could transform the community.

Thirteen: Carry the tension. If there is ongoing debate concerning library development, hold the tension and wait for it to subside. Ponder the issues carefully. Try not to take premature actions that exacerbate the situation. If one acts too quickly, the problems may be transmitted throughout the community. By waiting for a better time, it may be possible to transform the tension into the desired outcome. Know your position along the continuum between those who support library development and those who may be resistant.

Fourteen: Live with ambiguity. Be aware that all the dimensions of standard library development may not be possible or desirable within the tribal community. For example, charging fees for Internet access may be the norm in some public libraries. However, fees may not be perceived as acceptable in tribal communities. Try to achieve a healthy balance between the spirit of the community and economic imperatives.

Fifteen: Take the initiative. Ask to be placed on the agenda of tribal council meetings. Sometimes serendipity provides opportunities to enhance library development. More often than not, a proactive approach is more effective.

Sixteen: Be confident. Understand that if you have followed the guidelines and are resolved to provide outstanding library services, you are likely to succeed. Enthusiasm and knowledge joined with astute community development practices are powerful means of enhancing self-confidence.

Seventeen: Anticipate changes. Planning for change and accepting its inevitability are essential if the library is to be a vital presence in the community. Looking toward the community's future, coupled with a strong sense of the present position of the library, helps one manage the library's direction, thereby accomplishing the stated mission.

Eighteen: Simplify. It is of great value to articulate all aspects of the library's development, including its mission, services, and programs, in lay terms. When presenting a proposal to a tribal council, it is helpful to use terminology that is familiar to the council. Include local examples to illustrate your points. If you simplify your language, it may clarify your position and demonstrate the relevance of your proposal.

Nineteen: Be organized. An orderly way of presenting a library development plan not only indicates efficiency, it also demonstrates respect for the community. Given the busy schedules of most decision makers, especially governing and administrative bodies, they are likely to appreciate an organized plan.

Twenty: Work. Honor the position you have been given in the tribal community by doing the actual work of developing library services. Examine your motives, evaluate your effectiveness, and see yourself as perpetually learning. This process includes reflecting on the progress involved in developing the library. Provide high-quality work that is relevant to the achievement of the stated mission and vision. In short, when you work, work well but toward the accomplishment of larger goals, those related to the mission and vision.

Twenty-one: Maintain a sense of humor. If you do not have one, get one. Laughter is an essential gift for survival, may be critical if the library is to flourish, and may put the people with whom you deal at ease.

In conclusion, developing a tribal library is both an honor and an opportunity to participate in the nation-building process. This process is part of the unfolding of the community's story. The library, translated as a house of wisdom, may be central to the story. Work hard to ensure that the center of the story holds true for future generations.

21

Advocacy and Marketing for the Tribal Library

Sandra Littletree

One of the biggest challenges of tribal libraries is getting decision makers to provide unwavering support for the library. "How do I get my tribal council to support the work we do in the library?" is an often-asked question, and it is not simply answered. By learning how to assert your value, you can begin to turn others in your community into library advocates and supporters.

Advocacy is the combination of marketing, publicity, and public relations, as well as lobbying and professionalism. It is about being visible and asserting your value. It is also about providing the best services possible and telling people about it. Advocacy may be targeted to a specific campaign, such as when there is a specific need. But it can and should also be an everyday activity. It includes the things done on a daily basis, both inside and outside of the library, to become visible and to get the support needed from decision makers.

Support for libraries in Native communities tends to be different from non-Native communities, where institutional memories of libraries and schools are often positive. If people have had positive experiences with libraries, or if their families have had positive experiences with libraries, then the job becomes easier. However, if memories of libraries are tainted by negative experiences with education and schooling, as is the case with many Native peoples, then the job of the library advocate becomes more difficult.

One of the major hurdles that tribal libraries face is convincing the community that libraries today are more than book rooms. Community members may have to be convinced that the library's services are complementary to the growth of the community and its future generations. They may not see the librarian doing all of the tasks that keep the library viable and serve the community, such as providing services for the youth, teaching people how to use technology to find needed information, researching reference questions, or collecting oral histories and tribal knowledge. The skills and training of librarians often go unnoticed.

Resistance may also come from people who believe that knowledge and history should be passed down by the traditional oral/aural means. Although there is no substitute for learning from elders and other family members, the library can serve as the holder of cultural knowledge through collections such as recorded oral histories and tribal documents. Once people understand this, they may be more likely to support the library.

Tribal libraries may face resistance from people who see other services as being more valuable than "a room full of books." They may say that it is more important to serve the people who need food, require assistance in housing, have health conditions, etc. The job of the tribal librarian is to prove to these naysayers that the library can help solve these problems and help move the tribe and its people in a positive direction.

Misconceptions about libraries are a problem for all types of libraries across the country, from academic libraries, to special libraries, to public libraries, to school libraries. Decision makers will not support something that they know little about or do not understand. Stereotypes about libraries and librarians negatively impact a library's attempts to gain more support in the community. In a recent study, perceptions of librarians have described them as unambitious, shy, resistant to change, and adhering to work that is boring and routine.[1] If patrons think that the librarian's job consists of reading books all day and occasionally stamping a book for checkout, then they will need information to understand the value of the library and librarians.

If you are facing some or all of these issues, now is the time to speak up. With budgets always shrinking, decision makers are looking for ways to cut back. Though decision makers may support the library in spirit, they may find it difficult to do so when there are other programs in need of financial assistance. You do not want your community to dismiss the value of the library. What can you do to get the support you need, to get your community behind you so that you can continue the work of the tribal library? It is time to make a plan, get involved, and speak up for the tribal library.

Often the terms *advocacy, marketing, lobbying, public relations*, and *publicity* get confused and are used interchangeably. In *The Visible Librarian: Asserting Your Value with Marketing and Advocacy*, Judith Siess defines marketing as "determining who you serve and with what products"; publicity as "getting the word out that you can help people do their jobs better-cheaper-faster"; and finally, public relations as "talking to people about their needs and your strengths."[2] These distinctions are useful as you begin to think about strategies to become more visible.

Before diving into an advocacy campaign, a library can make use of planning strategies to better understand community needs, goals, needed resources, and communication strategies. This is what Siess calls marketing, otherwise known as understanding your users and determining your products. Even though you may think you know all there is to know about your community, taking time to make a plan to understand your patrons (as well as your nonpatrons) and the need for your services will save time and resources later, and you may be surprised at some of the results.

Tribal libraries may find Sandra Nelson's *The New Planning for Results: A Streamlined Approach* or Fisher and Pride's *Blueprint for Your Library Marketing Plan* good sources to gain some practical library planning skills.[3] Including stakeholders in a strategic planning process may be one of the first steps in gaining their buy-in, as they become more aware of the library and its services through the process.

If you are not doing so already, you will need to gather relevant data and statistics about your services, patrons, and community to share in annual reports and presentations about the library. By collecting data over time, you can demonstrate growth, trends, and needs. For instance, if reference transactions have tripled over a period of time and the number of visitors has significantly increased, you might be able to make the case that the library is certainly being used more by the community, and thus ask for increased financial support. Other data that you can collect include circulation statistics, the number of registered card-holders, program attendance, a daily head count, and website hits. Collecting and sharing relevant data with stakeholders may be one of the most significant activities a tribal library can do to gain support.

At the heart of all advocacy plans, from the simplest to the most elaborate, is getting your message to key decision makers to get them on the side of the tribal library. There are many ways to do this. Following is a short list of tips:

- Get others to speak for the library. Their stories become powerful as they relay how the library has impacted their lives.
- Use every opportunity to tell people about the library and about what you do. This includes taking opportunities to make formal presentations at group meetings or informally mentioning the library at the grocery store, for example.
- Practice becoming a better public speaker. Good formal presentation skills will make a better impression on decision makers.
- Know your stakeholders and their interests. If you are in a smaller community, take advantage of the fact that everyone knows everyone else, and make an extra effort to know the priorities of government officials and decision makers. It is likely that the library can contribute to the goals of the stakeholders.
- Create a relevant and effective publicity campaign. As funds allow, you may find that it is worth investing in some eye-catching and memorable promotional materials.

Advocating and marketing is valueless if the services provided are not worth speaking up for. Strive to provide the best services. Be the best professional you can be. Have the best staff. Provide innovative and useful services. Be seen as *the* place to go for information. Be known as *the* professional for information services, reference services, and public services. Give as well as receive. As a librarian, one of the best things you can give to your patrons and community is the gift of information, which includes information literacy skills, recommendations of books, and showing people how the library can enhance their lives.

Listed below are several recommended readings.

Alman, Susan Webreck. *Crash Course in Marketing for Libraries.* Westport, Conn.: Libraries Unlimited, 2007.

Karp, Rashelle S., ed. *Powerful Public Relations: A How-To Guide for Libraries.* Chicago: American Library Association, 2002.

Reed, Sally Gardner. *Making the Case for Your Library.* New York: Neal-Schuman, 2001.

Turner, Anne M. *Getting Political: An Action Guide for Librarians and Library Supporters.* New York: Neal-Schuman, 1997.

NOTES

1. Shaheen Shaheen and Azim Haider, "Image Problem Even Haunts Hi-Tech Libraries: Stereotypes Associated with Library and Information Professionals in Singapore," *Aslib Proceedings* 60, no. 3 (2008): 229–41

2. Judith A. Siess, *The Visible Librarian: Asserting Your Value with Marketing and Advocacy* (Chicago: American Library Association, 2003), xvi.

3. Sandra Nelson, *The New Planning for Results: A Streamlined Approach* (American Library Association, 2001); Patricia H. Fisher and Marseille M. Pride, *Blueprint for Your Library Marketing Plan: A Guide to Help you Survive and Thrive* (Chicago: American Library Association, 2005).

22

Developing a Staff Development Plan for a Tribal Librarian

Loriene Roy and Janice L. Kowemy

All information professionals are facing great changes—in their patron demographics, patron expectations, resources, and services. To meet these demands, librarians need to constantly refresh acquired skills and retool. This refreshment is important not only for the individual librarian but also for all staff, the library, and its patron services.

The need to continually update skills is seen in competency documents developed by many professional organizations and their units. In the "Competencies for Librarians Serving Youth," the Young Adult Library Services Association (YALSA), one of eleven divisions of the American Library Association (ALA), states that the young adult librarian will be able to "plan for personal and professional growth and career development."[1] The Reference and User Services Association (RUSA) suggests similar continuing education for the reference librarian, who "actively contributes to improving professional practice through engaging in projects with colleagues and enhancing individual skills through independent learning."[2]

A special librarian is "committed to lifelong learning and personal career planning."[3] A law librarian "actively pursues personal and professional growth through continuing education."[4] The continuing education responsibilities for a public librarian working with children are even more explicit. This librarian not only "pursues professional development and continuing education opportunities throughout her/his career," he or she also "participates in local, state, and national professional organizations to strengthen skills, interact with fellow professionals, promote professional association scholarships, and contribute to the library profession" and, specifically, "stays informed of current trends, emerging technologies, issues, and research in librarianship, child development, education, and allied fields."[5] An art librarian is involved in "continuous and proactive learning" as well.[6] Music librarians in management positions are to "ensure that staff continue to receive training by providing access to continuing education and other opportunities for improving skills and knowledge."[7]

Although these competency documents illustrate librarians' individual responsibilities for continuing their education, they only provide general advice, encouragement, and sometimes a requirement to do so. Some professional organizations offer mentoring opportunities and/or leadership training to assist librarians. These include the TALL Texans Leadership Development Institute and Snowbird Leadership Institute.[8] Still, most librarians develop their own plans for keeping up to date. For many, their response is to join and participate in a professional organization. Education and continuous learning is one of ALA's seven key action areas. Its commitment is stated in "Goal Area: Building the Profession" of the organization's latest strategic plan, "ALA Strategic Plan 2011–2015": "through its leadership, ALA ensures the highest quality graduate and continuing education opportunities for librarians and library staff."[9] One of five strategic objectives in this goal area is to "[i]ncrease the availability of and access to continuing education, career development and certification opportunities for librarians, library staff, trustees and library advocates."[10]

Some state library associations, such as the Alaska Library Association, have continuing education plans for their members.[11] In 2005, members of the Texas Library Association (TLA), one of the largest chapters of ALA, stated that their main reason for joining TLA was for continuing education. They identified top content areas for their needs. Many were traditional areas—collection development, reference, public programming, library instruction/information literacy—but they also sought to upgrade their knowledge in management issues, such as personnel/human resource development and technology, especially web design.[12]

The format for continuing education has traditionally included formalized classes and face-to-face attendance at conferences. These approaches still exist and are often preferred, but they only reach those who can afford the time to travel, attend, and pay for such participation. These options are more challenging with tribal librarians working in remote locations, often in single-librarian work settings with limited funding.

Librarians are increasingly turning to other delivery formats—blogs, online seminars, podcasts, online chats, webcasts, and multi-user virtual environments such as Second Life. Librarians have access to other providers of continuing education. These have grown to include vendors, such as SirsiDynix and its offering of the SirsiDynix Institute, and large service initiatives, such as WebJunction.org.[13]

The need to keep up with technology, especially Web 2.0 applications, is a common theme across library literature and conferences. There is far less coverage and advice for librarians on how to organize one's continuing education needs into a concerted plan. Tennant summarizes the typical advice on continuing education: (1) take time to learn, (2) try something new, and (3) stop doing something.[14]

What would a tribal librarian continuing education plan look like? It would be a written document that affirms the mission of the library and identifies the objectives for supporting a library-wide continuous education plan. Such objectives would be time sensitive and measurable. They would describe how continuous education would benefit the tribal community and identify key content areas that staff should explore in furthering their job-related skills and knowledge.

The plan would identify strategies for how the library staff would accomplish this. It would also identify the partners to whom the librarian would turn for this education—such as library and information science programs, state libraries, specific organizations, and continuing education providers. And finally, the plan would summarize how staff would evaluate their learning experiences and share them with their colleagues.

Janice Kowemy, director of the Laguna (K'awaika) Public Library at Laguna, New Mexico, prepared the following staff development plan, which is used as a model document for other tribal libraries in the state of New Mexico.

STAFF DEVELOPMENT PLAN LAGUNA PUBLIC LIBRARY 2008

Purpose
The Laguna Public Library recognizes the important roles played by each staff member and is committed to providing the support and encouragement for library staff to achieve educational opportunities through degreed programs, trainings, workshops, conferences, and networking. It is important to enhance knowledge and the necessary skills of libraries and information to better serve Laguna Pueblo and surrounding communities.

Current staff positions include:

- Library Director/Librarian
- Library Aide (two)

Objectives

1. To provide staff development training that is relevant to the needs of the Laguna Public Library and Laguna Pueblo community.
2. To maintain a current knowledge of emerging technologies, library issues, trends, and community changes.
3. To discover new perspectives in programming and services.
4. To maintain a high standard of customer service and ethics.
5. To maintain staff communication.
6. To add additional staff members as programs and services expand.

To achieve these objectives, the Laguna Public Library will provide staff members with a list of actions that will be beneficial to meeting our vision in staff development.

These specific activities will be provided by the Laguna Public Library with help from the New Mexico State Library and other library associations. They include:

1. Encouraging the use of online databases to read publications on library trends, programming, and services.
2. Providing training on efficient and effective customer service skills and ethics.
3. Visiting local libraries to obtain a perspective of what other librarians are doing in their libraries.
4. Involvement in collection development and strategic planning.
5. Providing emergency response training and evacuation plans for unexpected emergencies.
6. Encouraging travel to local and national conferences, trainings, workshops, and meetings.
7. Taking advantage of resources provided by the New Mexico State Library and Tribal Libraries Program.
8. Participation and commitment to library programs and activities.

To ensure the Laguna Public library is meeting the needs of its staff and their developments while working with the library, periodical meetings will be held to listen to concerns, comments, and answer questions, and engage in new ideas and activities.

NOTES

1. Young Adult Library Association, "YALSA's Competencies for Librarians Serving Youth: Young Adults Deserve the Best," 2010, http://www.ala.org/ala/mgrps/divs/yalsa/profdev/yacompetencies2010.cfm (accessed 16 January 2011).

2. Reference and User Services Association, "Professional Competencies for Reference and User Services Librarians," 2003, http://www.ala.org/ala/mgrps/divs/rusa/resources/guidelines/professional.cfm (accessed 16 January 2011).

3. Special Library Association, Special Committee on Competencies for Special Librarians, "Competencies for Special Librarians of the 21st Century," 2003, http://www.sla.org/content/SLA/professional/meaning/competency.cfm (accessed 16 January 2011).

4. American Association of Law Libraries, "Competencies of Law Librarianship," 2010, http://www.aallnet.org/prodev/competencies.asp (accessed 16 September 2011).

5. Association for Library Service to Children, "Competencies for Librarians Serving Children in Public Libraries," 2009, http://www.ala.org/ala/mgrps/divs/alsc/edcareeers/alsccorecomps/index.cfm (accessed 16 January 2011).

6. Heather Ball and Sara Harrington, "ARLIS/NA Core Competencies for Art Information Professionals," 2009, http://www.arlisna.org/resources/onlinepubs/corecomps.pdf (accessed 16 September 2011).

7. David Hunter, "Core Competencies and Music Librarians," 2002, http://musiclibraryassoc.org/uploadedFiles/Employment_and_Education/Music_Librarianship/Core_Competencies.pdf?n=7658 (accessed 31 August 2008).

8. June Berry, "Texas Accelerated Library Leaders: TALL Texans," *Public Libraries* 39, no. 6 (November/December 2000): 311–13; Teresa Y. Neely and Mark D. Winston, "Snowbird Leadership Institute: Leadership Development in the Profession," *College & Research Libraries* 60, no. 5 (September 1999): 412–25.

9. American Library Association, "Strategic Plan 2011–2015," 2010 http://www.ala.org/ala/aboutala/missionhistory/plan/strategic%20plan%202015%20documents/cd_36.2_2015_strateg.pdf (accessed 16 January 2011).

10. American Library Association, "Strategic Plan 2011–2015."

11. Alaska Library Association, "AkLA Handbook Section VIII: 2 Documents Adopted and/or Endorsed by AkLA: Continuing Education Plan," 2006, http://www.akla.org/handbook/viii-2ce-plan.html (accessed 16 January 2011).

12. Ted Wanner, "Why You Should Check Out Neal-Schuman's Professional Education Network," *Texas Library Journal* 83, no. 4 (Winter 2007): 158–60.

13. "SirsiDynix Institute," 2010, http://www.sirsidynixinstitute.com/ (accessed 16 January 2011); "WebJunction.org," http://www.webjunction.org/1 (accessed 16 January 2011).

14. Roy Tennant, "Three Hard Things," *Library Journal* 132, no. 11 (June 15, 2007): 30.

23

Time Management for the Tribal Librarian

Loriene Roy

Regardless of where the tribal librarian is employed, he or she probably is carrying an excessive workload. He or she serves multiple roles—as collection developer and organizer, program planner and creator, fund-raiser and grant writer, library services evaluator, literacy officer, and Native language facilitator, to name a few. Success often breeds more responsibility, as community members will increasingly turn to a hard-working, productive colleague with requests for more assistance. If he or she is working on tribal lands, the librarian is likely a key participant in cultural events and is on call to provide any assistance requested by the tribal council. Time management becomes a necessity and is even more imperative if the tribal librarian is running a one-person operation. It is more than a matter of arriving at work earlier, staying later, or taking work home; it is a matter of employing strategies for success.

Heike Bruch and Sumatra Ghosal identified three traps that prevent managers from being productive: demands, constraints, and nonaction.[1] They observed that only one out of ten managers acts in purposeful ways, that is, achieves his or her purpose. Those who are successful rely on two personal characteristics: the energy to accomplish the task and the focus to concentrate on it. And it is their view that managers can train themselves to be more productive.

Time management is a planning process that library employees can use to prioritize needed work tasks to make the most efficient use of time. The goal of time management is to assist the librarian in spending his or her time on key areas while avoiding wasting time on less productive tasks. It involves seeing the big picture. Time management not only helps the librarian get work done, it helps conserve human energy, allowing for a personal life as well. Thus, time management is a boon to staff retention through helping individuals avoid burnout.

What does time management encompass? It is a philosophy and action plan to

1. organize your work area,
2. organize your tasks,
3. organize your library public spaces,
4. organize your staff,
5. organize your patrons, and
6. organize your future.

People often follow their own time management strategies, the most common of which is list making. People set limits on the items on their daily to-do list—some indicate that the list should have no more than two items, while others recommend listing five daily tasks. Coupled with a calendar of due dates and lists of weekly and monthly objectives, these simple methods help keep the librarian on track and attentive to daily assignments, while being mindful of longer range responsibilities.

Develop a strategy for dealing with paper, especially incoming mail. J'aimé Foust recommends separating paper areas: the daily planner, the address book or rolodex, action files, and disposal in the wastebasket. Action files have content that is needed often, including the to-do file with an action pending subfile, a file of outgoing papers, a business file, a file of items that need to be read and then saved in reference files, and files that contain content related to special projects or activities.[2]

Pamela Bacon recommends using three baskets on a rolling cart to sort incoming material. One basket is for items "To Do Now," another basket for items "To Do Later," and the third basket with material "To File."[3]

Time management also involves becoming aware of oneself. Productive individuals are attentive to their energy levels and are mindful of whether they are morning, afternoon, or evening people. They attempt difficult, complicated tasks when their energies are high. They attend to more routine, generalized tasks when their energies lag. Make effective use of small units of time. You may find that you can accomplish a great deal by devoting even five minutes to a difficult task. This may be a better use of time than devoting an hour or more to the same activity. Thus, part of the process of time management is organizing your workday. You can minimize being buffeted from one emergency or interruption to another while focusing on accomplishing your day-to-day objectives.

Be aware of time-wasting activities. If you frequently lose your keys, for example, then routinize the steps in storing your keys. If you spend time searching for misplaced passwords, then incorporate a strategy for recording them in a safe place for easy access. Much successful time management is really effective information retrieval.

Sometimes librarians need help reflecting on how they spend their work time. A simple workflow analysis involves setting a random alarm mechanism such as a beeper to sound at various times during the day. The librarian then records what he or she is doing at the time that the alarm goes off. Years ago, a busy law librarian gathered these data over a six-week period for a student in a graduate class I taught. In analyzing the results, the librarian found that she was often photocopying or walking to deliver items. She reflected that these often time-wasting activities were part of her comfort patterns and then adjusted her work activities to batch trips or delegated these tasks, finding other ways to deliver material or satisfy photocopy requests.

Just saying "no" is also a strategy that one can learn. It is sometimes difficult to ascertain which offers one should accept, which offers will come again, and which are once-in-a-career, not-to-be-missed opportunities. Bacon recommends that the best strategy is responding to a request by saying, "Let me think about it—I'll get back to you."[4]

Time management also means reserving some time for yourself. Organizing includes scheduling your time. An open door policy sometimes results in an open interruption policy. Make sure that you attend to some necessary work before you meet with staff or the public. This will give you the boost and encouragement that you have accomplished some important background steps during your day in addition to meeting and working with people.

Consider time management part of your workplace wellness strategy. Save time for refreshment: stay hydrated, eat healthy, and exercise. Be aware of your library's sick leave and health benefits. Stay home when you are sick. It is better to recuperate over a short time than to have a lingering health concern. Make sure that your workplace is conducive to staff health. Review the workplace wellness materials, including the workplace wellness inventory, available through the ALA-Allied Professional Association (ALA-APA).[5]

Modern work life is often full of scheduled meetings. Consider how to make your meetings more effective. Members of the American Library Association can receive assistance at "Making the Meeting."[6] This content includes podcasts and text tipsheets in English and Spanish on topics including foundation building; planning and agenda design; the roles of the meeting chair; avoiding chaotic, adversarial, and aimless meetings; and key points related to rules of order and taking minutes.

Some time-saving tips are simple and can be incorporated overnight if not immediately. The following tips are just a sample of energy-saving tactics that some librarians employ:

1. Circulation history is your friend. According to F. W. Lancaster, past use or circulation of an item in a library's collection is an excellent predictor of future use.[7] Take advantage of this adage by placing newly returned items on a book cart near the circulation desk. Add a sign on the book cart that reads, "Good Reads!" You then only need to shelve the books when the cart fills.
2. Place newly donated paperbacks on a table under a sign that reads, "Paperback exchange! Take a book, leave a book." This serves as a continual book

sale of sorts without money changing hands or needed storage or organization of donations.

3. Save filling out overdue notifications. Construct a "wishing well" donation drop. Add a sign that reads, "Please leave a donation if you think your books are overdue."
4. Plagued by continual visitors who want to socialize during times you need to work? Save some task for your visitors. They will decide to help or will decide to cut their work-time visits short!
5. Build work coalitions. A high school or community group can volunteer to set up a display or exhibit in the library. A technologically skilled student may volunteer to teach computer classes. This saves you time and resources and is a good way to draw more people into the library.
6. Leave a "next to do note" on your desk or calendar. This will help you to immediately orient your thinking to the next task.

In his landmark book *Look to the Mountain*, Dr. Greg Cajete describes how indigenous peoples find fulfillment in life through a cycle of actions. These actions start with being and move through asking, seeking, making, having, sharing, and celebrating.[8] Do not forget to celebrate your continuing success.

NOTES

1. Heike Bruch and Sumatra Ghoshal, *A Bias for Action: How Effective Managers Harness Their Willpower, Achieve Results, and Stop Wasting Time* (Boston: Harvard Business School Press, 2004), 90, 111.

2. J'aimé L. Foust, "Dewey Need to Get Organized? Part 2," *Book Report* 19, no. 3 (November/December 2000): 23–25, 86.

3. Pamela Bacon, "Quit Playing Catch-Up," *School Library Journal* 45, no. 6 (June 2000): 35.

4. Bacon, "Quit Playing Catch-Up."

5. ALA-APA, "Join the Circle of Wellness@ Your Library," 2008, http://ala-apa.org/wellness/ (accessed 8 September 2010).

6. ALA, Association of College & Research Libraries, "Making the Meeting: Resources for Conducting Effective Meetings," 2008, http://www.ala.org/ala/mgrps/divs/acrl/resources/makingthemeeting/index.cfm (accessed 9 September 2010).

7. F. W. Lancaster, *The Measurement and Evaluation of Library Services* (Arlington, Va.: Information Resources Press, 1977), 181.

8. Gregory Cajete, *Look to the Mountain: An Ecology of Indigenous Education* (Skyland, N.C.: Kivaki Press, 1994), 71.

24

Accreditation Through the Lens of a Tribal Museum

Anne McCudden

INTRODUCTION

The Seminole Tribe of Florida's Ah-Tah-Thi-Ki Museum opened August 21, 1997, after almost ten years of planning. The facility sits on sixty-six acres of land within the Big Cypress Seminole Indian Reservation in the middle of the Florida Everglades. The majority of the property is taken up by a fifty-five-acre-plus Cypress Dome that is accessible by visitors along a raised mile-long boardwalk. We employ, on average, fifty full- and part-time staff and host an annual college-level intern program in four subdisciplines. The museum holds approximately 12,000 permanent collection items. Its archives operates a non-lending library and a research facility that is open to the public. The material culture collections are also available for research purposes. They represent the history and culture of the Seminole people and, in a broader sense, the Native American cultures of the southeastern United States. The museum's programming includes permanent and traveling exhibits, community outreach, and educational activities for all ages.

In early 2005, the staff of the museum decided to apply for accreditation from the American Association of Museums (AAM). In April 2009, the Seminole Tribe of Florida's Ah-Tah-Thi-Ki Museum was granted the honor of being the first tribally owned and operated museum in the United States to have achieved full accreditation from the AAM. As is commonly known, the process of achieving accreditation is no easy task. Regardless of whether you are talking about a hospital, a law enforcement agency, a school, or any other institution, the steps involved are numerous and rigorous. I would like to take the opportunity in this chapter to illuminate some of the major steps our institution took to complete the process and why we decided to embark on such a journey. I have broken down these steps to indicate the areas that we needed to address most urgently or with which we needed the most assistance. I would also like to point out that without three things—humility, patience, and determination—the staff of the museum and the governing authority of the Seminole Tribe of Florida would likely never have met this goal.

EMBRACING TECHNOLOGY

Without a doubt, one of the biggest challenges we faced during this process was the effort needed to get us into the twenty-first century. It may be indicative of people over forty years of age, or it may be more of a personal choice, but we found out fairly quickly that one area in which our institution needed to change was our grasp and use of technology. Most people might think that this would pertain mostly to the areas of collections and exhibits, but in reality, each and every division within the museum realized that there was a need for some sort of hardware and/or software in order to operate more efficiently. We implemented software and hardware in our operations, collections, exhibits, development, retail, and membership divisions, and each for separate reasons. In table 24.1, I have outlined some of the technological tools that we introduced or are now using. The learning curves and implementation schedules for each item varied and depended greatly on the staff who were directly involved with the project and whether the item was a perfect fit for us or not. I have found that as much help as these things are, there is always a degree of customization for each institution so that the product works at its highest capacity and the staff can and want to make use of it.

It also became apparent to us that the final decision about whether we would purchase and put into use a new technology depended on whether our old process (if any) was sufficient as well as how much the new endeavor would cost. We also considered such questions as whether it would be obsolete in the near future. Given that it has taken us almost five years to implement all of the above items, it should be clear that these things take considerable time and effort to initiate and implement.

What is not so clear, however, is how these products affect the bottom line of the museum. As far as return on investment goes, each product differs greatly. It is difficult to argue against putting items like this into use, but there are those who will try. There will always be naysayers who insist that the time and energy needed to transition from one system to another far outweigh the benefits gained, but even as those battles continue, it is important to not lose sight of the ultimate goals of any area: collecting accurate data, storing those data, and using those data to run the most efficient, productive operation possible.

Table 24.1. Ah-Tah-Thi-Ki Museum Implemented Technology 2004–2009

Technology	Use	Previous Process
	Development Division	
MarketingPilot	Tracks accounts, ad space, source codes, budget	Excel
PastPerfect	Membership database (funds, demographics, retention)	FileMaker Pro
BusinessMap	Tracks zip codes (demographics, occurrences)	Word of mouth
Quicken POS	Point of sale software (sales, inventory, sales trends, vendors)	Manual cash register
	Operations Division	
Access	Tracks pest occurrences across the property	None
IFAS	Pest identification analysis	None
	Collections Division	
PastPerfect	Collection management (accessions, loans, exhibits, oral histories)	Embark
Distakka	Physical storage of DVDs/CDs, with electronic retrieval capabilities	CD binders
	Programming Division	
SmartDraw	Autocad based design software for laying out galleries and rooms	Hand drawings
Artifax	Scheduling software (personnel, resources, room use, group type)	Paper files
SurveyMonkey	Web-based survey design and response tracking	Paper files
	Administration	
Access	Employee database (disciplinary actions, reviews, personal info)	Paper files
SkillPath	Tests potential applicants on various software programs	None
StatsTrek	Tracks web statistics	None
Google Analytics	Tracks web statistics	None
RedBeam Asset Tracker	Asset management tracking software	Excel
Shared network folders	All Access document storage	Individual hard drives
Shared network calendars	Accessible calendars	Individual calendars

ORGANIZATIONAL SHIFTS

One of the most emotionally charged issues that came up as we plowed our way through the accreditation process was the organizational reshuffling that was needed. When we first started this process, the museum had a strategically impaired "flat" organizational chart that hampered communication and went against a proper chain of command. There are essentially two functions to an organizational chart: showing who reports to whom and helping the staff understand delegation of authority and chain of command.

Although most people seem to fully understand why organizational charts exist, fewer people are comfortable with what happens when changes occur to these charts. Besides a person's job title and salary, the next most important value to an employee is where he or she sits on an "org" chart and, yet more important, who sits above and below. However, what employees should be focused on is what areas are being delineated by the chart and whether the workflow and structure are functional.

Upon first inspection of our existing organizational chart, our incoming executive director noticed that the sheer shape of the chart indicated a problem. Organizational charts should not be flat! There are very few businesses (for profit or not) that can function efficiently when more than seven people report to any one person. Using the knowledge that we gained from our Incident Command Structure (ICS) training, we accepted the fact that the optimal number of direct reports for any one supervisor is between five and seven. Of course this did not mean that we just moved positions and staff so that each supervisor had the optimal number of people. First we had to condition ourselves to look at the structure of the museum *not* as it had been laid out but as it *should* be. Let me give you an example. For years prior to this organizational overhaul, we had a high-level position that was responsible for everything from hiring a plumber to keeping time sheets. From this, we came to realize that one person should not be responsible for such disparate tasks, and we changed the position. Stepping outside of our comfort zone and looking at what each position was *supposed* to do instead of what it *had been* doing, we started down the road toward change. No longer was the answer "because that's the way we've always done it" acceptable. Once we backed away from our prior bad habits, we were able to realign people into the right position.

As we looked at what the main "divisions" (this term undoubtedly varies from museum to museum) should be, we realized that our chart was becoming more of an equilateral than an isosceles triangle. Over the next two to three years, we altered our chart at least five or six times, although we never did so because of personalities or attitudes. I found out rather quickly that to make an organizational move based on whom someone works well with or who likes to do certain tasks is a monumental mistake. Organizational shifts and restructuring should always take place because of either planned growth or, under more unfortunate circumstances, budget shortfalls. In the last year or so, we have made only minute changes to our organizational flow. Now when we consider making a change, we always ask ourselves if the move makes sense or, as we like to ask ourselves, "Round peg, round hole?" We try to make sure that we are moving positions around because we have to rather than because we want to.

Now that we have a fully functional organizational chart, I do find that we refer to it more and more often. Whether it is a new employee orientation or an outside agency wanting to see the chart, we use it often as a tool. Another point is that the accreditation process didn't tell us *how* to design an organizational chart; it simply asked for a copy of the present version. Looking at our version made us reflect on how it was not functioning very well. I found it very interesting that what the accreditation process does is simply ask you to provide what you have. It does not tell you how to assess what you have or design and implement what you need. An institution has to go through that process on its own.

LONG-RANGE THINKING

Planning is not an area that most professionals look *forward* to, no pun intended. You would think, however, that museum professionals might naturally have an inclination to look toward the future and back at the past, since they are so often responsible for recording both views, but that is not always the case. Too often, we found that the staff had an adequate knowledge of what their daily duties were in order to meet minimal functions, but that long-range goals were harder for them to bring into focus. One of the first things that our division-level staff did as a newly organized institution was to meet off-site and tackle the existing mission statement. We soon found out that the museum had in fact had two previous versions of a mission statement, but that no one knew what they were, and in fact it took some time to locate them. We also discovered that they had not always been referred to as "mission" statements, but rather as "museum philosophy" or "statement of purpose." I realize that there will be those who think that minutiae such as this could not possibly cause an institution to run poorly or inefficiently, but they could not be more mistaken. I myself had only limited exposure to the ideas of planning, mission statements, internal analysis, etc., before coming on board at this museum, and the rest of the executive-level staff was similarly unprepared. This of course made for a slightly bumpy road.

Strategic planning as a whole is not an easy or smooth process. It requires a lot of introspection, self-analysis, transparency, and humility, and there is no one agreed-upon way to go about the process. Once again, the AAM inquires whether a museum is engaged in active planning but does not dictate how it should occur. The AAM asks that a museum have a long-range plan, but that can be a very broad concept. I have seen long-range plans that were a couple of paragraphs long and others that were voluminous and had detailed work plans accompanying them. As was the case with so many other changes that we went through, the planning process evolved over a three-year-plus period. We are now at the point where we have a functional fiscal work plan and a three- to five-year strategic plan.

A QUESTION OF GOVERNANCE

One common misperception about the accreditation process is that if you are not a large common type of museum (art, science, childrens, etc.), you will struggle with answering the questions or will not have the appropriate types of staffing, budget, or facilities to fit the bill. In our case, we are a good example of a mix of common and uncommon. We fit the bill of a small museum as far as collections, exhibit space, and overall scope, but we are along the lines of a larger museum in terms of our staffing, facilities, and programming. Then there was the question of governance. In this part of the accreditation process, our museum was most definitely not going to be able to simply check a box and move along. It took a bit of explaining, but eventually we were able to succinctly explain how we operate as a tribal department within the entire tribal government. Again, just a slight deviance from the normal questionnaire, but the process provides for this. When accrediting bodies say "attach additional pages as necessary," they mean exactly that. In fact, taking the time to really think through how we are governed has proved invaluable. To this day, I have referred back to that description countless times when asked the same question.

ACCEPTING THE CHALLENGE AND LOOKING AHEAD

I believe that the accreditation process as a whole has enlightened our staff and our governing authority about what it is we do on a daily basis and what we plan to do for the next three to five years. When it was all said and done, we had spent almost four years taking a very inward look at ourselves. We thoroughly inspected every area of the museum, from collections, to operations, to membership. This has provided us with the tools to get these things done and, more important, it has prepared us for keeping up with our assigned goals. The reactions from staff and outsiders to these upcoming goals and how we are to achieve them have varied. What follows after accreditation is a real sense of commitment, and that has undoubtedly been a stumbling block for some involved. It appears that might also be one of the things that keep museums from seeking accreditation. In reality, there is no commitment that the AAM specifically asks of the museum. Rather, it is more of an internal commitment that is made between the staff and the institution. Everyone must agree to do the work in the allotted time, within an approved budget, and to meet the overall mission of the museum. Once that agreement has been made, what remains is for the policies and procedures to be adhered to. Within any museum, there is always a struggle with staff keeping their eyes on the overarching, long-range goals while still making sure the exhibits are current, the lights are on, and the collections are safe, but it can be done.

PERCEIVED AND REAL VALUE

Why bother? That seems to be the most common question I run into when speaking about the accreditation process and what it meant to our museum. When confronted with this, I usually spout off about how beneficial and challenging the process was and how much more professional and efficient we are because of it. But the more I think about it, the more I feel that the answer should be a bit more personal. I can say with a fair degree of certainty that all levels of our staff have been introduced to substantive ways to go about their work duties and, in a broader sense, their careers as museum professionals. There is also the value that the tribe and its members receive by supporting the museum in this goal. One way that the Seminoles make a statement about their history and culture is through the museum—*their* museum. By allowing the museum staff to take on this challenge, we took that to mean that the tribal government and members were in support of us using this tool to protect and preserve their heritage. It is a tool that was most definitely worth using.

25

TLAM: Creating Student-Driven Indigenous LIS at the University of Wisconsin–Madison

Christina L. P. W. Johnson, Catherine H. Phan, and Omar Poler

In the summer of 2008, we set off on our first trip to Red Cliff. A small Anishinabe (Ojibwe) reservation, the Red Cliff community is Wisconsin's northernmost place. A six-hour drive from Madison, it is nearly surrounded by Lake Superior's south shore on the tip of the Bayfield Peninsula. As graduate students at the University of Wisconsin–Madison (UW–Madison) School of Library and Information Studies (SLIS), we had recently received word that the community's library faced imminent closure. With the support of Red Cliff's director of tribal operations, we started a summer-long community interest assessment that drifted through the fall and into early winter. On our trips, we met dozens of community members and listened to their thoughts about the library's future. Our project culminated in a well-attended community meeting and a written report presented to the tribal council.

At the time, however, we could not have predicted how much the Red Cliff experience would ultimately reshape our education. A new course eventually blossomed from our initial service learning experience. Known as the Tribal Libraries, Archives, and Museums (TLAM) Project, ten graduate students, three academic advisers, and dozens of experts came together over a semester to help each other better understand the questions initially posed by our work with Red Cliff's library. Through both the conventional university classroom and lots of visiting, we patched together a new course on tribal information issues that emphasized learning through personal experience and relationships. This chapter describes the ongoing story of TLAM—and hopefully provides one potential learning model for library and information science (LIS) programs interested in incorporating tribal libraries, archives, and museums in their curricula.

FROM THE UW–MADISON TO RED CLIFF

Located at the UW–Madison, SLIS is a two-year, forty-two-credit master's degree program in all areas of librarianship. SLIS produces a new cohort of academic, public, special, and school librarians every year. It also offers a small, yet extremely successful, certificate program in archives and records management. Though small compared to many, SLIS nevertheless consistently ranks within the top ten American Library Association (ALA)–accredited LIS programs. This is not by happenstance. Until August 2009, Dr. Louise Robbins, a former small-town mayor with a fiery passion for social justice, directed the school. During her twelve years of leadership, SLIS was committed to diversity issues in LIS education. It was Dr. Robbins's activism and willingness to experiment that allowed for our course on tribal libraries, archives, and museums. The support of faculty and staff was essential.

The TLAM journey began, so to speak, in service learning. Following a presentation on the Red Cliff library and its likely closure, Dr. Robbins invited Jim Trojanowski, the director of the Northern Waters Library System, and Joe Bresette, Red Cliff's director of tribal operations, to discuss its future. In the talks, Bresette described their library as a "cookie cutter model" that provided no more than "stereotypical services." With the support of Tribal Chair Rose Gurnoe-Soulier and other community leaders, the conversation eventually turned to an interest assessment designed to gauge Red Cliff's own vision. After securing funds from the Kauffman Entrepreneurship Community Internship Program and the SLIS Second Century Fund, the SLIS team—three graduate students and two faculty advisers—traveled eight times from June through December to conduct interviews. The project culminated in a well-attended gathering in October 2008 at which community members laughed, teased, and shared their respective dreams for the library.

In the short term, Red Cliff community members expressed hopes to reopen their library in its current location and secure funding for a librarian who could advocate for its importance within the community. In the long term, though, they expressed a desire for an entirely new facility to better serve their needs and interests. The envisioned facility would not only function as a library, but include an archive and museum to provide reliable storage, maintenance, and access to community documents and artifacts. In addition, a new building would incorporate a large gathering space to accommodate various programs, functions, and ceremonies—including serving as a wake house. The possible inclusion of a wellness center and art gallery was also discussed. We compiled the findings in a written report and then presented it to the Red Cliff tribal council. A new library committee was appointed shortly afterward.

TLAM BEGINS

Though our presentation to the community marked the completion of the assessment project, it was only the beginning of our learning process. As individual graduate students and as representatives of SLIS, we were fully committed to continuing the relationship established between Red Cliff and the UW–Madison to assist the tribe in attaining their vision. Inspired and energized by the excited tribal members embracing the image of a library that served as the vibrant center for the community, we discussed how we could continue building upon the momentum of the previous months. In our discussions, we realized there was much more to learn and understand to better serve the unique needs of the Red Cliff community. What kinds of library models already exist that might help Red Cliff in its vision? How are other Wisconsin bands and tribes serving their communities? How have tribal libraries come to exist and operate within the framework of the conventional public library system? How have the unique histories and cultures of American Indian nations affected the way that library services are delivered and used in their communities?

Our service learning experience with Red Cliff exposed the gaps in our knowledge and understanding of indigenous information issues. Moreover, it illustrated a missing component of our LIS education. A course on tribal libraries, archives, and museums had never been offered before at SLIS—so why not propose a course of our own? Our proposal was heartily approved by Dr. Robbins, and the course was created for the following 2009 spring semester as a group independent study. It would be not only a self-education on tribal cultural institutions, but also an opportunity to develop a new course for the school. The class was driven by the knowledge and backgrounds of our original core group of students—two of whom had certificates in American Indian studies and preexisting relationships with indigenous communities. One was a Sokaogon Chippewa Community tribal member. The course succeeded and grew in multifaceted ways because of the diversity of our entire group—including the members who had no previous experience with American Indian issues at all.

Our work started well before the beginning of the semester and was an ongoing process throughout the term. After securing additional funding to support our travel to the various communities in the state, we dove into the difficult task of condensing an expansive topic into a sixteen-week syllabus. We researched and reached out to experts for advice on key materials and resources, drew on the knowledge of campus experts on American Indian issues, and initiated new relationships with Wisconsin tribal communities to learn about their cultural institutions. We designed the course to incorporate class conversations, community visits, and participation in relevant campus, local, and national events. Though it was student-led, SLIS faculty and staff fully supported TLAM through their willingness to experiment. Developing this strong relationship with the department was essential in advocating for the importance of indigenous information issues at SLIS. Utilizing existing relationships, as well as encouraging the creation of new ones with tribal cultural institution professionals, community members, professors, and potential funding sources, also proved important to our success.

In fact, relationships have been indispensable for TLAM. We realized that the continuation of these relationships—and the outcome of the entire project—would require more than an independent study. In a two-year LIS program, the course had to be supported by more than a group of enthusiastic students; it had to be endorsed at an institutional level. We made a presentation to the SLIS Curriculum Committee, advocating for the permanent institutionalization of our new course. It was overwhelmingly well received. The committee approved TLAM as a topics course, and it was placed on the course schedule for the following spring. Topics courses at SLIS address important issues not addressed in sufficient depth elsewhere. They also often function as a segue for relatively new classes in the curriculum or those not offered every semester. Inclusion of TLAM in the course schedule was an immensely satisfying recognition of the importance of the topic; we were thrilled by the enthusiastic support. Moreover, its approval as a topics course was an important first step toward full acceptance of TLAM within the curriculum. Its approval not only marked our department's commitment to American Indian information issues, but the possibility of the wider university's recognition of tribal cultural institutions.

PEDAGOGY

Our success in creating TLAM was not necessarily unique; we believe it can be done anywhere. The knowledge, resources, materials, and enthusiasm all exist to develop a similar course, but incorporating an unconventional pedagogy will likely be necessary. We used two approaches: conventional coursework that incorporated weekly readings and lectures as well as personal relationships. Without being fully aware of it, we employed service learning methodologies to learn. Our classroom work often only supplemented our experiential learning. This was necessary for many reasons. Tribal libraries, archives, and museums exist within a tremendously complicated context; few LIS faculty have the academic background to teach American Indian history, law, language, art, and current issues. And perhaps even more important, working with indigenous peoples from within a university setting is inescapably a cross-cultural experience. Students should strive to understand, respect, and practice a pedagogy more appropriate for American Indian information issues, a pedagogy that emphasizes *process* and *protocol*.

Unexpectedly, the dispersed nature of class materials and resources proved to be an opportunity to reach well beyond LIS education. As library educators Yontz and de la Peña McCook have observed, service learning "facilitat[es] meaningful collaboration across disciplinary lines."[1] This is especially true regarding tribal libraries, archives, and museums. To understand them, it is necessary to know a little about a lot—especially for those who lack previous experience with American Indian issues. With the help of professors and graduate students from disciplines and departments across the UW–Madison, TLAM began with a crash course on American Indian history, epistemology, language, law, and art. With students themselves coordinating and scheduling the classes, a panel of speakers offered their expertise on salient topics such as treaty rights, boarding schools, self-representation in art and museums, oral history, and the health information needs of American Indian communities. The creation of the class not only allowed students to work collaboratively in locating the pertinent resources and scheduling speakers, it brought together a new network of individuals interested in tribal libraries, archives, and museums. Importantly, LIS functioned as the interdisciplinary center. As one guest speaker remarked with surprise, "Who would have thought that the best American Indian Studies class on campus was in the Library School?"

In learning about tribal libraries, archives, and museums, we also had to look far beyond the UW–Madison. In preparing the class, we had the opportunity to correspond with Kelly Webster. A cataloger at Boston College and past president of the American Indian Library Association, she reinforced our desire to incorporate travel and relationship building with the other communities. She urged us to pay attention to more than just books and journal articles. Paraphrasing Loriene Roy in the introduction to *Library Services to Indigenous Populations: Viewpoints & Resources,* she advised us to "continue learning about tribal librarianship through the oral history, lives, and actions of the many brilliant and visionary indigenous librarians who are maintaining, developing, and extending Native library services."[2] It was true. Our most meaningful learning occurred as we traveled to the communities. Sometimes over snow-covered and slippery highways, we visited six of eleven federally recognized nations in Wisconsin. Each trip helped us better understand and contextualize the services that tribal libraries, archives, and museums provide their communities. But perhaps even more important, the visits showed us that "living part." As Gregory Cajete has written, "understanding the depth of relationships and the significance of participation in all aspects of life are the keys to traditional American Indian education."[3] Through our new relationships, we not only intellectually comprehended the importance of tribal libraries, archives, and museums; we felt it.

Personal relationships are more important than a semester-long class. They require special care, consideration, and sometimes even long-term planning. For TLAM, an unconventional course that relied almost exclusively on a non-hierarchical informal network of learners and teachers, this was especially true. Every experience provided a new opportunity to be a grateful host or respectful guest. Our teachers' time was a gift to be respected and reciprocated to the best of our abilities. We attempted to express our thankfulness and appreciation through small gifts, meals, and just simply by keeping in touch after our visits. It is important to think about the long term. To be valuable community partners, we wanted our relationships to exist well beyond a single semester and for tribal librarians, archivists, and museum professionals to benefit from their relationship with SLIS for years. Relationships demand a commitment to each other's mutual needs.

CONCLUSION

TLAM has had long-term benefits. We are convinced that an unconventional course on indigenous information issues is critical to recruiting more Native students to LIS education. Among many things, our experience provided a semester-long argument about how libraries, archives, and museums are crucial within tribal communities. Moreover, it showed that LIS can be culturally reinterpreted to appropriately serve American Indian communities. Our experience also proved that LIS can interest more than graduate students. Undergraduate students—even high school students—have expressed strong interests in being involved. The course also provides an enduring framework for the mutually beneficial sharing of skills and resources between tribal cultural institution professionals and LIS students. For instance, following our first semester, two TLAM students spent the summer volunteering and working with the Oneida Cultural Heritage Department's archival collection. Other tribal librarians and archivists across Wisconsin have also expressed an interest in student assistance.

In hindsight, we now see our experience as an opportunity for LIS students to take ownership of their education. Moreover, the partnerships between LIS schools and tribal libraries, archives, and museums can ensure that tribal information professionals have a persistent voice in the education of future librarians and archivists. Taking learning out of the classroom and into communities makes LIS more relevant, more engaging, and ultimately more meaningful. We hope our story might inspire students to advocate for the creation and implementation of their own successful TLAM. Also, we hope that by sharing our story, more discussions will emerge to help improve and sustainably continue this work, not just here but in LIS schools everywhere.

NOTES

1. Elaine Yontz and Kathleen de la Peña McCook, "Service-Learning and LIS Education," *Journal of Library and Information Science Education* 44, no. 1 (Winter 2003): 62.

2. Kelly Webster, "Re: Suggestions on Tribal Library Resources?" e-mail to Omar Poler, 18 November 2008; Loriene Roy and A. Arro Smith, "Preface," in *Library Services to Indigenous Populations: Viewpoints & Resources*, ed. Kelly Webster (Chicago: American Library Association, Office of Literacy and Outreach Services, 2005).

3. Gregory Cajete, *Look to the Mountain: An Ecology of Indigenous Education* (Skyland, N.C.: Kivakí Press, 1994), 26.

Index

About the Contributors

Karen Alexander served as the library/legacy archives director for the Miami Tribe of Oklahoma from October 1989 to January 2010. As part of her job there, she administered grants from the U.S. Dept. of Education, the National Archives and Records Administration, and the Institute of Museum and Library Services, and served as the Tribe's U.S. Department of Housing and Urban Development (HUD) director for three projects, resulting in additional knowledge in remodeling, construction land reclamation, and water well drilling. She wrote the first language grant that was funded for the Miami and began their first archives. With grants in 1995, she founded the Connecting Help and Resources Linking Indians Effectively (CHARLIE) Library Network, which connects seven of the tribal libraries in northeast Oklahoma. In 1997, she graduated with a master of library and information studies from the University of Oklahoma and continues to benefit from her professors' advice there. With Teresa Runnels, she cofounded Oklahoma Issues, a statewide tribal library advocacy group that strives to encourage all tribes to network on common library issues through a listserv, maintained by Ms. Runnels. A second group, also cofounded with Teresa Runnels with the assistance of Jan Bryant, then president of the Oklahoma Library Association (OLA), and continued by the next two presidents of the organization, is the OLA Tribal Libraries, Archives, and American Indian Collection Ad Hoc Committee. Its focus is to assist tribal staff, primarily in libraries, who may wear many hats to work together, providing training, sharing information, and mentoring as needed to better serve populations that are underserved. Appointed by two governors, she currently serves on the Oklahoma Historical Records Advisory Board.

Daniel Alonzo is the photo archivist at the Austin History Center in Austin, Texas. Before returning to Austin, Daniel was the archivist and librarian at the

Old Jail Art Center in Albany, Texas. The Old Jail is a converted museum space from an 1877 limestone jail built on the western frontier of Texas. The jail opened in 1980 as a fine arts museum and has expanded many times to include an art research library as well as the local historical archives. Prior to his experience in Albany, Daniel was in graduate school getting his master of science in information studies from the School of Information at the University of Texas at Austin. While in school, Daniel was a teaching assistant for Dr. Loriene Roy and spent a summer digitizing archival material at the National Museum of American History in Washington, D.C.

Sarah Arriaga recently received her master of science in information studies from the University of Texas at Austin's School of Information, where she was Dr. Loriene Roy's teaching assistant (TA). She has completed projects establishing company archives at the OCLC Corporate Library in Dublin, Ohio; at Southwest Airlines in Dallas, Texas; and at ExxonMobil Upstream Research Company's Technical Information Center in Houston, Texas. As Dr. Roy's TA, Sarah had the opportunity to visit seven tribal libraries in New Mexico in preparation for Operation Teen Book Drop.

Victoria Beatty coordinated the Instruction/Distance Library Services program at Diné College from 2004 to 2008. She joined the Diné College Libraries in 2004 as instruction/distance services librarian, a new position created to bring the nascent information literacy program, as well as basic library services, to five community centers that lacked access to a physical library. Equipped with little more than a map and the insights gained from Cheryl Metoyer's book *Gatekeepers in Ethnolinguistic Communities*, she traveled a circuit of nearly five hundred miles, working with students, faculty, and staff at the college's Arizona centers in Window Rock, Ganado, Chinle, Kayenta, and Tuba City. Within a year, she had earned her place as the students' personal librarian at the community centers as well as on the main campus at Tsaile. She developed a culturally relevant information literacy curriculum and worked collaboratively with faculty to design assignments that integrated information literacy in relevant ways. The position of instruction/distance services librarian was unique among the tribal colleges during the three years she held the position. As of this printing, there is no comparable position at Diné College or at any of the other tribal college libraries. Beatty is currently a librarian with the Albuquerque/Bernalillo Library System, and she blogs about her experiences at http://www.victoriabeatty.org/.

Anjali Bhasin is currently a graduate student at the University of Texas at Austin School of Information. She has worked with If I Can Read, I Can Do Anything and Operation Teen Book Drop to help with the distribution of books to Native teenagers. She is the recipient of a University of Texas at Austin Diversity Mentoring Fellowship and an American Library Association (ALA) Spectrum Scholar. Prior to attending graduate school, she worked as the assistant director of the Associated Students of Madison at the University of Wisconsin–Madison and as a community organizer for the League of Conservation Voters.

Bonnie Biggs is professor emeritus and was a founding librarian at California State University–San Marcos. After her retirement from the Library, Biggs served as the university's tribal liaison to help strengthen relationships between the university and local tribal communities, establishing a Tribal Communities Task Force and Native Advisory Board to the President. Biggs worked for over twenty-five years in the area of tribal library development. As project director of the Library of California Tribal Library Census and Needs Assessment, Biggs brought tribal library needs to the attention of the California State Library. She developed a library graduate school internship program that serves tribal libraries, founded the Native Libraries Round Table within the California Library Association, and organized the first State Library–sponsored California tribal library workshop. She served as President of the American Indian Library Association (AILA) and in 2006 received AILA's Distinguished Lifetime Service Award. In 2005, Biggs was awarded the Distinguished Service Award by the eighteen tribes of the Southern California Tribal Chairmen's Association. In retirement, Biggs still serves on the university's Native Advisory Council; helps others with her therapy dog, Koshi; and is Board Vice President of Love on a Leash, the Foundation for Pet Provided Therapy.

Educated by many tribes and countries, *Dr. Shayne Del Cohen* has a BA in community development, an MA in international administration, and a PhD in international law from Columbia Pacific. Development activities as a VISTA for the Fallon Paiute-Shoshone Tribe, the Talent Search Director and later Resource Developer for the Inter-Tribal Council of Nevada, and a planner for the Reno-Sparks Indian Colony led to twenty-five years as an independent consultant. Her related activities have included being the Nevada coordinator for a Five-State Tribal Library Development project, the Ak-Chin Him Dak; the Zuni Archives; and several private collections. She is a member of the Nevada State Historical Records Advisory Board and President of Nevada Press Women and publishes a daily *Journal to Indian Country*, an eclectic gathering of resource information. In a forty-year career of assisting with tribal development efforts, Del Cohen has found that "paper" is often the basis for proving oral traditions to reestablish property and intellectual rights, the basis of cultural lifeways.

Amelia Flores is the library/archives director for the Colorado River Indian Tribes (CRIT), where she has worked for the past twenty-five years. She resides on the CRIT reservation near Parker, Arizona, and is an enrolled member, as a descendant of the Mohave tribe. Flores earned a BS in education from Northern Arizona University and a master's degree in Linguistics at the University of Arizona, Tucson. As an activist for her language, she has been teaching Mohave language classes in the tribal community for adults and children. She also actively supports tribal libraries on the local, state, and national levels. She was instrumental in forming an Arizona Tribal Libraries group called Gatherings of Arizona Tribal Libraries and served as its first co-chairperson. These gatherings are held twice a year at various tribal library sites throughout Arizona. In addition

240About the Contributors240 *About the Contributors*

to her work with the library, Ms. Flores is also a strong advocate for tribal archives and is a founding member of the First Circle of Tribal Archivists; in 2006 she was a contributor to the Protocols for Native American Archival Materials document. Throughout her career she has served on local and state boards and is currently the Northern Arizona Representative for the Arizona Library Association's Executive Board. In 2007, she was awarded a Guardians of Language, Memory, and Lifeways Medal of Honor for Libraries, and in 2008, a Revitalization, Implementation, and Preservation of Tribal Language Award at the Sixth Annual Yuman Family Language Summit for her dedication in revitalizing the Mohave language.

Mary Anne Hansen is an associate professor and Reference Librarian at the Montana State University (MSU) Libraries. She also serves as The Libraries' Distance Education Coordinator and as a Montana liaison to the National Network of Libraries of Medicine/Pacific Northwest Region in Seattle. In addition, she co-coordinates The MSU Libraries' annual Tribal College Librarians Institute (TCLI) with her colleague James Thull; TCLI is a weeklong professional development opportunity for librarians serving the information needs of Native college students and faculty. Mary Anne earned her MLS through the University of Arizona's distance program in library and information science. In addition, she has a master's degree in adult and higher education with a counseling emphasis and an undergraduate degree in modern languages, both from MSU. Her research interests include health information, American Indian education, leadership, mentoring, information literacy, and distance education. She is active in the American Library Association (ALA), the Association of College and Research Libraries, the Montana Library Association, the Pacific Northwest Library Association, and the Pacific Northwest Chapter of the Medical Library Association. A native of Bozeman, Montana, Mary Anne is married to a jazz musician, with whom she loves to spend time on hiking and cross-country ski trails with their two red labs.

Dr. Kristen Hogan is a literary activist writer, teacher, and workshop director based in Austin, Texas. She has worked as a book buyer and co-manager at the Toronto Women's Bookstore and as a core staff member at BookWoman in Austin, Texas. Drawing on this work and over thirty original oral histories, Hogan is completing her manuscript *Queer Marginalia: Feminist Bookstores' Literary Activism, 1970–2010.* At the University of Texas Libraries (UT Libraries), in collaboration with women's and gender studies subject specialist Lindsey Schell and faculty member Matt Richardson, Hogan created the proposal for the new Black Queer Studies Collection in the UT Libraries catalog; this local note designation improves accessibility and visibility of black diasporic LGBTQ materials. As a visiting assistant professor of women's and gender studies at the University of Texas at Austin, she conducted workshops for student organizers and transnational activists on feminist organizing and advocating for antiracist, feminist literature. As an assistant professor of women's and gender studies and English at Louisiana State University, she cofounded Under the Radar: A Speakers Series Celebrating Queer Issues and Diversity. As a graduate student at the University of Texas at

Austin School of Information, Hogan believed it is a responsibility of libraries to advocate for diverse literatures and to work against systems of oppression.

Christina L. P. W. Johnson received a master's degree from the School of Library and Information Studies at the University of Wisconsin–Madison. Along with classmates Catherine H. Phan and Omar Poler, Christina launched a for-credit graduate course on tribal libraries, archives, and museums. Christina currently is librarian at the Green Bay Campus of Globe University/Minnesota School of Business in Green Bay, Wisconsin.

Norma A. Joseph, Cultural Resource Director for the Sauk Suiattle Indian Tribe, is charged with the responsibility to care for the tribe's archive records, archaeological reports and items, tribal enrollment, teaching the Lushootseed Language Sauk Suiattle dialect, and preserving tribal culture. Norma is an enrolled member of the Sauk Suiattle Indian Tribe of Darrington, Washington. She earned her language teacher certification in May 2009 to teach the Lushootseed Language, Sauk Suiattle dialect after several years of study and research. She achieved her MA in 1985 from UCLA in American Indian studies; her BA dual major in political science and ethnic studies was earned at Western Washington University in 1982. Norma served on the Sauk Suiattle Tribal Council for twenty-one years, with several brief breaks in her elected term in office. She was reelected to Tribal Council as the Vice Chairman in January 2010 for another three-year term. During her employment with Washington State University as the Native American Student Retention Counselor from February 2006 through August 2009, Norma worked closely with Gabriella Reznowski in bringing awareness to concerns of language revitalization and preservation. She continues to work diligently to preserve her tribe's language and teaches in a community-based language program while teaching and preserving the tribe's culture.

Janice L. Kowemy is currently the director at the Laguna Public Library in Laguna Pueblo, New Mexico. She is a Laguna tribal member from the village of Seama. She received her master of science in information studies from the University of Texas at Austin in December 2007 through the Honoring Generations program. She also earned a bachelor's degree from the University of New Mexico in business administration with a concentration in marketing and a minor in Native American studies. Janice is involved with various library organizations that include AILA and New Mexico Library Association and Native American Libraries Special Interest Group, where she is the chair (2009–2010 and 2010–2011) and past secretary (2008–2009). She was named a 2010 Library Journal Mover & Shaker and received the 2010 New Mexico Library Association Library Leadership Award.

Janice was introduced to the field through a grant the Laguna Public Library received from the Bill and Melinda Gates Foundation's Native American Access to Technology Program. Today, Janice has updated and expanded collections, promoted services in the community, provided programs for all ages, updated technology, and forged community collaborations. Janice is an advocate of tribal libraries and believes they play significant roles in tribal communities by providing information and literacy resources, new technologies, and cultural language programming. These information and cultural resource centers should be supported by tribal governments and community members.

Sandra Littletree is the program manager for Knowledge River at the University of Arizona's School of Information Resources and Library Science. Knowledge River is a nationally recognized education program focusing on library and information issues from Hispanic and Native American perspectives. Sandra comes from the Eastern Shoshone Tribe on her mother's side and is an enrolled member of the Navajo Nation on her father's side. She developed advocacy resources for tribal libraries and oversaw the revision of the third edition of the *TRAILS Tribal Library Procedures Manual*. She was a Fellow at North Carolina State University Libraries (2007–2009), where she worked as a Collection Manager and a member of the Research and Information Services department. She was an ALA Spectrum Scholar from 2005 to 2006, an Honoring Generations Scholar from 2005 to 2006, and a participant in the 2008 Minnesota Institute for Early Career Librarians from Traditionally Underrepresented Groups. She served as a member of the Spectrum Special Interest Group (2008–2010), secretary of the Gathering of Arizona Tribal Libraries group, and is a member of the advisory board for Greenwood's "The American Indian Experience." Sandra has a master of science in information studies from the University of Texas at Austin and an MA in curriculum and instruction from New Mexico State University. She is originally from the Four Corners region of New Mexico.

Kawika Makanani is the librarian of the Hawai'i-Pacific Collection, Midkiff Learning Center, of the Kamehameha Schools Kapalama (Honolulu campus). He is a graduate of the Schools and returned to teach Hawaiian studies for more than two decades before moving to his current position. He is enhancing the print-dominated legacy collection by adopting electronic technologies to provide a wider range of Hawai'i and Pacific knowledge resources, particularly those created by the Aboriginal peoples and not often or easily found in the mainstream. Kawika has been active in educational and cultural affairs within the Kamehameha Schools and the community, serves on the editorial board of Kamehameha Publishing, is a member of the ALA and Hawai'i Library Association (HLA), and, when possible, participates in the International Indigenous Librarians' Forum (IILF) and World Indigenous Peoples' Conference on Education (WIPCE). He is assisting with the formation of a Native Hawaiian librarians' association.

Dr. Robert Sidney Martin is professor emeritus in the School of Library and Information Studies at Texas Woman's University, where he was Professor of Library Science and Lillian Bradshaw Endowed Chair until his retirement in 2008. He currently serves on the National Council on the Humanities and the Executive Board of the Urban Libraries Council. From 2001 to 2005, he served as Director of the Institute of Museum and Library Services. Previously he was

Professor at Texas Woman's University, Director and Librarian of the Texas State Library and Archives Commission, and Associate Dean of Libraries for Special Collections at Louisiana State University. He has authored or edited numerous books and journal articles on library management, the history of libraries and librarianship, and the history of the exploration and mapping of the American West. He has been elected and/or appointed to numerous positions of leadership in service organizations for library and archives professionals. His work has been recognized with numerous honors and awards, including Distinguished Service Awards from both the Texas Library Association and the Society of Southwest Archivists, and the Justin Winsor Prize from the American Library Association. He is a Fellow of the Society of American Archivists and a Distinguished Alumnus of Rice University. In 2008, he was awarded the Presidential Citizens Medal, the second highest civilian honor conferred in the United States. He earned a BA in history from Rice University, an MLS from the University of North Texas, and a PhD from the University of North Carolina at Chapel Hill.

Born and raised in Evanston, Illinois, *Anne McCudden* attended Loyola University in Chicago and graduated cum laude in 1992 with a bachelor's degree in history. In 1994, Anne moved to South Florida, where she worked for seven years at the Archaeological and Historical Conservancy, Inc., as a field technician completing Phase I and II archaeological work in Florida. In 1996, Anne began her graduate work at Florida Atlantic University (FAU); she received her master's degree in history in August 2002. Between 2002 and 2004, Anne worked as the Lab Director for the FAU Anthropology lab as well as an adjunct professor in the Anthropology Department at the University of Miami. Since 2002, Anne has worked for the Seminole Tribe of Florida's Ah-Tah-Thi-Ki Museum on the Big Cypress Reservation. She began her work as the Curator of Education, then moved to the position Curator of Collections in 2003. Since March 2004, she has been serving as the Museum's Director. During her tenure as Director, the Ah-Tah-Thi-Ki Museum was awarded full accreditation by the American Association of Museums. Anne also serves on the boards of the Florida Association of Museums Foundation and the American Association of State and Local History.

Dr. Cheryl A. Metoyer (Cherokee) is currently an associate professor and associate dean for research at the Information School and adjunct associate professor in American Indian Studies at the University of Washington, Seattle. In addition, she is a Senior Researcher at the UCLA American Indian Studies Research Center. Cheryl was a faculty member at the UCLA Graduate School of Library and Information Studies, and from 1993 to 1997 she held the Rupert Costo Professorship in American Indian History at the University of California, Riverside. In 2006, she was awarded a Rockefeller Fellowship in the Humanities for her research on Native American systems of knowledge.

Cheryl's research interests include indigenous systems of knowledge; the design of American Indian libraries, archives, and museums; and information-seeking behaviors. Her work has been published in major research journals, including *College & Research Libraries, Library and Information Science Research,* and *American Indian Culture and Research Journal.* The Association of College and Research Libraries honored her book *Gatekeepers in Ethnolinguistic Communities.*

Beginning as the Library Project Director at the National Indian Education Association, Cheryl has continued to assist tribes in developing information services. She has worked with the Mashantucket Pequot, Cahuilla, Yakama, Navajo, Seneca, Mohawk, and Lakota nations. Over the years, she has served on several advisory boards, including the National Commission on Libraries and Information Science, the National Endowment for the Humanities, the National Museum of the American Indian, the U.S. Department of the Interior, the Southwest Museum, and the D'Arcy McNickle Center for American Indian History.

Sam Olbekson is an enrolled member of the White Earth Band of Minnesota Chippewa and an active participant in the Native American community in Minneapolis. Sam has a deep commitment to researching and promoting the academic and professional discourse of culturally sensitive design and planning issues for contemporary Native communities, focusing on tribal housing, museums, cultural centers, and libraries. Sam holds a master of architecture in urban design from Harvard University and a bachelor of architecture from Cornell University. He has served as a guest architectural design critic at Harvard University, the Boston Architectural Center, Wentworth Institute of Technology, and the University of Minnesota. Sam's professional work includes tribal museums, Native American art galleries, sustainable Native American housing development, and planning projects for Native urban communities. He has worked on numerous commercial, housing, arts facilities, performance spaces, environmental centers, and academic projects and enjoys working closely with organizations to create spaces that capture the unique cultural, aesthetic, environmental, and physical opportunities of each project. Sam is currently the Board Chair for the Minneapolis American Indian Center and a member of the Minnesota American Indian Chamber of Commerce, the American Indian Council of Architects and Engineers, and the American Indian Library Association.

David Ongley has been the director of the Tuzzy Consortium Library in Barrow, Alaska, since 1996. He is an active member of the Alaska Library Association (AkLA), where he is currently serving as president (2010–2011), and previously served eight years as the AkLA chapter representative to the American Library Association (ALA). He was the chair of the ALA Committee on Rural, Native, and Tribal Libraries of All Kinds from 2007 to 2009. He served as president of the American Indian Library Association in 2003. He was honored in 2004 by *Library Journal* by being selected for inclusion in their Library Movers and Shakers. In 2009, he received the Distinguished Service Award from the American Indian Library Association. A graduate of the School of Library Science at Western Michigan University in 1983, David has worked in libraries for nearly thirty years, specializing in reference and technology. Since moving to Alaska in 1991, he has become an advocate of library services for indigenous people.

Dr. Susan D. Penfield is currently the program director for the Documenting Endangered Languages Program at the National Science Foundation. She received her PhD in linguistic anthropology from the University of Arizona, where she has been a senior lecturer in the English Department and a faculty affiliate for the Second Language Acquisition and Teaching PhD Program and the Department of Linguistics. She has been working with U.S. indigenous communities for over thirty years and is actively involved in research on language documentation, language revitalization, indigenous languages, and technology and community-based language/linguistic training. Susan frequently teaches for the American Indian Language Development Institute, where she has initiated courses in indigenous languages and technology and more recently in grant writing and language documentation. Her work with language and technology was supported by the Bill and Melinda Gates Foundation and resulted in a book, *Technology-enhanced Language Revitalization*, with Philip Cash Cash, and a listserv titled "Indigenous Languages and Technology (ILAT)," which now has over three hundred members worldwide. She is currently a consultant for a number of communities where language documentation is forming the basis for strong revitalization activities, notably the Colorado River Indian Tribes in Arizona and the Coushatta community in Louisiana.

Catherine H. Phan currently works as a metadata librarian at the University of Wisconsin (UW) Digital Collections Center (UWDCC) in Madison, Wisconsin. The UWDCC works collaboratively with UW System faculty, staff, and librarians, as well as cultural heritage institutions and public libraries throughout Wisconsin, to create and provide access to digital resources that support the teaching and research needs of the UW community, uniquely document the university and state of Wisconsin, and provide access to rare or fragile items of broad research value. Resources within the collections are free and publicly accessible online. Catherine received her MA from the School of Library and Information Studies at the University of Wisconsin–Madison, where she also received a bachelor's degree in Chinese language and literature.

Omar Poler is a recent graduate of the School of Library and Information Studies at the University of Wisconsin–Madison, where he also received a bachelor's degree in history and a certificate in American Indian studies. An enrolled member of the Mole Lake Sokaogon Chippewa Community in northeastern Wisconsin, he learned to love reading and libraries from his parents—especially his father, Dan, who helped start one of Wisconsin's earliest tribal libraries. Before attending college, Poler worked as a labor union organizer and an environmental activist opposing sulfide mining in northern Wisconsin. He was an American Library Association (ALA) Spectrum Scholar from 2008 to 2009, an LIS Midwest Access Program (LAMP) Scholar from 2008 to 2010, and in July 2010 began serving as an intern for the ALA Committee on Rural, Native, and Tribal Libraries of All Kinds. His interests include American Indian history, Ojibwe language revitalization, and learning about regional traditional music of all kinds.

Gabriella Reznowski, librarian for Languages and Cultures at Washington State University, became interested in language revitalization through the endangered languages of the Pacific Northwest and her friendship with Norma Joseph. An affiliate of Washington State University's Plateau Center for Native American Studies, Gabriella graduated with an MLIS from the University of Alberta in 1998. She has since worked in public, school, and university library settings, gaining a rich and varied view of the field. Gabriella's other areas of research include the librarian's role in motivating language learners and the role of libraries in supporting linguistic diversity. She is currently working on her forthcoming book, *Canadian Literature: Strategies and Sources*, from Scarecrow Press.

Dr. Loriene Roy is professor in the School of Information at the University of Texas at Austin. She is Anishinabe, enrolled on the White Earth Reservation, a member of the Minnesota Chippewa Tribe. In addition to her role as the advisory editor for The American Indian Experience, she serves on the boards for the Academic Solutions Database for American Indians, Outreach Connections, the International Children's Digital Library, WebJunction.org, and TexShare. Loriene is founder and director of "If I Can Read, I Can Do Anything," a national reading club for American Indian students. She served as 1997–1998 President of the American Indian Library Association and the 2007–2008 President of the American Library Association. Her professional awards include the 2009 Leadership Award, National Conference Tribal Archives, Libraries, and Museums; 2007 State of Texas Senate Proclamation Number 127; 2006 ALA Equality Award; 2007 *Library Journal* "Mover & Shaker"; Outstanding 2002 Alumna from the University of Arizona's School of Information Resources and Library Services; the 2001 Joe and Bettie Branson Ward Excellence Award for Research, Teaching, or Demonstration Activities that Contribute to Changes of Positive Value to Society; two Texas Exes Teaching Awards; and two James W. Vick Texas Excellence Awards for Academic Advisors.

Dr. Rhonda Harris Taylor is an associate professor in the School of Library and Information Studies (SLIS) at the University of Oklahoma (OU), where she teaches graduate courses in the organization of information and knowledge resources, multicultural librarianship, management of information and knowledge organizations, and academic library administration. She is the Director for the IMLS-funded "Partnering to Build a 21st Century Community of Oklahoma Academic Librarians" (2009–2012) Project at OU SLIS, whose goal is to recruit and educate new academic librarians prepared to fill leadership roles in providing services to underserved and minority groups. She has previously served as president of the American Indian Library Association (AILA) and as editor of the AILA newsletter. She is an enrolled member of the Choctaw Nation of Oklahoma.

James Thull has a master of arts in history and a master of library and information sciences from the University of Wisconsin–Milwaukee. He currently works as a reference librarian and assistant professor at Montana State University–Bozeman and has been the Junior Coordinator of the Tribal College Librarians Institute since 2005. He can be reached at jjthull@montana.edu.

Kelly Webster, an enrolled member of the Oneida Tribe of Indians of Wisconsin, has been active in the American Indian Library Association (AILA) for twelve years, serving in a wide variety of capacities, including president from 2004 to 2005. She is currently head of Metadata Services at the O'Neill Library of Boston College. She is active in supporting the American Library Association's Spectrum Initiative, which aims to increase the representation of librarians of color in the profession. In 2003, she coordinated a program at the ALA Annual Conference titled "What YOU Can Do for Tribal Libraries." She is editor and compiler of *Library Services to Indigenous Populations*, a resource that combines important contributions from several AILA members with a comprehensive bibliography.

Amy Ziegler is a certified archivist in Special Collections at the Pikes Peak Library District in Colorado Springs, Colorado. She came to Colorado Springs from Austin, Texas, where she completed her master of science in information studies from the University of Texas at Austin in 2006. While in Austin, she worked at the Dolph Briscoe Center for American History as an intern for the Professional Touring Entertainment Industry Archive. Also while in graduate school, she was a part of Honoring Generations, an Institute of Museum and Library Services funded program, under Dr. Loriene Roy's mentorship. She has a BA in history from Oklahoma State University in Stillwater, Oklahoma. Amy is Yuchi, enrolled in the Muskogee (Creek) Nation, and grew up in Kellyville, Oklahoma. She currently serves as Secretary on the board of the Society of Rocky Mountain Archivists and is also a member of the Society of Southwest Archivists and the Society of American Archivists.

CPSIA information can be obtained at www.ICGtesting.com
Printed in the USA
BVOW070021290212

284035BV00002B/4/P